The Welfare State Generation

The Welfare State Generation

Women, Agency and Class
in Britain since 1945

Eve Worth

BLOOMSBURY ACADEMIC
LONDON • NEW YORK • OXFORD • NEW DELHI • SYDNEY

BLOOMSBURY ACADEMIC
Bloomsbury Publishing Plc
50 Bedford Square, London, WC1B 3DP, UK
1385 Broadway, New York, NY 10018, USA
29 Earlsfort Terrace, Dublin 2, Ireland

BLOOMSBURY, BLOOMSBURY ACADEMIC and the Diana logo are trademarks of
Bloomsbury Publishing Plc

First published in Great Britain 2022
This paperback edition published 2023

Series design: Liron Gilenberg | www.ironicitalics.com
Cover image: Dr Maura Stafford writing notes with midwife,
Royal United Hospitals, Bath, Somerset 1988. Homer Sykes/Alamy Stock Photo

A catalogue record for this book is available from the British Library.

Library of Congress Cataloging-in-Publication Data
Names: Worth, Eve, author.
Title: The welfare state generation : women, agency and class in
Britain since 1945 / Eve Worth.
Description: London ; New York, NY : Bloomsbury Academic, 2021. |
Series: New directions in social and cultural history |
Includes bibliographical references and index.
Identifiers: LCCN 2021029979 (print) | LCCN 2021029980 (ebook) | ISBN 9781350192065
(hardback) | ISBN 9781350192072 (pdf) | ISBN 9781350192089 (ebook)
Subjects: LCSH: Women–Great Britain–Social conditions. | Public welfare–Great
Britain–History. | Welfare state–Social aspects–Great Britain–History. |
Great Britain–Social conditions–1945-
Classification: LCC HQ1593 .W65 2021 (print) | LCC HQ1593 (ebook) |
DDC 305.40941–dc23
LC record available at https://lccn.loc.gov/2021029979
LC ebook record available at https://lccn.loc.gov/2021029980

ISBN: HB: 978-1-3501-9206-5
         PB: 978-1-3501-9210-2
         ePDF: 978-1-3501-9207-2
         eBook: 978-1-3501-9208-9

Series: New Directions in Social and Cultural History

Typeset by Integra Software Services Pvt. Ltd.

To find out more about our authors and books visit www.bloomsbury.com
and sign up for our newsletters.

For my mum, Jan.

Contents

Figures

Acknowledgements

First and foremost, I would like to thank the women who were interviewed for this project. I feel incredibly honoured that you shared your life stories with me. You have helped me to think in much more interesting ways about women's lives in recent history.

I am grateful to the AHRC (grant no: AH/K503198/1) and Queen's College, Oxford, for funding the first stages of my research. Thank you also to Women in the Humanities and St Hilda's College, Oxford, for providing such a stimulating and supportive intellectual environment in which to write this book. Extra special thanks are owed to Sheila Forbes, and to my incisive supervisor Selina Todd. It has been a pleasure to share and develop ideas with both Helena Mills and Laura Paterson at various stages of this research. Christina de Bellaigue has come to be a great friend and intellectual collaborator. The Rags to Riches network at The Oxford Research Centre in the Humanities, that I have been a part of since its inception, has been so valuable to my research on social mobility. There is a community of women scholars in the Oxford History Faculty who have always been so supportive of my research; these include Kathryn Gleadle, Senia Paseta and Siân Pooley.

This research has been enriched by the opportunities that I have had to engage at conferences and talks with the amazing set of historians currently working on the recent history of Britain. NACBS, SHS and MBS were particular highlights in pre-Covid times. I would like to especially thank Pat Thane and John Davis, who encouraged me to write a book out of this research, and Jon Lawrence and Helen McCarthy, who have helped me so much as a postdoctoral scholar. My thinking has also benefitted from the rich resources of the Bodleian Library, the Mass Observation Archive at the University of Sussex, and the Labour and Conservative Party archives.

Bloomsbury, and particularly Abigail Lane, have made the book writing process so smooth. I am indebted to the editors of the *New Directions in Social and Cultural History* series who have really believed in this book. Thanks also to the reviewer who offered such thoughtful comments on the manuscript.

Finally, thank you so much to my family. Ella is the warmest person yet the sharpest critic, and Ethan always manages to bring the fun. My dad has helped me get through years of study with much-needed patience, eye for detail and for the arc of history. My partner, Martin, offers me endless support and makes every single day better. And my mum, who is the brightest person I know – without her insight this project would not have been possible. She has been there to challenge and encourage me every step of the way. This book is dedicated to her.

Introduction: *The Welfare State Generation*

This book argues that the welfare state has been so fundamental to the life histories of women born in Britain between the late 1930s and early 1950s that these women should be considered the 'welfare state generation'. The post-war expansion of the welfare state was one of the most transformative political changes of the twentieth century, yet we know comparatively little about its development in practice or its long-term impact on those who grew up within it. This is an important historical moment to assess whether the Beveridge promise of 'cradle to grave' welfare provision was achieved because the first generation of women to benefit are now in older age, and they occupy a central role in contemporary debates about the future of the welfare state, rising inequality and intergenerational equity. *The Welfare State Generation* foregrounds these women and examines the welfare state from below through the lens of their experience. This approach shows that their lives were intertwined with the history of the state as provider, educator and employer in post-war Britain.

Historians of modern Britain have acknowledged the significance of the welfare state expansion on the early lives of post-war children.[1] This premise is often illustrated by Carolyn Steedman's statement on the impact of increased state intervention in welfare provision during her childhood: 'I think I would be a very different person now if orange juice and milk and dinners at school hadn't told me, in a covert way, that I had a right to exist, was worth something.'[2] Steedman was born to a working-class family in 1947 at the height of the post-war increase in births. Her path-breaking experimental auto/biography, *Landscape for a Good Woman*, explores her mother's life and her own childhood growing up in post-war London. Steedman's autobiography is an important text within a wider trend of post-war women writing about their experiences of childhood and youth in the 1950s and early 1960s. She suggested that this trend was a result of the welfare state, in terms of both recognition of the significance of the political moment in which they grew up and the changes to schooling inherent in the 1944 Education Act.[3] Steedman's account originated in a collection of autobiographical stories about the girlhood of women born in Britain between 1943 and 1951, reinforcing this point.[4] For Liz Heron, born to a working-class family in Glasgow in 1947, 'two great landmarks' broadly shaped the post-war girlhood of the contributors: 'the Education Act and the founding of the welfare state'.[5] Heron argued that these changes offered 'a sense of possibilities' and a 'sense of our self-worth' to this generation of women, pointing to the tangible and intangible impacts of the welfare state that this book examines.[6] In both Heron's and Steedman's accounts, the significance of the political moment into which they were born was brought into even sharper relief by the contrast with the recent horrors of the Second World War. Women felt compelled to write about their post-war girlhood because it seemed such a unique historical moment. As a result, their autobiographies often stopped once they reached young adulthood.

This book goes beyond post-war women's well-known autobiographical writing to develop a detailed and wider-ranging study analysing the ways in which girls born between the late 1930s and early 1950s related to the welfare state. Important as the accounts produced by Steedman and Heron are, these autobiographical sources shed little light on our understanding of how the welfare state continued to impact the lives of women beyond childhood and youth or the range of women's differing experiences of the state. *The Welfare State Generation* addresses this lacuna by using an original life history methodology, centring upon my sample of oral testimonies from thirty-six subjects, to analyse women's experiences from their birth in the long 1940s to retirement in the mid-2010s. This produces a much-needed social history of the welfare state in the midst of the broader turn towards social history in British historiography.[7] In the wake of the financial crisis of 2007–2008, there has been a return to vital questions of material and economic change.[8]

As part of the ascendancy of cultural history in the later twentieth and early twenty-first centuries, oral history interviews were primarily analysed by historians for insights into cultural discourses and as forms of narrative constructions – and reconstructions – of the self. Feminist oral historians such as Penny Summerfield and Lynn Abrams have developed a sophisticated body of oral history theory, which offers specific modes of analysis for understanding women's subject position and relationship to wider cultural scripts in their interviews.[9] The interviews were taken as texts, which could be analysed for meanings ascribed to the past rather than for evidence of what actually happened in a material sense. This approach to oral history interviews embraces and makes use of what could be perceived as inaccuracies such as omissions, dissonances and mis-remembering. This was a reaction to the oral history methodology of the 1980s, which drew on the traditions of social and economic history. Interviews were rigidly structured, with each meeting consisting of the same questions, often asked in exactly the same order, so that they could be directly comparable to each other. Interviewers would even occasionally abruptly change the subject to return interviewees to the set of pre-written questions or time period. Elizabeth Roberts's research on the lives of working-class women in twentieth-century Britain is very much in this tradition.[10] Her studies produced a wealth of material on the social and economic minutiae of women's lives and argued for social class as a vital prism of analysis.[11] However, Roberts expressly ruled out drawing broader conclusions from her interviews: '[A]s the book is chiefly based on oral evidence, it is primarily concerned with the local and the personal. It would be unwise to draw from it too many conclusions about a wider society.'[12]

This book is a contribution towards the developing analytical framework for oral history interviews. The turn towards social history requires a new methodological approach to oral history which incorporates cultural history analysis and appreciation for the value of the glorious messiness of oral interviews but also revitalizes and extends social history methods. The social history approach to oral interviews in this book returns to a conceptualization of personal testimony as *evidence* but asserts that this can be evidence of more than the 'local and personal'. Experience, defined as the dialectic between the individual and the social, is the key analytical concept here and it brings the material world back into the heart of our understanding. This approach builds on the work of Selina Todd who has recently argued that classed and gendered experience can be accessed in personal testimony in a meaningful way, and doing so helps to 'refine and challenge' existing historical interpretations and narratives.[13] When we analyse interviews in this framework, it is possible to reorient our perspective not only on women's lives, but also major themes in contemporary British history. It is especially bold to treat women's voices in this way, and my original oral history praxis reflects this elevation of women's testimonies.

Each argument that I make emanates outwards from analysis of the oral history interviews with women of this generation. Their personal testimonies are not used as illustration or supplementary to other research but instead form the foundation of this book. What makes the centrality of the welfare state so powerful here is that its significance emerged organically in my oral histories with women. I did not set out to have the welfare state as the primary way in which to understand their lives. My aim from the beginning of the research project was to interview women born in the mid-twentieth century and to analyse the ways in which their experiences interacted with broader political, social and economic change. The criteria for recruitment were broad, limited only by self-identified gender, birthdate and (at least initially) place, and the project was framed as simply about women's lives. At the beginning of each interview, I explained to the women that the interview would be structured around the life course, but that I wanted to take seriously how they viewed their own experiences and the turning points that they felt were meaningful. People, and the twists and turns of their lives, are fascinating and surprising, and they often describe, connect or contradict things in ways that are not possible to predict in advance. The welfare state arose during the course of the open-ended life history interviews as a structure which not only defined their early experience but continued to shape their lives into middle age and retirement. Oral testimony reveals that the welfare state sits at the heart of a nexus of issues that are significant in the study of women's experience and in recent history more broadly, including changing educational and labour market participation, shifting marital relationships, and political ideologies of class and gender.

Despite often involving collecting data on the whole life course, the analysis of oral history tends to focus on memories from earlier in life, and interviews with women born around the 1940s are therefore primarily used to illuminate the 1950s and 1960s. This means that oral history can inadvertently perpetuate a lack of interest in middle age and older women. It can also lead to an underappreciation of the dynamism of women's lives. Women generally have far less linear life trajectories than men and are more likely to enter different occupational and educational arrangements at different points in their lives, particularly during their childbearing years. Analysing the experiences of women of the welfare state generation late in their lives challenges the discourse of progress – both personally and socially – that is often associated with this generation of women. We do not yet have a detailed history of these women's experiences after the 1970s or research into how the history of that period might look if we foregrounded women. This is particularly important when considering the impact of the profound social and political change that occurred in Britain as social democracy began to falter in the later twentieth century.

There is no settled definition of the welfare state, and as Nicholas Timmins argues the phrase itself 'suffers the drawback of being static' when in fact it is a fluid entity whose boundaries expand and contract over time.[14] He chose to define the British welfare state as representing "the five giants on the road of reconstruction" which Beveridge identified, the policies created to combat Want,

Disease, Ignorance, Squalor and Idleness'.[15] This definition has the benefit of encompassing both the sense of the welfare state as a holistic change to society but also the questions of morality and deservedness which continued to underpin the provision of many services. Thus, from the beginning, the post-1945 settlement was characterized as much by liberal political philosophy as social democracy.[16] This produced a number of contradictions and tensions in the way that the welfare state functioned, particularly between universalism, means testing and the role of the market. These contradictions only intensified as the twentieth century progressed. The shape of the state began to change rapidly from the 1980s onwards, which influenced women's experiences of employment and then retirement. Living through these changes has led these women to hold, perhaps surprisingly, complex attitudes to welfare in older age. Pat Thane has stated that intergenerational tensions are defining features of Britain's contemporary politics and that historians need to challenge popular caricatures of the post-war generation as selfish in their old age.[17] *The Welfare State Generation* provides a nuanced discussion of post-war women in retirement and makes connections between their earlier lives and their experiences of old age.

Social class and mobility were important aspects of experience in Modern Britain, especially in the wake of the Second World War.[18] Women of the welfare state generation who had grown up during this historical moment were au fait with the terminology of class and the power relationships it invoked. The rise of the social sciences in British universities led to class being elevated as a worthy subject of study, and, by the early 1960s, working-class life was increasingly represented in cultural outputs such as books and films.[19] The post-1945 decades represented a symbolically significant period in British history of social mobility. The terminology of 'social mobility' did not even fully emerge until the post-war years and David Glass's 1949 study *Social Mobility in Britain* is considered the first research to explicitly utilize the term. The emerging study of social mobility was at the heart of the rise of the social sciences in the post-war decades. Social mobility was the subject of influential post-war sociological investigations, and many of the male sociologists carrying out this research had themselves experienced social mobility.[20] The period between the late 1940s and the early 1970s is generally considered a 'golden age' of social mobility, during which large proportions of the British population experienced upward mobility from their class of birth.[21] Social mobility has generally been understudied by historians, but they have recently begun to complicate what the 'golden age' actually means and thus have started to challenge key 'myths of mobility' associated with this moment. Todd's research has dismantled the 'myth' that selective education in the form of the grammar school was the main driver of social mobility in this period.[22] Building on John Goldthorpe's research, Peter Mandler recently stated that, despite the fact that there was increased mobility, it was absolute rather than relative.[23] There was more 'room at the top' because of a changing occupational structure rather than because society genuinely became more equal.

Across all disciplines, women have been neglected in the study of social mobility and – to a lesser extent – of class in general. The dominant models of social mobility since 1945 have taken the male-employed adult as the norm and have made use of snapshots of quantitative data. Both of these tendencies function to obscure women's differing processes and experiences of mobility. The authors of one of the few sociological monographs dedicated to women's mobility in Britain concluded that 'women experience distinctive kinds of mobility ... the traditional framework simply cannot accommodate female social mobility'.[24] The influential 'head of household' model of class presumed that a woman's class was derived from their father's occupation during their childhood and then later by their husband's position in the occupational structure. In this model women do not have a social class position in their own right and by extension cannot be socially mobile of their own accord.[25]

In this analysis, women's mobility was incorporated through the study of 'marital mobility', an idea based on what Gill Jones termed 'fundamentally sexist assumptions'.[26] Jones gives the example of a quotation from a male fellow researcher in 1971: 'what a man "does" defines his status, but whom she marries defines a woman's. In meeting strangers one can "place" a man socially by what he does, a woman by asking what her husband does'.[27] This was the established view until women's own occupational and educational mobility slowly began to be examined in the mid-1980s. The continued predominance of social science methodology and a focus on quantitative data has not captured the complexity of women's social mobility because it relies on a linear life course where careers have become fixed by the mid-thirties, and also excludes complicated familial factors. The linear post-1945 male career model is not especially useful for understanding careers more generally in the twenty-first century, when holding multiple jobs at once has become commonplace and maximum flexibility on the part of the worker is required, incorporating the need to retrain for different employment. Women's experiences in the post-war period represent a more useful prism through which to understand the development of working life in the twenty-first century. My life course approach and use of qualitative data from oral history interviews demonstrate that social mobility should be conceived of as a continuous process with moments of upward and downward mobility across the lifetime.

Historians should restore women's agency in their own class positioning, particularly in the post-war period, when the expanded welfare state opened up new educational and occupational opportunities, which were essential for providing mobility routes to women of this generation. Paid employment is increasingly viewed as a significant aspect of women's experience and identity through the twentieth century,[28] and this importance only intensified in the post-war decades. Dolly Smith Wilson has suggested that even a part-time routine job in the 1950s could make a significant impact on women's economic power within marriage.[29] Research on middle-class university-educated women in the post-war decades has placed more emphasis on the disappointment of female careers in the wake of completing prestigious higher education.[30] Historians of women in the post-war period have undertaken crucial research into the rise of part-time work, the increase in married women's employment, and the dual role of work and motherhood. However, these trends have not been studied much beyond the 1960s, even though the structure of the workplace has changed so fundamentally – with the notable exception of Helen McCarthy's recent work on working motherhood which takes aspects of this history into the twenty-first century.[31] There is still the need for work that makes connections between the changes in women's employment, the role of the welfare state and processes of social mobility.

Women's concerns and activism in the early twentieth century were central to the creation of the welfare state, although by the Second World War provision remained patchy and was not yet professionalized.[32] The post-war move towards a comprehensive and professionalized welfare state was significant in shaping the lives of women born between the late 1930s and early 1950s. Feminism is one of the primary political ideologies that contributed to the social belief that the state should hold responsibility for welfare. During the early decades of the twentieth century, feminists criticized the idea that the family and marriage represented sufficient welfare for women. Feminist activists campaigned for 'direct assistance' to be given to women and mothers. Susan Pedersen has outlined the 1910s campaign for endowment of motherhood in Britain, which, although it ultimately failed, developed the concept of the 'citizen mother' as 'worker for the state'.[33] Seth Koven and Sonya Michel have also made the case that women activists were influential in the rise of Western welfare states.[34] They explicitly connect this to maternity, arguing that 'female reformers demonstrating a strong commitment to motherhood did not necessarily limit or weaken their political participation but instead transformed the nature of politics itself'.[35] Consideration of women's relationships with the welfare state brings these questions of how politics should be defined to the fore of historiographical debate.

During the 1970s and early 1980s, there was a wave of pioneering feminist scholarship on the expanded post-war welfare state and its impact on women's lives. Prior to this, scant consideration had been given to the particularities of women's experiences of the welfare state or the ways in which the ideology of welfare influenced private and public relationships. Much of the feminist scholarship sought to demonstrate that the ways in which welfare programmes were set up and administered were discriminatory against, and detrimental to, women. Such studies focused primarily on women as receivers of welfare provision and as economic dependants and largely took a policy approach to these issues. Feminist scholars such as Elizabeth Wilson posited that the Beveridge Report, which laid the foundations for the post-war welfare state and the expansion implemented by the Labour government, enshrined restrictive ideas about women's role in society and the family through the way it chose to administer services and benefits.[36] This body of scholarship is valuable, and Chapter 5 sets out a detailed analysis of their insights. However, I suggest that women not only were subjects of the welfare state but also acted as agents of change, particularly as workers, within its structures.

The approach taken here to women's relationship to the welfare state chimes with the work of Frances Fox Piven on welfare in mid-to-late twentieth-century America.[37] She argued that the expansion of the welfare state in the mid-twentieth century, and the 'new relationships' that women developed with the state, yielded significant opportunities for women, as well as patriarchal constraints. For the purposes of this book, one particular aspect that she highlights as important for women is their role as 'employees' of the welfare state.[38] She argues that 'the political potential of these organizations cannot be dismissed because they are part of the state apparatus'.[39] In an article that sought to complicate feminist interpretations of the Beveridge Report and the welfare state, Sheila Blackburn similarly implored British historians to consider the benefits of the post-war welfare state for women, particularly the impact of the 'expanded social and health services', which 'offered increased and secure work opportunities for women'.[40] She points to the National Health Service (NHS) as the 'largest single employer of labour in Britain and [it] employs predominantly women'.[41] However, she continues, '[A]lthough the senior positions in health and security are dominated by males, whilst women occupy the majority of the lower-paid jobs, the possibilities should not be brushed to one side'.[42] Thus, in a similar manner to Piven, Blackburn argues that identifying issues with the welfare state should not obscure discussion of the positive improvements for women. These arguments speak to why it is so important to analyse women's particular relationships with the welfare state and why these affected this generation so profoundly.

The concept of 'generation' is central to this project, although it is used in a flexible rather than determinist sense. In his formative essay on 'the problem of generations', Karl Mannheim argued that not every age cohort forms a coherent generation, but it is more likely to occur when 'the tempo of social and cultural change' is 'quicker'.[43] Mannheim noted that sharing a common overarching experience did not necessarily mean that each member of a generation would have the same response to the historical context.[44] As the pace of change was especially rapid across Europe in the post-war period, this moment has been particularly associated with the concept of 'generations' and the tradition of 'collective biography', which 'uses multiple life stories in order to tell the story of a collective who travelled through similar institutions, localities or eras'.[45] This research tends to be primarily focused on the paradigm of 1968, which takes as its subjects the young people, often university educated, who were involved in the moment of political and cultural radical activism that challenged the authority of governments and social norms such as the nuclear family during the late 1960s and early 1970s. Recent studies exemplify the tendency to prioritize activism in understanding the post-war generation. Celia Hughes has analysed oral history interviews with 1968 activists to explore their gendered political formation and experiences in activist networks from childhood to the mid-1970s.[46] George Stevenson analyses women's liberation activists during the 1970s, and Jonathan Moss similarly emphasizes women's workplace activism in this period.[47] This can limit our conception of this generation as frozen in time during this moment, and historical studies of their lives tend to end during the 1970s. This can also limit our conception of the political. Generation is such a useful framework for those working on 1968 precisely because it is a way to theorize the interaction between personal and political experience. Here, though, I take a much more expansive definition of what is 'political' than these previous studies, instead arguing that life experience is inherently politicized, that the boundaries are often blurred between activist and non-activist, and that the key political framework for understanding their lives was the welfare state.

Defining a generational cohort is a complex task. Mannheim stated that a fifteen-year time span is a common estimate of a generational cohort, which maps onto my birthdate range of 1938 to 1952.[48] I originally started out with a wider birthdate range of twenty years (1935–1955).[49] I narrowed this in the wake of my pilot interviews, as I found that this age range did not have a shared experience, in the same way researchers of women's lives found with those born in the long 1940s. Phillida Bunkle has argued that women born between 1938 and 1949 form a generation. She drew the connection through second-wave feminism and the written word.[50] Abrams has used oral history evidence to suggest that women born in this decade (1939–1949) formed a coherent generation, which she termed the 'breakthrough' or 'transition' generation.[51] For her terminology, she drew on sociological research by Betty Jerman and Mary Ingham in the late 1970s and early 1980s.[52] Abrams's research does valuable work in shifting the focus away from 1968 activism and self-identified feminists. Abrams has also suggested that, since the advent of second-wave feminism, women of the post-war generation have become more confident in centring themselves in their own oral testimonies.[53] She has argued that, even if women were not feminists, the movement provided them with the language to discuss aspects of their experience and their significance within the life story in ways that may not have previously been available to them. Abrams makes use of memory – often considered a flaw of oral history – to demonstrate that interviews can offer invaluable access to historical experiences that women may have lacked the language to articulate contemporaneously. For Abrams, what defines the post-war generation is the changing nature of the modern female self in the long 1960s. Her approach is more focused on 'selfhood' than the experience of material and economic change, and she therefore does not emphasize the significance of social class or the welfare state.

The women in my oral history sample hail from a variety of social-class backgrounds. Three-fifths of the women self-defined as working class during childhood, one-fifth clearly described themselves as middle class and the final one-fifth saw their family as on the cusp of working and middle class. By the time of our interviews, around half of the women had experienced social mobility across the life course, primarily upwards from manual working class to lower professional middle class. Working for the welfare state often functioned as the primary instrument of this social mobility, and all but two of the women I interviewed were employed by the state in some form for at least part of their careers, despite the fact that this was not a criterion of participation in the project. Short biographies of each woman are provided in Appendix One, with details of key life events. This mixed-class sample is different in nature to previous oral histories of mid-twentieth-century Britain. Moreover, some of the women captured in the sample had quite high public profiles – this is not a demographic generally represented in social history studies. This range of experiences makes it possible to draw more robust conclusions about a shared generational experience.

The interviewees were originally intended to be recruited from the residents of Sheffield and Oxford. Sheffield is a relatively neglected post-industrial city in terms of oral history, with historians preferring to focus on the north-west of England or Scotland instead.[54] More work has been done on Oxford, largely carried out by researchers at the University of Oxford.[55] However, as my call for interviewees diffused outwards through avenues such as adverts in local newsletters, institutions such as the University of the Third Age, and attendance at community centre events, many women got in touch who wanted to speak about their experiences but lived elsewhere. In the spirit of the more flexible nature of the project, I made the decision to interview these women. The percentage of the women in the final sample that live in Sheffield or Oxford is 60 per cent, although notably, only one-third of the sample was actually born in either of those places. The rest of the sample reside in various places across the UK, including London, Liverpool and Birmingham. I interviewed women who grew up in all four nations of the UK, although England predominates. The range of women in my sample from Sheffield and other large industrial cities has influenced my arguments, specifically in relation to the changing relationship of women to the state from the late 1980s onwards. Instead of putting forward a male focus on de-industrialization in these places, I have developed a meta-narrative of work in this period, which centres women's experience of employment in these cities with large public sector employers. Place is not one of the primary analytical frameworks of this book. Yet the wider scope of place in my study highlighted the rise in spatial mobility in the later twentieth century, which led to women living in a number of different locations across the life course and weakened their connections to particular localities.[56] This raises interesting questions about whether fixed locations for interviewee recruitment should continue to be a key feature of oral history studies of contemporary Britain.

There are two notable gaps in the sample. First, all of the women that I interviewed are white. This was not intentional and can be partly explained by a smaller sample of potential interviewees born in Britain during this period, especially prior to the wave of Windrush immigration from the Commonwealth in 1948. However, it was especially striking as one interviewee Brenda (b.1938), who was involved in the Commission for Racial Equality in Oxford during the 1980s, contacted some women of colour in the age range she knew personally about the project, but none of them responded to her. Steph Lawler faced the same problem when she was recruiting women of a similar age for her project on mothers and daughters, finding that even on a project with a wide-ranging theme women of colour were far less likely to volunteer for participation in interviews.[57] I argue throughout the book that women's experiences of the welfare state were contradictory from girlhood to retirement, particularly for working-class women. However, black women's scholarship has shown that state intervention in Britain has a disproportionately complex and often more coercive impact on their life experience. The authors, Beverley Bryan, Stella Dadzie and Suzanne Scafe, of *Heart of the Race* termed the welfare state 'the uncaring arm of the state'. They argued that black women's relationship to welfare state services, particularly as users, has a different tenor in some respects to that of white women, which should be acknowledged in research on the post-war period.[58] Second, women who attended grammar school after passing the eleven-plus examination are over-represented in the sample compared to secondary modern school students. Stephanie Spencer noted a similar type of imbalance in her interview sample of women who attended school in the 1950s.[59] As I demonstrate in this book, this was a consequence of the ongoing influence of the eleven-plus examination on the lives of post-war women, and thus the under-representation of secondary modern students offers historians an important insight into who thinks their experience is worthy of discussion.[60] I contend that the 1944 Education Act was one of the most significant pieces of twentieth-century legislation, not only because of the opportunities it provided, but also because of the understudied divisions it created within families.

The oral history interviews are contextualized using a variety of rich material, including personal testimony collections, political policy documents, sociological texts and census data. I bring different types of primary source materials together that are usually viewed separately – such as qualitative and quantitative and personal and political material – because individual experience should not be divorced from its interrelationship with the wider historical context. As Mike Savage has emphasized, the rise of the social sciences and the desire of governments to hold more data on their citizens in the wake of the Second World War led to a significant amount of research being produced on social policy and its impact on everyday lives.[61] Alongside this, the interview as academic research method developed and proliferated. Steedman has connected this focus on production of knowledge about individuals to the introduction of creative writing in primary schools during the post-war years.[62] I make use of neglected sociological texts about women's lives published in the 1970s and

1980s, often written by women of the welfare state generation. I also analyse the responses to three Mass Observation directives: one titled 'Going to University' from spring 2004, a later directive on 'Social Mobility' sent out in spring 2016 and finally a 2018 directive on the welfare state.[63] These three directives have provided me with insights into themes and time periods where little personal testimony material has been produced by women born between the late 1930s and early 1950s. Mass Observation is a social research organization that was established in 1937 to create 'anthropology of ourselves'.[64] The organization was especially active during the war years but wound down in the 1950s, before being revived following the establishment of the Mass Observation archive at the University of Sussex in the 1970s.[65] The powerful responses to the directives produced in the second phase of the project have not yet been fully utilized by historians of contemporary Britain.

The Welfare State Generation is structured around the life course of women. Chapter 2 focuses on the childhood experiences of women born between *c.* 1938 and 1952. Thus, I examine women's engagement with three key welfare state institutions during childhood: the NHS, council housing and secondary schooling within the selective education system. Chapter 3 builds on this, analysing the advice given to and choices made by women of this generation as they left compulsory secondary education in the late 1950s and 1960s. I outline the shifting occupational structure in Britain during the post-war decades and demonstrate the centrality of welfare state expansion to the change. I also consider the more intangible impacts of the welfare state on women of this generation. Taken together, these chapters lay the foundations for understanding women's relationships to the welfare state as they grew up.

Chapters 4 and 5 both cover the period from the late 1960s to the early 1980s – a significant decade for women of the welfare state generation both politically and economically. Chapter 4 shows that this was a period when women experienced upward social mobility, prompted by an expanding welfare state labour market and increased levels of public sector higher education provision. Chapter 5 focuses on the political potential of women as employees of the welfare state during the 1970s. The chapter also analyses the interrelationship between the priorities of second-wave feminism in this period and the collective biography of women of the welfare state generation.

Chapter 6 turns to the period from the 1980s onwards when the welfare state was under threat from successive Conservative governments. I argue that women's testimony reveals a process of 'de-professionalization' in the public sector, which negatively affected the welfare state generation and produced a moment of class intensification. Finally, Chapter 7 analyses the experiences of women born between the late 1930s and early 1950s as they transition to retirement in the twenty-first century. Older age was a disruptive moment for women of this generation, both in terms of their own personal identity and because of the political context that brought their relationships with the welfare state to the forefront of the social imagination.

2

'Daughters of the state': Girlhood in post-war Britain

The welfare state was the framework that defined the early lives of girls growing up in the post-war period. In this chapter, material circumstances, personal experience and the broader political environment are intertwined to produce a new account of girlhood in the expanded welfare state. A particular focus is placed here on three key aspects that emerged in the oral history interviews as the areas of social policy with which girls of this generation had the most contact: the NHS, council housing and secondary schooling. The 1944 Education Act is conceptualized as central to the project of welfare state expansion. This act made secondary education free and compulsory for the first time, and this particularly mattered for girls because they lost out more than boys when families had to make choices about educational cost and the family economy. As one interviewee stated, 'I think it was the 1944 Education Act that really changed things.'[1] The eleven-plus examination, which was introduced by this act as a tool to determine which secondary school each pupil should attend, loomed especially large in the memories of women of this generation. Sitting the eleven-plus was one of the life experiences shared by all women, and passing or failing could be a defining moment. The state intervened directly in children's lives and sorted them into different school types with enduring consequences.

Historians have understudied children's relationships with the state in this period. In the late nineteenth and early twentieth century, concern for the material and intellectual vitality of children as avatars for the future of the nation represented an impetus for some early welfare legislation. Laura King has suggested that the Second World War intensified this concern, and the conception of children as 'future citizens' became central to a political rhetoric aiming to create consensus for expanding the welfare state.[2] However, she notes that the image of the future citizen was 'often male … and the values to be instilled in such children were middle class'.[3] This idealized image had consequences for the way in which girls, particularly working-class girls, experienced state expansion of welfare provision. The place of children within family life also changed in the post-war years. Social reconstruction involved the creation of a new 'normality' in Britain, which saw couples marrying younger and having children earlier.[4] Access to birth control also made it possible for women to have more control of their own fertility, and, on average, they chose to have fewer children than during the interwar period. This meant that they could direct more attention and resources towards each child.[5] The few histories we have of girls and young women in the post-war period tend to focus on the significance of the mother–daughter relationship in isolation,[6] but this chapter expands this to include fathers and siblings, making the connection between changing family dynamics and the welfare state.

This chapter teases out the varied intergenerational and intrafamilial influences of the state. Hints of these differences arise in women's autobiographical writing. While Carolyn Steedman's famous quotation, mentioned in the previous chapter, from *Landscape for a Good Woman* is about the positive impact of the welfare state on her childhood, different versions of the state loom as a spectre throughout. In the opening vignette, the state is represented by a 'dumpy' health visitor who condescendingly tells her mother that 'this house isn't fit for a baby'.[7] Steedman vividly remembered this incident and the tears and shame it provoked in her mother. The experience is pinpointed as the moment Steedman first understood her family's position in the class hierarchy, igniting her desire never to be in a position to be spoken to in the way the middle-class health visitor spoke to her mother. By passing the eleven-plus examination, Steedman was one of the few working-class girls 'allowed to travel through the narrow gates at the age of eleven, towards the golden city'.[8] Her younger sister did not pass and left her secondary modern school aged fifteen. Steedman now finds herself again trying to reconcile different impacts of the welfare state: 'We're both daughters of the state, but she's poor and I'm not.'[9] Meaningful class differences also exist between working- and middle-class girls' experiences of the expanded welfare state that need to be explored. An example of this is Angela Carter's discussion of the state.[10] Born in 1940 to middle-class parents, who themselves experienced social mobility, Carter expressed similar sentiments to Steedman about the welfare state: 'We'd got the full force of the Attlee administration behind us and all that it stood for … all that free milk and orange juice and cod liver oil made us big and strong and glossy-eyed and cocky and we simply took what was due to us whilst reserving the right to ask questions.'[11] There is a subtle difference between Steedman according the state the power to make her feel like she had a 'right to exist' and Carter's assertion that she 'took what was due'. These girls were the welfare state generation, but to speak of a generation is not to flatten their experience.

Material change: NHS and housing

Bridget (b.1951) began our interview by showing me the coupons she had saved for 'the orange juice and the vitamins that kids got in those days, it was only soon after the war'.[12] She explained that 'it wasn't that we were hard up or anything, it's just the way it was then, everybody got them'. This was a powerful indication of the significance of the material change for children ushered in by increased welfare provision. The impact of welfare state expansion was transmitted to children through its two most prominent material aspects: the NHS and council housing. The NHS was dominant in childhood recollections of the welfare state largely because it was perceived as universal. In addition, changes to council housing provision had a more positive effect than was suggested by contemporary studies, although analysis of its impact on children draws out class divisions.

The NHS was introduced on 5 July 1948 and 'within three months of its establishment it was being hailed in a Gallup Poll as the greatest achievement of the Labour government. Indeed, so dominant a position did the NHS command in popular perceptions of the welfare state that the two terms were commonly regarded as synonymous'.[13] This type of slippage between the welfare state as a whole and the NHS was made frequently by women in my sample. The NHS represented a substantial change to the way in which healthcare was provided in Britain, but much of its social history is yet to be written. According to George Gosling, the NHS replaced 'a complex and constantly evolving mixed economy of healthcare, within which hospital services had been provided by a combination of public and voluntary services'.[14] The decades prior to the Second World War were the high watermark of payment being required for medical treatment.[15] Gosling has argued that healthcare between the wars operated as a two-tiered system. The middle class had largely been able to afford the healthcare they needed and were treated with respect by practitioners even though the complex system of providers was not ideal.[16] Working-class people did have a degree of access to free, especially emergency, treatment, but this often depended on charitable organizations or the good will of practitioners. The creation of the NHS shifted the conception of healthcare to a universal right, and this was crucial in increasing post-war women's sense of their own value within society.

The introduction of the NHS is a prime example of how the significance of welfare changes was communicated to children. Parents told their children stories of how difficult it had been to access good-quality healthcare in the interwar years. Forms of intergenerational transmission varied depending on social class. Working-class girls were told stories by their parents of family members being unable to afford healthcare. Jean (b.1950), adopted by a working-class family as a baby, recalled being told 'tales of not going to the doctors because you couldn't afford to go. My mother had two siblings that died because of diphtheria'.[17] Jean explained that she was 'always made aware of how fortunate we were to have the NHS … that you didn't have to worry, if you were ill you were going to get cared for'.[18] The recurring symbol of the shift was parents recounting the 'queues' in the summer of 1948 for 'glasses and dentures'.[19] The contemporary social policy scholar Richard Titmuss noted in his early writings on the NHS the 'pent up demand' that was unleashed in 1948 for dental and ophthalmic services.[20] As Sandra's (b.1946) mother told her as a child: 'You suddenly found that half the world thought they needed dentures or glasses. There was a big uptake and we saw the benefit of that'.[21] This mattered because it demonstrated that the NHS not only provided care in moments of crisis but also improved day-to-day quality of life. These quotidian health needs were more likely to have been neglected in the interwar years as it was harder to justify spending money on them. Working-class parents wanted to make sure that their children were cognizant of what healthcare was like prior to the war so that they understood the importance of the NHS.

Intergenerational transmission in middle-class families was different in nature. Middle-class children mostly noted their parents explaining the impact of the NHS on others or on themselves in their professional capacity. Fathers in middle-class families often worked as professionals in the health service, local government or schools, and conveyed a sense of public duty to their daughters. Diane's (b.1946) father set up a dental practice in Slough after the war, and he enthusiastically supported the NHS from its inception.[22] He had grown up in Glasgow and practised there in the 1930s and made it clear to Diane as a child how difficult he had found it as a young dentist before the war because of the sheer number of 'people who needed medical or dental treatment and just couldn't pay for it. If you were a medic, you were endlessly having to make decisions about whether you were going to treat people for free or not, and how many people you were going to treat for free'.[23] Diane explained that he was glad to be relieved of that responsibility and remained committed to the 'post-war settlement' throughout his life. Similarly, Susannah (b.1940) recalled her father, who worked as a physician in a local hospital, telling her about the difficult decisions his own father had to make as a general practitioner (GP) in Sheffield during the early twentieth century.[24] Her father explained that he was initially 'ambivalent' about the NHS but, ultimately, felt relieved that he did not have to make this type of decision and that he had more time to focus on medical research. These parents passed on to their children the view that a national health service was important, alongside the role of the professional within it.

Many of the parents who expressed support for the NHS were staunch Conservative voters. Both Diane's and Susannah's fathers were Conservatives, as were the mothers of Jacqui, Joy, Jean and Sandra, although their fathers voted Labour, and this difference could be a 'bone of contention'.[25] This configuration of political allegiance was common in working-class families in the post-war period. The Conservatives recognized that even their supporters were mostly in favour of the NHS. In the elections of the early 1950s, the Tory party felt that they had to state their commitment to the NHS. For example, they specifically pledged in their 1950 manifesto 'to maintain and improve the Health Service'.[26] Having Conservative family members endorse the social right to healthcare reinforced post-war girls' support for the NHS. Jean demonstrated this when she stated that she knew that her mother had not voted Labour in 1945 but still told her positive stories about the changes in health provision, making her 'more aware' of how significant it was.[27]

It is striking that only one interviewee made a criticism of the NHS in the post-war years. This relates to the changing relationship of the family to their doctor. One of the most substantial debates about the NHS in the 1950s and 1960s was whether 'state healthcare [had] undermined the doctor–patient relationship and exacerbated the decline of family doctors'.[28] Dawn's (b.1945) family were, in her words, 'on the cusp' of the working and middle classes.[29] Her father was a foreman at a building firm and her mother a housewife. Dawn stated that, after the war, her mother missed the 'very personal relationship' she had developed with the 'family doctor' even though she had to pay to see him. When Dawn was a baby, the doctor would 'call in just to see how we were both doing – wouldn't happen now!'[30] However, Dawn tempered this criticism by saying that, overall, she felt that the NHS 'gave us better healthcare'.[31] In contrast to Dawn, Joy (b.1939) recalled her mother being 'incredibly grateful' for the NHS in part because it changed the tenor of her relationship with the family doctor.[32] Joy was an early wartime baby hailing from a working-class family. She described herself as a 'sickly child' who had 'bronchitis every winter'.[33] Joy remembered her parents worrying about the cost of the numerous home calls and the way the doctor would often insist on waiting for her father to come in from work to discuss the diagnosis. This was stressful for her as a child: 'It was bad.'[34] The difference in attitude reflects the class differential in treatment prior to the war.

Working-class women gave examples of how their own childhoods would have been fundamentally altered without the NHS. Kathy was born in 1950 to a close-knit working-class family in London.[35] Her mother was a housewife and her father a postman. Kathy believed that the creation of the NHS saved her grandmother's life:

> Labour's victory 1945 – Bravo! There was a particular slant in our family on the NHS because when I was a baby in 1951 – so very early days of the NHS – my dad's mum got bowel cancer. She was expected to die – then she had one of the very first colostomies ever performed in this country and lived until she was nearly 90. They were poor as church mice – she'd never have afforded that sort of surgery so you know, in a way, I, we, sort of owe our existence to that bit of surgery.[36]

This latter comment, that she 'owes her existence to that surgery', is especially interesting because, just a few seconds earlier (as shown in the quotation above), she had noted that she was already born by the time of the surgery. Likewise, Rita (b.1952), who hailed from a working-class background, spoke about living with her mother's long illness when she was a teenager.[37] She described witnessing the frightening deterioration of her mother's health – as her mother was consistently wrongly diagnosed with mental health issues, it took a particularly observant psychiatrist to realize that she had heart problems. Rita remembered the normalization of living with her mother in bed in the front room with an oxygen tank on one side and a thinly disguised commode on the other. Eventually, after a plea from her father for some action to be taken, she was finally operated on and a tumour in her heart was discovered. At this point, Rita stated that her mother received the 'very best of expert care and consideration and went on to live until her nineties'.[38] Although she believed that 'entrenched attitudes to women' arguably delayed her mother's diagnosis, she was convinced that her mother would not have survived at all without access to a universal healthcare system. This demonstrates the profound impact that the NHS had on the childhoods of women born in the long 1940s, echoing Steedman's statement about the 'right to exist'.

The NHS substantially improved maternity care, specifically benefiting women and their children. Infant mortality fell rapidly between 1941, when fifty deaths were recorded per 1000 deaths, and 1955, when this figure had fallen to twenty-seven deaths.[39] Interestingly, women were keenly aware if they (and

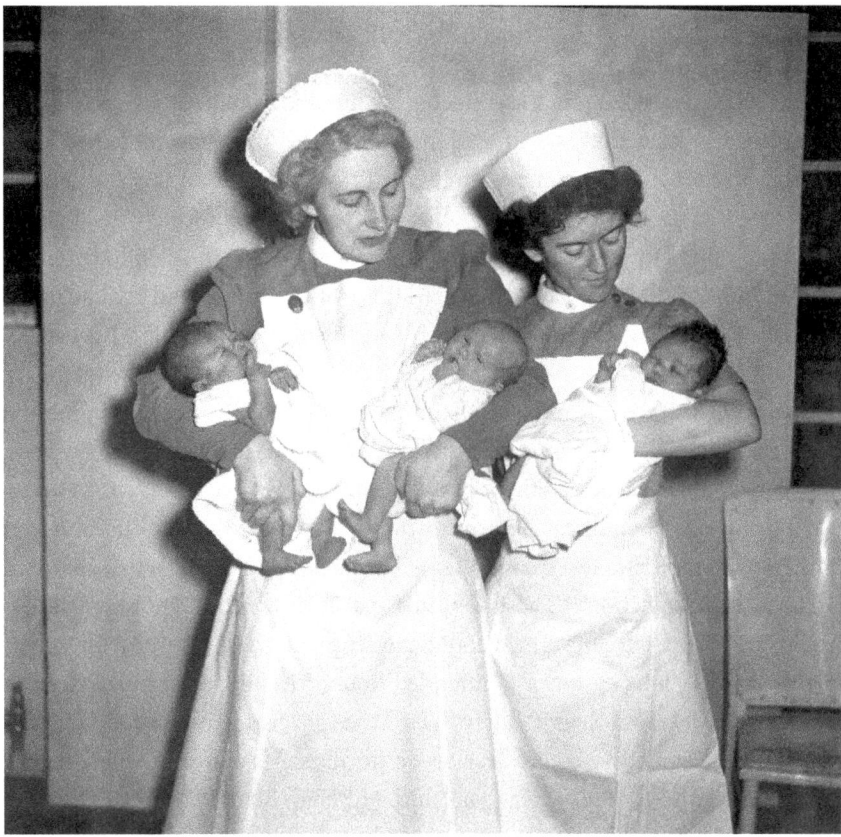

Figure 2.1 Nurses holding some of the first babies born on the National Health Service, 5 July 1948. © Alamy images.

their siblings) had been born into the NHS. Sandra (b.1946) declared it 'the most important change the Labour Party brought in after the Second World War', primarily because she recalled her mother telling her stories of how much easier the birth of her younger sister had been in the 'new NHS maternity unit'.[40] The harsh winter of 1947 was deployed as a means to dramatically heighten the division between being born pre- and post-NHS. Lois described being 'born before the NHS ... mum had to pay the doctor, I cost two and sixpence ... our Jack [brother] was born after the NHS in 1949, so he came free'.[41] She continued:

> It was the winter of 1947. Dad was still in the army. Mum and Nan were having to struggle with a newborn baby. It was a severe winter; they had to dig themselves out every morning and there was a problem with my birth. The midwife couldn't get her to hospital because of the weather conditions. So, there was the doctor and the midwife having to struggle with a breech birth at home and the midwife

said to mum, 'You've been very lucky, we could've lost you both' …. so I'm lucky
to be here!'[42]

Liz Heron made similar remarks, opening her autobiography with the statement:
'I was born in May 1947, when the whole of Britain was thawing out of long,
freezing winter … a year too early to benefit from the NHS at this stage in my
life.'[43] One interviewee in particular demonstrated the way in which this division
could seep into stories of the self. She commented that her sister, born in the
early months of 1948, 'reluctantly entered this world, battered and bruised, long,
hard labour, mewing and moaning passive aggressive from the off', whereas she,
born in the spring of 1952, was always told that she had 'sailed into the world, no
bother at all, my face covered with a shimmering veil that meant I can never die
from drowning, blessed by magic, born gifted'.[44] This is an example of the ways
in which children embodied the promise of the welfare state.

Housing was a significant aspect of the welfare state because 'the modern
home and its inhabitants were represented as the symbolic, and actual centre of
post-war reconstruction'.[45] These were the spaces in which the new generation
would grow and develop. The Labour government's desire to provide better
quality council housing was also intended to improve the material standard of
living for families and their children. The Attlee government had wide-ranging
plans to build expansive council estates on the outskirts of towns, where the air
was cleaner and more space was available. Although housing was considered a
critical plank of welfare state expansion, it was one of the areas to falter from the
beginning. The Labour Party had planned to build 4 or 5 million new houses in
the life of the parliament but, by 1951, only 1 million had been built.[46] The cost
was higher than expected, and cutbacks were made on good-quality materials,
stringent regulations and the rate of building in the late 1940s. The Labour
government's prioritization of council housing ensured that the incoming
Conservative government continued to build at record levels in the 1950s, but
their decision to cut standards gave the new government the political space to
further reduce the quality and size of this housing.[47]

The delay in house building caused real problems for working-class families.
Both Sandra's and Nancy's (b.1940) families lived in poor-quality, privately
rented flats but were not able to access council housing because there was not
enough stock available to meet demand in their areas.[48] Nancy stated that, in
the late 1940s and early 1950s, she experienced 'an endless movement from one
rented house to another, to a flat, to a boarding house, to my father's aunt … it
was really quite bad, and I was quite ill'.[49] Some families were forced to remain in

prefab houses framed as only a temporary solution to housing problems caused by the war. Jean's father resorted to building his own house for the family so that they could leave the prefab.[50] Moving house was recommended by a doctor, who stated that the thin walls and damp were making Jean's asthma much worse. Carol's experience epitomized the negative impact of the delay. Born in 1948 to a working-class family in Swansea, Carol's was an insecure and chaotic childhood and this played out in her self-narrative in a sequence of metaphors of spatial dislocation, beginning with the image of the family's prefab house:

> I was born at home, and home was a prefabricated house, it was made of cardboard essentially … so I was born into a very much working-class family that was homeless after the war because Swansea was bombed … these prefab homes were meant to be temporary for five years, we were left there until I was twelve, and there was a hole in the wall through to the outside.[51]

It didn't help that her father was traumatized by fighting in the war and struggled with 'PTSD and alcoholism' throughout Carol's childhood.[52] The local building trade was stagnant in post-war Swansea, and this meant that her father often had to go away for extended periods of time in search for work. She recalled that her father did not want her mother to work outside the home because he feared that this would undermine his status as breadwinner.[53] Carol and her sister were often left at home with their 'frustrated' mother, who was 'tied to this confined space' and prone to violent outbursts.[54] There was a similar housing shortage in the part of Glasgow where Heron grew up in the early 1950s. She wrote in her autobiography about 'larger families around us being rehoused at a steady rate, but we were doomed to wait forever'.[55] One of the defining features of the 'welfare state generation' is that, unlike for those born from the mid-1950s onwards, the war cast a shadow over their everyday existence. Having to continue living in a prefab was a symbol of this and of being left behind from some of the gains of post-war society.

Much of the scholarly debate surrounding council housing in this period has focused on the issues faced by families from inner-city slums moving to out-of-town estates. This paradigm has begun to be challenged, with historians arguing that influential researchers such as Michael Young and Peter Willmott held pre-existing assumptions about the nature of the working class, and gender roles within it, which led them to emphasize the negative effects of slum clearance in their conclusions.[56] Richard Hoggart lamented what he perceived as the loss of the 'traditional' working class he had grown up in in the interwar period.[57] His work is in agreement with social policy scholars that state expansion was at least partly responsible for 're-engineering' working-class communities. However, women in my sample who moved to council estates during their childhood mostly remember this positively. The delay in building meant that younger members of the cohort tended to benefit from the move. The percentage of the population living in council housing in the 1950s rose from 18 per cent in 1951 to 25 per cent by 1961.[58] In 1952, five-year-old Lois moved from a slum house in the centre of Sheffield to an out-of-town estate. Her one memory of the slum with a 'strong effect' on her was watching her mother kill a rat in their kitchen. She described the incident in detail:

> My mum grabbed the shovel. Bang, bang, bang, bang, bang – 'do you think it's dead, love?' – bang, bang, bang. And she put it down the loo … well I didn't understand how toilets work at four or five years old, and I wouldn't go to the toilet because I was so frightened it would jump up and bite me![59]

This was the defining moment of living in the slum for Lois and she found it a relief to move. Living in these estates from a young age may have eased the experience for post-war children in a way that did not happen for their parents. Ruth (b.1949) remembered having lots of friends on her estate and all being able to play outside together and roam the nearby countryside.[60] When she was just a few months old in 1952, Rita's family moved to a three-bedroom council house with a garden and indoor toilet in an estate on the outskirts of town, which bordered fields and farmland.[61] She felt that 'this was a turning point that marks the different expectations for me … I never experienced being a slum child'.[62]

Women did not express nostalgia for older forms of inner-city housing, nor did they describe their mothers as doing so, although assumptions about working-class women's roles within local networks informed contemporary scholars' arguments that they missed the 'community' of the slums.[63] Maureen (b.1944) recalled her mother having a nervous breakdown after they moved from living with her maternal grandparents (because of the impact of the Blitz) to a council estate.[64] However, her mother's distress arose from her disappointment that they had been housed in 'an old estate with an outdoor toilet' rather than the new estate – '*the* place' – where Maureen's aunt and uncle had been provided with semi-detached houses. Her mother 'was obsessed with a bigger house' and 'more facilities'. She understandably did not want to settle for poor-quality housing.

Council housing remained a class issue in the wake of welfare state expansion. None of the women from middle-class backgrounds lived in council housing during their childhoods. Unlike on other aspects of the welfare state, such as the NHS and schooling, middle-class women were largely silent on the topic and it appeared to be much further outside their experience. Ben Jones has highlighted that, during the interwar period, council housing tended to be occupied by the middle class or affluent working class. In the 1950s, the Conservative government 'aggressively encouraged' affluent tenants to move out of council-owned housing because they 'aimed to turn a social divide into a spatial one'.[65] Throughout the 1950s, Conservative Party rhetoric continued to suggest that private property ownership remained the ideal in society – for example, stating in 1951 that 'the more people who own their own homes the better'.[66] By the late 1950s even the Labour Party had begun to buy into the aim of a 'property-owning democracy', though they continued to prioritize improving council housing.[67]

Some working-class girls internalized the idea that it was more desirable to own property than to live in a council house, and this related to charged gendered – and politicized – ideas about aspiration. There were instances in working-class families in this period of mothers supporting the Conservative Party and fathers supporting the Labour Party.[68] Girls were often kinder in their assessment of their fathers' politics. Joy's family lived in a council flat in London during her childhood. She explained that she got on better with her father than her mother because he was 'a socialist ... and just wanted me to be happy', whereas her conservative mother had 'middle-class aspirations' and so applied a lot of 'pressure' on Joy to succeed.[69] Joy noted that, although she agreed much more with her father's perspective:

> My mother's middle-class aspirations rubbed off on me because when I was a child and went to primary school and I was about nine or ten, all my friends were always middle class, and we lived in a flat and all my friends had houses with stairs. And I used to say to my mum, 'Why haven't we got a house with stairs?' They used to read books like Peter Rabbit and stuff. Incredibly middle class. And I was always aware that their way of life – even my best friend when I was eleven or twelve – her father was a detective in the police force and they were higher up the social scale than we were. I always wanted to own a house with stairs ever since – so if that's not being aspirational, I don't know what is![70]

Jean had a similar experience with her mother. She praised her father's 'socialism' and engagement with workplace politics but critiqued her mother's 'Tory' politics, for being 'deferent' and connected to her experience in the 'home'.[71] Jean demonstrated this using an anecdote about housing, stating that, after her parents were able to buy their own house, her mother 'was quite snooty. If people asked us where we lived she would make it quite clear that we lived in the village not on the council estate'.[72] Although Jean was uncomfortable with this, she recalled feeling envious when she visited middle-class friends as a child because they had 'the kind of things we just didn't have in our house'. The mothers in the recollections are not the Hoggartian 'pivots of the home', passive and placid figures whose desires are only for their husband and children's happiness rather than their own.[73] Mothers are presented as much more formidable and wanting figures in women's narratives of post-war mobility than in the usual iconography of working-class motherhood. Disagreement sometimes exists around this because both mothers and daughters have powerful *wants* that could come into conflict and were not easily negotiated in this moment of historical flux. The role of women wanting more for their children is increasingly recognized as an important instrument of social mobility.[74] Women of the welfare state generation sometimes criticize their mothers but also often implicitly recognize the value of their mothers refusing to settle for less for their children and themselves.

For working-class girls who lived in out-of-town council estates, it was not until secondary school that they entered the homes of middle-class friends and questioned the normality of their own experiences. The phrase 'culture shock' was used by a number of women to describe discovering that families owned big houses and children had their own bedrooms furnished with items such as 'fluffy white rugs'.[75] Ruth, who came from a working-class family, recalled that, during her childhood, she thought that 'everyone lived like us' and was surprised to an extent to learn of her own position in the class structure.[76] This speaks to the rise in 'socio-spatial polarisation' outlined by Jones in his work on council housing in this period.[77] Another interviewee explained that she 'did not feel shame' about living in a council flat but nonetheless became acutely aware of this fact when she 'mixed with middle-class children for the first time' at the grammar school.[78] We now turn to the classed, and gendered, experience of secondary schooling.

The school system and the eleven-plus examination

The stated intention of the 1944 Education Act was to introduce a system of secondary education that provided schools suited to different 'ages, abilities and aptitudes'.[79] Local authorities were free to adopt a variety of structures and school types, but most opted for a broadly bipartite model whereby pupils who passed the academically competitive eleven-plus examination were sent to a grammar school and the close to 75 per cent of children who failed would attend a secondary modern. Throughout the time the examination was in place, working-class children had a statistically much lower chance of passing the eleven-plus exam than middle-class children: less than 20 per cent of the children of manual workers passed compared with over 50 per cent of children from professional families (rising to a 70 per cent to 80 per cent pass rate in certain areas).[80] While the language of the act was ostensibly neutral, throughout the post-war decades, parents of all social classes had a preference for grammar school places for their children over secondary modern places.[81] The desirability of grammar schools relative to secondary moderns has had enduring implications for whether people believe that their experience of post-war childhood has value and is worth discussing. There is a noticeable absence of autobiographies authored by those who failed the eleven-plus, and women who failed tend to be in the minority in oral history samples of the period.[82] Women who attended secondary modern schools often talked about their education in a matter-of-fact manner and wanted to move quickly through the experience onto a discussion of their adult lives. Theresa (b.1941), who grew up in Liverpool in a tenement block with her mother and grandmother, illustrates this tendency, stating simply, 'I did not pass the eleven-plus. Left school at fifteen.'[83] In contrast, grammar school girls frequently spoke in immense detail about their schooling even in cases where it represented a tough time in their lives.

Women with a variety of secondary school experiences were acutely aware of where their school had stood in the local institutional hierarchy and where they stood within that school. The 1944 Education Act was vague enough that, although most areas broadly functioned as bipartite, they built on a complicated patchwork of existing school types with their own histories within their communities. In some local authorities, a tranche of schools fell between secondary modern and grammar status, including central, technical and intermediate schools. A few select authorities also chose to hold a thirteen-plus (as well as the eleven-plus) examination for a select few pupils deemed likely to succeed.[84] Across classes, women retained a striking knowledge of the local secondary schooling structure. Maureen spent several minutes of our interview outlining fifteen different Sheffield secondary schools. She concluded that the grammar she attended was one of the best schools in the city. Girls who did not attend grammars shared this in-depth knowledge of school structure and often deployed it to make the case that their school was not on the lowest tier. For example, Barbara (b.1941), who grew up just outside Reading, explained that her school was a central school, and Lois gave reasons as to why her secondary modern was a particularly 'academic' version of that school type.[85] This intense stratification was compounded further by streaming within each school. Chrissie (b.1950) wondered whether, although she was upset she had failed the eleven-plus, it might have actually been better for her self-confidence in the long term to be in the A/B stream of her secondary modern rather than the lower C/D stream of a grammar.[86] Another working-class interviewee, Jean, was still haunted by being in the lower end of the A/B stream at her grammar school, stating, 'It has had a big impact on my self-esteem.'[87] The education system ushered in by welfare state expansion paradoxically worked to perpetuate the fine gradations of the British class system, even at a time when there was debate in the public sphere about meritocracy and whether the post-war settlement was evening out social divisions.

Middle-class parents knew how important it was that their children should pass the eleven-plus, employing any advantages at their disposal to try to ensure that this happened. As a result, the examination and the build-up to it loomed much larger and more vividly in the memories of middle-class girls. Lesley (b.1950), whose father was the headteacher at a boys' grammar school and helped her practise for the exam, recounted the experience in detail:

> I felt very nervous because it was such a big deal. Only we children who had to sit the eleven-plus were in school and I believe we had to sit it on two separate days. I think there were four papers. One day was English and intelligence paper, and one day either two maths or a maths and an intelligence. I do remember it very, very well.[88]

In many middle-class families, all of the siblings in a family would pass the exam, in contrast to perhaps one child in a working-class family. Having at least one professional parent and access to money for extra tuition if needed helped middle-class children to pass.[89] Lesley highlighted the naturalness of middle-class children passing the exam when we discussed why she thought all her siblings had sailed through the eleven-plus: 'Well, why wouldn't we? We were all middle-class children who came from two highly intelligent, educated parents.'[90] Mary Evans, who hailed from a middle-class background, wrote a short autobiography about her time at a girls' grammar school in the 1950s. She argued that, as well as the more explicit reasons, such as coaching, which aided middle-class children to pass, there was an 'emphasis on the written word and a particular kind of Janet and John, petit bourgeois normality' that gave them an implicit advantage.[91]

Notably, two women who came from upper middle-class families were told that it was even more important that they passed the eleven-plus exam than their brothers. They both had a keen interest in science and their parents thought that it would be better to send them to a grammar rather than a private school. Elizabeth (b.1939) was very close to her father, who worked as the head engineer for the Central Electricity Board.[92] She explained that he was 'absolutely passionate' that she should receive a good education. Elizabeth stated that her brother went away to boarding school and 'the option for me would have been a local girls' private school, which would have had no science whatsoever in those days. There was no thought of me going to boarding school because it wasn't traditional'.[93] After she passed the eleven-plus, her parents chose a particular grammar school 'because it had not only a very charismatic headmistress but also a very good science department'.[94] Her experience was very similar to Susannah's, whose brother went to boarding school while she attended a grammar.[95] The movement of middle-class girls away from fee-paying to state schools may have contributed to the declining proportion of students at private schools in the post-war decades.[96] This model of girls who wanted a better science education being sent to grammar schools is linked to a longer history of private girls' schools often functioning more as finishing schools than rigorous academic institutions.[97] Making use of grammar schools in this way is an example of how middle-class girls benefitted from the welfare state.

Some middle-class children did, of course, fail the eleven-plus, but their parents often went to great lengths to protect them from attending a secondary modern and the downward mobility this could represent. Three middle-class women in my sample did fail, but none spent more than a year or so at a secondary modern school. Brian Jackson and Dennis Marsden also found that middle-class parents were able to support their children in the education system in a 'host of small but telling ways', which included stepping in when 'things went wrong'.[98] This usually meant parents paying for their child to attend a private school.[99] For example, Beth (b.1955), the youngest interviewee, was sent to a private convent school.[100] This was despite the fact that Beth, whose birthdate places her just outside the welfare state generation, 'didn't really mind failing'.[101] Neither Sadie's (b.1943) nor Anita's (b.1952) parents could afford to pay school fees for them even though the girls were devastated when they did not pass.[102] Although they were both from middle-class backgrounds, it is notable that they described their position within that class as 'on the cusp' or 'lower middle class'. Sadie's parents divorced when she was a child, and she lived primarily with her mother, who ran a guesthouse. Her father was an RAF squadron leader, which meant that he was away a lot. During their brief time together, he would help Sadie with her homework because he 'wanted me to do well'. When she failed the eleven-plus, he was 'upset' and this in turn made Sadie feel as though she had 'disappointed' him.[103] Sadie's parents arranged for her to go to an 'intermediate school' and to sit the thirteen-plus a year after she arrived. She passed the thirteen-plus and was moved to a grammar school. Anita remembered 'crying in the shed for weeks' after finding out she had failed.[104] Her parents were also shocked and made the decision to move the whole family to Shropshire, where the first comprehensive schools were just being built. This solution was only possible because Anita was born at the younger end of the generation.

Working-class girls' relationships with the eleven-plus examination were more complex. Although parents encouraged their daughters' education, they did not necessarily focus on specificities such as preparing for the eleven-plus. In a similar way to the stories they told about the NHS, parents often told their daughters stories about their lingering regret of being unable to take up secondary school places in the interwar years because of cost.[105] In 1949, David Glass recorded that only 12 per cent of the adult population received a secondary education.[106] Sylvia (b.1945) grew up in a small Lancashire town, and her father was a shop steward at the primary local employer – an auto factory.[107] She stated that he instilled in her and her sisters that 'education counted' because he always wondered what might have been if he had been able to take up his scholarship at grammar school.[108] Even with a scholarship, the uniform was prohibitively expensive and the family also needed his wages from quite a young age. Sylvia also compared their approach to education to her own as a parent: 'They were not half as aware [of education] as myself as a middle-class parent bringing up our daughters with my husband. So, they were outside the system, but they valued education.'[109] For example, there were books in the house but they 'never said, "Are you working hard for your exams?" or anything'.[110] Rose (b.1945) made a similar statement about her working-class father's attitude towards her education, although she expressed much more anger because she failed the eleven-plus. She made an explicit connection to her generation and the heightened role of the state. Rose noted that her sister (who also failed the selective examination) was still 'bitter' about their father's lack of interest in his daughters' education, but she felt that this was not an accurate characterization:

> What was true was that [Dad] was a socialist, and he thought 'leave it to the state'. Even thought charities shouldn't exist actually. Leave it all to the state, and that'll be alright, and that is doing well. And he hated private schools; he just hated them … But I understood where he was coming from. It wasn't he was not interested, it was just that he thought that he was doing his best – to leave it to the state. I mean, I totally disagree with him. I never left any of my children's education to the state I'm afraid.[111]

A contemporaneous sociological study, *The Affluent Worker*, argued that working-class parents did not lack educational aspirations for their children but rather did not have an intimate knowledge of how the system functioned.[112]

As a consequence, there was a prevailing sense of disorientation surrounding the eleven-plus among working-class girls. Maureen recalled going on holiday to Torquay when she was ten years old and the woman running the boarding house saying to her, 'Best of luck with your eleven-plus.'[113] This exchange prompted confusion. Maureen remembered thinking 'what's she on about? What does she mean? And it never registered until years later.'[114] Eileen (b.1945) missed the exam altogether because it fell on the same day as her older sister's wedding. Neither Eileen nor her parents were even aware the eleven-plus had happened that day until one of her friends turned up at the wedding reception talking about it. She then had to sit the exam at a later date scheduled by the local authority for children unable to take it when originally planned. Rita was not even sure precisely what a neighbour was referring to when she called out the window to her on the way home from school that 'the letter had arrived' and Rita had 'passed'.[115]

Experiences of schooling

Sociologists such as A. H. Halsey and Jean Floud were quick to identify in the 1950s that the grammar school intake was disproportionately middle class and upper working class.[116] They also found that working-class grammar school pupils were more likely to leave earlier and be in lower streams than their middle-class counterparts. Halsey and Floud argued that this largely owed to 'the unequal distribution of measured intelligence between social classes', thus characterizing it as a personal rather than social failing.[117] They questioned whether this could really be described as 'equality of opportunity', especially as intelligence could be affected by environmental and genetic variables.[118] Not until Jackson and Marsden's 1962 study *Education and the Working Class* were some of the underlying assumptions about lack of intelligence or ambition among members of the working class comprehensively challenged by researchers.[119] They made a more subtle argument about the ways in which grammar schools were constructed as middle-class spaces, which could make working-class pupils feel out of place.

Working-class girls certainly portrayed the grammar school as a middle-class space. Sylvia noted that 'there were many little rituals, which were about distinction, [such as] standing up when the teachers came into the room'.[120] The recurring trope of the grammar schoolteacher sweeping through the corridors wearing their academic gown is another example of this.[121] Kathy described her girls' grammar school having 'public school pretentions, you know, in the East End of London, but, they all wore the gowns and you know – mad stuff like that, really'.[122] Jackson and Marsden recorded a headmaster stating: 'I see grammar school education very strongly as a matter of communicating middle-class values to a "new" population.'[123] Being in this space produced complex feelings in working-class girls. Both Kathy and Sylvia described the value of 'gaining access to the cultural activities and artefacts of the dominant class'.[124] Others remembered holding onto the fact that grammar pupils were repeatedly told by their teachers, 'you are the top ten percent' or 'you are the elite', even if they struggled with the overall experience.[125]

Attending a grammar school could be an alienating experience. Carol stated that, at her prestigious grammar school, the headteacher 'had a real downer on working-class kids, you didn't have to do anything, just be who you are – your address was enough'.[126] She also felt removed from her family both metaphorically and literally – when they moved to a new estate in 1960 her parents put a bureau and a 'useless' set of *Readers' Digest* books in the tiny cloakroom, and 'I was sent to this room to do my homework when everybody else was getting on with family life, I felt pushed out'.[127] As a result, Carol described herself as in 'no person's land … I thought I just want to get away from these people'. Heron outlined the same disjuncture between her working-class 'home life' and school, 'which was underlaid by class differences, snobberies about who had what and who lived where'.[128] She too 'just wanted to be somewhere else'.[129] Girls did not have cultural texts to reach for to understand their own experiences. Hoggart coined the term 'scholarship boy' in the 1950s – the 'organising paradigm'[130] of how we conceptualize social mobility in mid-twentieth-century Britain. According to Steedman, this term had extremely gendered connotations: 'in curious language that connects the intellect to the sexual organs, Hoggart described the boy's "problem of self-adjustment", claiming "[it] is, in general, especially difficult for those working-class boys who are only *moderately endowed*"'.[131] Hoggart's centring of masculinity and male agency created a dissonance between his experience of social mobility and that of female writers. As Heron explained, 'the experience of class mobility … was given expression during the fifties and sixties in both fictional and sociological form. But the protagonists were almost exclusively male (the working-class hero), their conflicts and dilemmas assumed as masculine by their very nature'.[132]

The outcome of the eleven-plus was described by working-class girls as powerful enough to impact on family dynamics and, to a certain extent, decide (or at least confirm) the fate of post-war siblings. In working-class families where it was rare for all siblings to pass the exam, it could be a divisive moment. Brenda (b.1938), born into a working-class Jewish family in London, felt a lot of pressure when she sat the exam because three of her four older siblings had previously passed.[133] However, she failed the exam and described how tough this was for her in the family: 'Chip on my shoulder! My mother was terrible. She said, "Well, I don't know what you're going to do now that you're a failure!" Eleven years old – it was awful!'[134] Brenda had recently made a short autobiographical documentary and related that she had talked about the significance of failing. She said, 'It was very polariz[ing]. My siblings passed the eleven-plus and it's on the film how I bore this cross – I didn't think I was able to do anything.'[135] Lois also found that the close relationship she had developed with her older brother started to splinter after he passed the eleven-plus and intensified when she failed a couple of years later.[136] She described feeling that she was now a 'failure' whereas he was on his way to 'becoming middle class'. We ended the interview discussing the continued 'distance' between them. From the opposing perspective of a sibling who went to grammar school, Sylvia similarly felt that a gulf opened up between her and her twin sister. She explained that, as soon as she went to the grammar school, the power balance between them shifted:

> Immediately I felt in a position of advantage over my sister. And in a way I've never discussed this properly with my sister because there are issues that she's quite bitter about, and so it's quite difficult. And she has flung it at me recently: 'How do you imagine I felt when you went to grammar school?' And going to the grammar school was really the stepping stone to entering, ultimately, what has been professional life.[137]

It is significant that both these women use recent examples here, which demonstrate that the effects of the selective examination are ongoing and hard to fully recover from. In the interviews, the divisions caused remained visceral and continued to impact sibling relationships into older age. Despite this, there is scant historiography on siblings in the post-war period. There is a hidden history here relating to the implications of these family divides on Britain after 1945 and on our understanding of the welfare state.

The impact of the eleven-plus, and which school a child attended, on sibling relationships was particularly intense for relationships between sisters and often talked about in gendered terms. Carol had always had a rivalry with her sister but this worsened after the eleven-plus. Carol found that her elder sister 'hated me even more after I passed … and was more horrible to me'.[138] One way this manifested itself was in her sister going after 'any boy I was keen on … they always liked her more than me, and she knew that'. Rita and her elder sister also always had a difficult relationship, but she described witnessing her failing the eleven-plus as a milestone in their divergence. She saw this as a clear indicator of a tendency, which she felt had already been causing tension between them: the idea in the family that her sister was 'domestic' and she was 'bright'.[139] She explained, 'It was always, she'll make a good wife ... I mean she was so completely framed in that wife way that I'm eternally grateful that I escaped that – that I wasn't the person who was supposed to be that. She was the stand-in mum, but what was the payoff?'[140] Linda's description of a relationship with her elder sister had many echoes of Rita's and Carol's experiences. Linda, although born just outside the main bounds of the welfare state generation, had an elder sister born in the late 1940s who failed the eleven-plus.[141] They had a turbulent childhood and moved around a lot as their mother tried to find work and a council house after their father unexpectedly left when Linda was just five years old. This tested their relationship, but Linda talked in especially fatalistic terms about the wake of the exam:

> Debbie resented me, she was always jealous of me because I got into the grammar school ... Debbie had a missed opportunity because schooling was so bad and she went and worked in a supermarket and then just got in with the wrong crowd. And our paths never met, and yes, I think she was a little bit resentful.[142]

Linda believed that her sister's experience at the secondary modern was not an education in any true sense: 'Debbie's education was just wiped out – I don't think she was ever asked to read a book, you know ... they did housecraft and baby care and lay the table, that sort of stuff. I mean I did a bit at my school, but it was just one hour a week.'[143] The belief that girls who attended the secondary modern school were confined to more traditionally female roles impacted on the self-definition of the grammar school girl.

This was connected to ways in which gender and the eleven-plus were themselves entangled. As Stephanie Spencer has argued, the welfare state was structured on the basis that male and female roles would remain largely the same, and this affected the education provided for the different sexes.[144] The secondary modern certainly reinforced traditional gender roles: '[D]espite increases in employment opportunity the prevailing ideology of domesticity as the ultimate goal for girls remained embedded in a gendered curricul[um] in a secondary modern.'[145] Women who attended a secondary modern (or a central school) recalled undertaking more gendered subjects and tasks than their grammar school counterparts. Barbara stated that, at her mixed school, boys and girls were often separated into 'specialist' subject areas, with girls taking 'needlework and shorthand typing' and boys 'doing woodwork and practical things like that'.[146] Barbara explained that she did not mind this so much because she had not thought she would pass, stating that 'the education was about right for me'.[147] Eileen felt similarly about her time at a secondary modern school as Barbara and was upset to be transferred to a technical school at fourteen because she found the subjects they taught her there 'useless' for life after education.[148] Lois, however, found the experience more difficult as she had been 'expected to pass' the eleven-plus and wanted to take more academic subjects. Lois described disliking the requirement at her secondary modern for girls to spend a school year being a 'dinner girl', which involved serving older students in the dining room. It was a 'traumatic' time for Lois because she 'suffered a lot of verbal abuse' in the role from her peers, who made fun of her commitment to school work.[149] For Rose, she struggled with the teachers at her secondary modern. She recalled the shame she felt at being labelled 'empty-headed' by one male teacher and her frustration that only boys were chosen to 'get creamed off to the grammar school'. Even more seriously, Rose said that the headteacher was a 'sexual abuser': 'He would feel down your back and twang girls' bras.'[150] She was angry that her mother was 'flattered' by the headteacher and did not step in to stop the abusive behaviour.

Girls who attended grammar schools in the 1950s and early 1960s did not wholly escape gendered connotations of schooling, but the way they experienced these was more contradictory. There were fewer grammar school places for girls. The results of the eleven-plus were adjusted so that girls had to achieve higher scores than boys in order to pass. Although, as Thane has explained, this was 'on the grounds that their assumed greater "maturity" at age eleven gave them an unfair advantage', it is notable that girls were penalized rather than boys assisted to do better.[151] An implicit assumption was built into the system that the more academic grammars were for boys rather than girls. Rita remembered that there was no discussion about whether her brother would go to the grammar when he passed, but when she did, 'My mum was mortified that she'd have to spend the money on the uniform, it was my dad the reason I went, not my mum.'[152] This was further symbolized by the fact that she entered not only classed but male territory to attend the grammar school – the school was an ex–boys' school that had become co-educational in the wake of the Education Act. Just as working-class pupils entered a middle-class space when they entered a grammar school, girls entered a gendered masculine space. However, it was still communicated to grammar girls that, in the longer term, marriage should be their priority, meaning that they needed to retain their 'femininity' alongside developing their intellect.[153]

An example of the gendered complexities of attending a grammar school involved the navigation of political discussion. British political history formed a key part of the curriculum, and the school environment did to some extent encourage formal political debate. In her autobiography, Margaret Forster (b.1938) wrote in much detail about the mock elections held at her grammar school during General Election campaigns.[154] Beyond this, it could foster a more general sense of entitlement to try out views. Jackson and Marsden highlighted that the grammar school was characterized at this time as 'being for that part of society that had opinions'.[155] This influenced girls' experience at grammar school – as Ruth noted: 'It gave me more opportunity to be vocal, to have an opinion – this is what really separated me from my sister'.[156]

This translated into many grammar school girls recalling a more confident approach to political discussion in the home. There was a sense of political distancing from the recurrent trope of the figure of the 'conservative mother' and 'domesticated sister' and a desire for interaction with the father. Joy said that there was no political discussion between her mother and father, but she was pleased that 'most of my conversations with [my father] as I got older were about politics'.[157] Sylvia experienced difficulties with being excluded from this dynamic, describing the feelings of 'jealousy' she felt towards her eldest sister when she and their father would 'talk earnestly' about serious events such as the Cuban Missile Crisis.[158] This was a cross-class phenomenon. A middle-class interviewee, Sally (b.1943), stated that, 'from the age of twelve or thirteen', she 'argued with [her] father through every issue from hanging through homosexuality, pacifism, CND'.[159] They never agreed but she felt a mixture of pleasure and distaste for his frequent remark during their arguments, 'You're too clever for your own good, Sally. Don't ever show your boyfriends how clever you are, love, or they won't marry you.'[160] This discussion arguably played an important role in developing an embryonic sense of self that identified with masculine involvement in the public sphere. Fathers often enjoyed these debates – as Phillida Bunkle recently argued, 'there is a slightly uncomfortable sense … that the fathers prefer these clever, bright, successful girls. These daughters are the people their mothers might have been'.[161] Sally's father's comments, though, underscore that this had to be negotiated alongside an awareness of the limits of being a young woman in post-war society: girls could only go so far before being contained.

The school uniform was a key symbol of girls' complicated and gendered relationship to schooling in this period. Evans recalled the confusing messages about femininity that the strict uniform represented to her as an adolescent. She explained that female pupils were supposed to take great care with their uniform but also not to have too much of an interest in the way they looked because studying should be their priority: '[T]he paradox of constant vigilance and policing (the endless watching for the non-regulation hair slide or the frilly petticoat) was that, as "good" girls, our appearance was not supposed to matter.'[162] Annette Kuhn (b.1945), a historian who was herself a grammar school girl, argued that, for working-class girls, the uniform represented two sets of paradoxes.[163] First, she echoed Evans's distinction of the uniform, simultaneously emphasizing 'femininity' but also 'keep[ing] the unruly feminine side in check' so that 'order could prevail' and girls could concentrate on their school work.[164] As a pupil from a working-class background, Kuhn also recalled the uniform 'stand[ing] on the one hand for security and the alienness of school life, and on the other for the first flush of pride and subsequent bitter conflict at home around my schooling'.[165] In this vein, Rita's most vivid memory of her time at grammar school was the shame of her second-hand blazer with a 'faded' blue rim, making her feel exposed. However, the uniform also marked Rita out for abuse in her area – 'you were hated … every day the secondary modern kids would wait outside the school gates with missiles to throw at us as we headed for home in our grey bowlers and prissy uniforms'.[166] Sylvia felt that, despite the abuse she received, when she went to meet her twin sister at the secondary modern, she would always 'stand at the gate thinking "I'm glad I'm in this uniform"'.[167] Yet the narratives also challenge the assumption that clothing can be used as a way to transform women's social class – that appearance is the instrument of social mobility. Kuhn eloquently summed this up:

> [Y]ou cannot lightly shed everything that has gone into your formation when you don the uniform of a 'good school'. You learn, through messages that are nonetheless forceful for being unspoken, that your clothes don't quite fit, that your voice doesn't quite ring true, that you don't belong.[168]

Kuhn defined class as 'something beneath your clothes, under your skin, in your reflexes, in your psyche, at the very core of your being'.[169]

The uniform is just one way the grammar school could function to bring together class and gender distinctions by impacting on the body.[170] Sociologist Diane Reay wrote very personally about the potential impact of elite educational experiences on the working-class female body in particular. Born into a large working-class family in the 1950s, after attending a grammar school (which she described as a 'battlefield'), she felt so alienated and exhausted that she developed anorexia and then bulimia.[171] Similarly, Carol's feeling of disconnection, discussed above, ultimately led to her becoming 'very very depressed'. When her academic performance suffered, and she did not feel she could talk to her parents about it, Carol made the decision to try and kill herself. She took a whole bottle of aspirin and then 'lay down on my parents' bed waiting to die'.[172] Angie (b.1945), the daughter of a miner, described her whole experience at a girls' grammar school through the body. She recalled being accused of 'smoking' because she used to have stained fingers from helping her mum peel shallots for pickled onions. They did not believe her when she denied it and was branded a 'liar' by the teachers.[173] The description of the way the other pupils treated her echoes that of an anthropological subject. They peered at her and asked her questions about her home life, making her feel in the same 'exotic and unusual' category as the 'ethnic minority girls who were the daughters of diplomats' – 'they were interested in me … you know, the idea of a coal mining village – and they actually thought that my dad used to come home in his pit black and be bathed in a tin bath in front of the fire'.[174] Her body also became the symbol of her fall from grace when she became pregnant at the age of fifteen and had to drop out of school. This demonstrates how tough grammar school could be for working-class girls in this period and how hard it was to make sense of their experiences.

Conclusion

For girls growing up in the post-war period, the political and the subjective intersected through the prism of the welfare state. In personal testimony sources, women expressed a clear sense that they were part of a distinct generation, defined by the post-war settlement. Children frequently juxtaposed their own experiences of the welfare state with their parents' or the previous generation's lack of access to decent healthcare, housing or secondary education. Awareness of physical and material improvements could impart a feeling of being valued in society. The NHS had an especially positive impact on girls' sense of value because it was perceived as universal, unlike housing and education, which were more conditional. Girls' understanding of welfare state expansion, and what it meant for their gendered and classed identity, developed in part through familial relationships. This chapter has uncovered a complex family dynamic, with changing relationships between fathers and daughters, and between siblings, taking on an increasingly important role in the development of gendered selfhood.

Benefiting from welfare state expansion at such a young age did produce a degree of entitlement among women born between *c.* 1938 and 1952, but this did not develop in the same way between classes or even within families. The welfare state had contradictory and differentiated effects on girls of this generation. Secondary schooling is the primary example of this contradiction. The selective effects of the eleven-plus were so potent in the interview testimonies as to function as a myth in the Roland Barthes sense of a single idea or image, which signifies and condenses a set of meanings beyond the exam itself.[175] Moreover, while the government expanded state education because it sought to increase equality of opportunity, the way the expansion was enacted helped to entrench class hierarchy. Within this revised education system, the curriculum and atmosphere were gendered to ensure that girls would retain the primary objective of becoming wives and mothers. By raising expectations of education for all pupils, however, and by increasing the number of girls in receipt of a grammar school education, the state opened up a space for young women to test the boundaries of prescribed gender roles. This made the experience of the working-class grammar school girl especially complicated – she had to negotiate her identity within a framework in which she was not a traditional girl or a boy and in which she was no longer working class but not fully middle class.

When historians seek to summarize the effects of the welfare state on childhood, many reach for Steedman's well-known comment on the symbolism of 'orange juice'. When we centre girls in discussion of the welfare state, though, it is perhaps more germane to deploy her term, 'daughters of the state', a phrase she uses to simultaneously draw together and differentiate her sister's and her own experiences of the state during childhood. This phrase captures the key idea that the experiences of women of this generation were tied up with the welfare state but not necessarily in the same way. The remaining chapters of the book seek to analyse how the varied influences of the welfare state during girlhood played out and developed over the life course of women.

Opportunity and constraint: The welfare state generation leaves school

Young women's opportunities after leaving compulsory education were shaped by the expanded welfare state. Women born between the late 1930s and early 1950s grew into young adulthood during the 'long 1960s' (defined as 1957–1973).[1] The extent to which young women's lives were changing during this decade is contested by historians, with differing perspectives offered on the possibilities available to women in education, employment and their personal lives.[2] This should be understood as a historical moment when young women were negotiating the competing influences of liberation and constraint – and the impact of the welfare state on their lives perfectly encapsulates this dialectical experience.

This chapter brings together the experiences of young women who left school and entered the labour market and those who continued in education. Throughout the 1950s and 1960s, the statutory school leaving age was fifteen years old, and the majority of women left school on or close to this age to enter paid employment. The 1961 census found that just under 60 per cent of women aged 15–19 left school at age fifteen and the proportion had reached almost 75 per cent by the age of seventeen.[3] In this period, only one in twelve students entered some form of higher education and just one quarter of these were women.[4] Women who attended higher education were much more likely to be middle class: as late as the 1960s, only one in 600 working-class girls went to university.[5] The percentage of young people in higher education remained largely static until the 1960s. In the immediate post-war decades, welfare state expansion led to an increase in places at post-secondary teacher training and nursing colleges.[6] In the early 1960s, the Robbins Report into higher education provision recommended 'that courses of higher education should be available for all those who are qualified by ability and attainment to pursue them and who wish to do so'.[7] Women born prior to the mid-1940s had largely already left education and entered employment by the time the Robbins principle came into effect. A persistent attitude remained, tempered by Robbins but not eradicated, that university was for the few with 'innate ability' rather than a universal right in the same way as healthcare and secondary education had become in the post-war period.[8] However, Carolyn Steedman did perceive her opportunity to attend university as a continuation of her filial relationship with the state.[9]

For women of the welfare state generation, labour market changes provided employment opportunities at this early stage of the life cycle. The British economy was experiencing the beginnings of what economists have termed an 'occupational transition' in the mid-twentieth century.[10] This transition involved a substantial expansion of white-collar and professional roles within the service sector and a concomitant contraction in industrial and manufacturing occupations. Clerical work was a popular destination of female school-leavers in the post-war decades. One survey recorded that, between 1959 and 1966, 40 per cent of all female school-leavers aged 15–17 entered clerical work.[11] Peter Mandler has emphasized that, during the 1950s and 1960s, 'the form that upward mobility took tended to bypass educational qualifications altogether. Women went straight into the intermediate classes at school-leaving age, into clerical and retail jobs'.[12] This was a significant form of social mobility in itself but does not represent the long-range mobility that we often associate with this generation.

The welfare state was one of the primary drivers of occupational transition, increasing demand for state workers. These positions were available to women in large part because men flocked to fast-growing, better remunerated employment in existing 'senior' professions or new private sector roles.[13] The professional roles available to women in this sector during the late 1950s and 1960s were primarily 'intermediate' or 'semi-professional', such as nursing, teaching and social work. The term 'semi-professions' was in fact coined by the sociologist Amitai Etzioni in 1969.[14] Etzioni provided a useful but underused framework for understanding semi-professions: that these jobs had shorter training times, lack of autonomy relative to fully fledged professions although, crucially, 'they were characterised by greater autonomy than blue- or white-collar work', and involving 'more communication and less creation of knowledge'.[15] The welfare state was premised on setting up a range of caring professions, which 'resembled the kinds of work that women had previously been expected to carry out either at home or on a voluntary basis'.[16] Working-class women benefitted from the new administrative and support roles in the welfare state that were available to girls without extensive qualifications. There is little existing historiography on these jobs, which limits our understanding of the expansive impact of the state on women's employment opportunities.

Career advice

There was a prevailing sense among women of this generation that, during their time at school, they were presented with a narrow range of gendered occupational choices, disconnected from their individual skill sets. This contributed to girls feeling alienated from the educational process. Kathy (b.1950) recalled that, at her grammar school, girls who were considered 'academic' were told, "'You'll be a teacher, won't you?" If you were perceived as not being particularly academic, you were placed in a department store. No one lasted long.'[17] Joy (b.1939) left school just after sitting her O-Levels. She stated that, despite her best subject being 'art', she was encouraged into 'teaching or clerical work' by both her school and her parents. By age sixteen, Joy felt 'ready to leave but I don't know why I was ready. At that age, and for a long time afterwards I didn't know what I wanted to do. I didn't even consider going to university'.[18] In her work on young women in the interwar years, Selina Todd questioned historians who criticize working-class women for 'drifting' in their educational and working lives.[19] Instead, she argued that this approach ignores the reality of a lack of opportunity for women. The terminology of 'drifting' arose in Maureen's (b.1944) testimony in her discussion of what was expected of working-class grammar school girls. A leaver at sixteen, she explained: 'I left school with eight good O-Levels with no idea of any career or anything about university – nobody told you – so you just kind of drifted.'[20] She repeated this idea as follows:

> It was either teaching or secretarial [Grumbling sounds]. So, you know, that was it – nobody gave you any kind of feel or vision or made me feel confident that I could do this or do that. You just – the word drift comes into it – you just sloshed through and came out.[21]

The authors of *Learning to Lose*, a semi-autobiographical collection of writings on sexism in the post-war education system, discussed their own experiences in terms of 'drifting'.[22] They outlined that 'there was virtually no career advice for women' and that 'the possibilities of female employment were presented within the confines of what was appropriate to the female sex'.[23]

In order to better understand the experience of social mobility, scholars need to pay as much attention to those moments when mobility might be expected to occur but does not fully come to fruition as to when upward movement does occur.[24] For working-class girls who attended grammar schools, lack of direction could produce a disjuncture between the personal significance of passing the eleven-plus and the material implications. Cynthia (b.1941) described doing well in her exams and passing seven O-Levels but decided to leave just after sitting them. She explained that 'I think had I been more encouraged by the staff … and had my parents been more familiar with the education system I might well have been persuaded to stay on'.[25] Attending the grammar school gave her an 'opportunity to have a wider education' but she was unsure what she could do with it in material terms. In class terms, she felt in 'limbo' between the working and middle classes. Rita (b.1952) expressed the same sentiment, explaining that entering the grammar school meant she was 'out of the working class really quite quickly', creating emotional distance between herself and her parents, but she felt 'a little cheated' that she had not become middle class.[26] She left school at age sixteen after sitting only a small number of exams with 'no real sense of what I could do'.[27] Ruth (b.1949), who left school at sixteen years of age and started a retail job, harboured regrets about 'throwing away the opportunities' provided to her by going to the grammar school.[28] She felt that this was partly her own fault but also voiced frustration with the lack of support from her mother and her school for failing to engage with her difficult home situation. Despite this, Ruth described the significance later in life of the idea that 'I must have been bright' for passing the eleven-plus in the first place.[29] Annette Kuhn (b.1945), who had a similarly difficult experience of grammar school, shared this feeling of having gained intangible 'tools' to 'draw on' later but little in the immediate aftermath.[30] In their early 1960s study of working-class children who attended grammar school, Jackson and Marsden found that many of their subjects had come to the end of their education seriously questioning 'what was it all for?'[31]

The individual attention of a teacher could make a huge difference in determining whether working-class grammar school girls felt that it was possible to stay on to sixth form and aim for higher education. Sylvia had little awareness of her education options until an art teacher took an interest in her work in the lower sixth and alerted her to the possibility that she could 'go to art school and get a grant'.[32] The teacher helped her navigate the application process. Sylvia said, without this intervention, 'I wouldn't have gone, I've often thought about this – the opportunity – when you have a bit of good teaching, and if you ask anyone in their history they'll say, "oh I remember such and such a teacher"'.[33] She took up a place at a prestigious art school in Manchester to do her foundation year followed by a degree. Likewise, India (b.1947) felt that without the support of a particular teacher she would not have obtained her place at the University of Warwick and would instead have left school at the statutory leaving age, like her younger sister.[34] India's social background was complicated – she described it as 'on the cusp' of working and middle class.[35] After training as a teacher in one of the post-war schemes run by the government for men leaving the army, her father moved the family from the south-east of England in the 1950s to take up a position as headmaster of a primary school in Northern Ireland. Her parents separated soon after India started at the local grammar school in 1959 and her mother moved back to England, taking her two daughters with her. However, India had a turbulent relationship with her mother and ended up moving in with a friend's family so that she could concentrate on her studies. She was grateful when her teacher offered to help her prepare for her exams and apply to university. Grammar schools as institutions often did not provide advice to pupils on applying for university because they presumed that middle-class parents would guide their children through the process.[36] This tendency amplified the significance for working-class grammar pupils of encountering a teacher prepared to encourage them into higher education.

University remained a minority experience during the post-war years. However, for women hailing from professional middle-class backgrounds at prestigious private and girls' grammar schools, university was presented as an achievable goal. Although for much of the post-war period only 2.5 per cent of girls went on to university, 69 per cent of the girls who stayed on at school to sit A-Levels were of middle-class origin.[37] Frances (b.1939), who came from a middle-class background, and whose father had gained a 'double first at Merton', noted that both her parents and school expected her to gain a place at Oxford or Cambridge: 'By the time I was that age, all my three brothers had gone to Oxford, so to be honest, I would have felt a bit of a failure if I hadn't got through.'[38] Elizabeth (b.1939) described her father 'being absolutely passionate' about her going to university, explaining that 'he knew that I should have an education and he supported me completely all the way through'.[39] She had been sent to grammar school by her father to make sure she received a good-quality science education and this enabled her to obtain a place studying chemistry. Likewise, Susannah (b.1940) had ambitions to follow in the footsteps of her father to study medicine and applied to the University of Cambridge.[40] She was given extra science tuition to prepare for the entrance exam. Even middle-class girls born at the very earliest end of my sample were more likely to speak of being encouraged to go to university than working-class girls attending grammar school in the wake of the 1963 Robbins report.

It was more common for girls leaving school in the late 1950s and 1960s to be encouraged into teacher training colleges. Seventy per cent of the students at teacher training college during this period were women.[41] Funding a place at training college only cost the government just over a third of the cost per annum of funding a university place.[42] Teaching was already the primary profession available to women, especially lower middle and middle-class women in the interwar years. Carol Dyhouse highlighted that, since at least 1914, women's post-secondary school education has been 'especially dependent on the fluctuations in demand for teachers'.[43] However, the sheer scale of the increase in the post-war period, rising from 13,000 students in teacher training in 1938/9 to 124,000 in 1970/1, meant that this was a career working-class grammar school girls could realistically aim for.[44] A 1963 Nuffield survey study titled *Women and Teaching* found that the link between women having at least one parent who had been a teacher entering the profession was much weaker in the post-war years than before the war, and showing signs of continuing to weaken.[45] The authors considered this a reasonable proxy for class and therefore concluded that there was 'a broader social basis for recruitment' than in the interwar period.[46] Girls, especially working-class girls, were directed towards teacher training colleges even in certain instances when they had the grades for university.[47] In her response to the Mass Observation directive titled 'Going to University', Alice (b.1950), who came from a working-class background, wrote about how important it was to her parents that she had the opportunity to be the first family member to go to university. However, she felt that the teachers at her girls' grammar school reacted condescendingly when she suggested this:

> The attitude towards girls was that they shouldn't worry their pretty little heads about university when there was teacher training college available … Only Oxbridge students were deemed worthy of university, the rest seemed to be channelled towards teaching, largely in infant and primary schools. So, when I said I was applying to university I was met with total negativity: 'If you're going to teach you don't need a degree.'[48]

The comments made by the teacher here suggest that university was seen as for an exceptional few throughout the post-war decades and that teaching was considered a more appropriate ambition for women.

Teaching was a potent symbol of the contradiction between expanding occupational horizons and continued feminine expectation for women of the welfare state generation. Carol (b.1948), who had experienced a difficult adjustment to grammar school, continued to struggle with depression in her final years at school.[49] She wanted to go to art school but poor A-Level results, including in art, made getting a place an unlikely prospect. This was compounded by the fact that neither the grammar school nor her parents were supportive of her desire to become an artist and instead encouraged her to apply for teacher training college. Teacher training college was considered aspirational by her parents, as Carol explained: 'That was going up in the world, you know, from where they were, that was it – no university, you don't even think that far up, you just go up the next little bit.'[50] Desperate to leave home, she took up a place in primary school teaching at a training college in a different town, although she did choose art as her teaching specialism. Carol found it bitterly ironic that she had 'fulfilled' her 'parents' ambition' despite having a very complicated relationship with them.[51] However, the possibility of teacher training college allowed her to leave her hometown and gain a qualification that was crucial to her eventual social mobility. Valerie Walkerdine (b.1947), a contributor to Liz Heron's *Truth, Dare or Promise* collection, described using teacher training college as a 'passport out of the suburbs' rather than a deeply held ambition.[52] Walkerdine stated that becoming a primary schoolteacher seemed 'acceptable' for working-class women and that no one offered her a sense of what else she could do but teach.[53] A Mass Observer, Gail, born in the early 1950s, outlined this contradiction most overtly when she wrote that, after receiving 'mediocre' exam results: 'I desperately wanted to leave home, I opted for teacher training college. I certainly didn't want to be a teacher.'[54]

Nursing was frequently presented to women born between the late 1930s and early 1950s as the primary career alternative to teaching. The introduction of the NHS had increased the need for nursing staff.[55] Cynthia (b.1941) explained that 'in the fifties girls went to be secretaries, nurses or teachers'.[56] Sandra (b.1946) had passed the eleven-plus and picked a 'prestigious' grammar school over an hour away from her parents' home.[57] She had a better experience at this school than many of the other working-class girls but still found that the 'main things' that she was encouraged into were 'nursing and teaching'.[58] Sandra was happy with her decision to apply to nursing college and her parents were 'very supportive' of this choice.[59] Jean (b.1950) was more frustrated with the narrow range of options and the dissonance between the advice given to boys and girls at her mixed grammar school: 'Whereas boys were doing medicine and going off to university, not many girls went. They went to teacher training or nursing – that was good enough for girls.'[60] When she tried to alter her ambitions from nurse to physiotherapist she was met with derision. Her parents' enthusiasm for the NHS and a stay in hospital after breaking her leg at an early age had inspired her to want to become a nurse, although by the time she was a teenager this ambition had become a little constraining. Jean's parents saw nursing as a

> suitable career, so everything was done to promote it ... I was going to be a nurse come hell or high water. When I was about fifteen or sixteen, I thought about doing physiotherapy. And I went as far as writing off and getting all the blurb and what I needed in O-Levels and A-Levels. And then I went to see the careers officer – she said oh what did I want to do and I said, 'Oh I was thinking physiotherapy'– and in my memory she looked me up and down and said, 'and what makes you think you're clever enough to do that?' and I said, 'Oh all right then, well, I'll be a nurse.'[61]

Jean did take up a place at nursing college but continued to question whether this was the right career for her. Another interviewee described nursing as one of the 'service roles' that were recommended to girls.[62] Research into women's career preferences in the post-war decades demonstrates that women rated nursing highly on a scale of preferred occupations but a rung below teaching.[63] The more physical nature of the work and lower average earnings meant it was considered of lower status than becoming a teacher.

Rather than an active decision about what they wanted to be, women from a variety of educational backgrounds put forward more of an idea about what they did *not* want to be. For instance, Lesley (b.1950) 'swore' she would 'never be a teacher', Angie (b.1945) 'was absolutely determined' she 'would not be equipped to be a secretary' and Rita stated all she wanted was 'not to be stuck in an office job. To keep out of this thing that was waiting to get me. I never thought of going to university'.[64] Despite teaching being considered a particularly aspirational profession for secondary modern pupils, Lois (b.1947) described firmly rejecting advice from her headmaster that she should become a teacher because she was 'able to see how difficult it was for some teachers to cope'.[65] In recent reanalysis of interviews conducted in the early 1960s with girls who were leaving secondary modern school, Henrietta O'Connor and John Goodwin argued that 'at every turn they were pushed towards low status and low skilled jobs ... many of the girls actively wanted to avoid taking the type of jobs held by their mothers and female friends ... [they] were attempting to resist the mechanisms of social and cultural reproduction'.[66] They observed that, even though the young women were not always successful in their resistance, the impulse was nonetheless historically significant.[67] The shared desire among women of this generation to reject what seemed to lie ahead is evidence of the impact of the welfare state. The daughters of the state felt they were entitled to at least try to aim for a different life than what was expected of them.

Figure 3.1 Teenage girls hurdling at a school sports day in Devon, UK, 1955.
© Alamy images.

Entering the labour market

The form of entitlement discussed above manifested itself primarily as movement between jobs. Analysis of their labour market choices adds to our understanding of the wide-ranging influence of the state. Welfare state expansion also necessitated a significant increase in administrative and support roles, which were staffed predominantly by women.[68] This is an aspect of state employment that has been seldom discussed by historians. According to Laura Paterson, the growth of local councils was a particularly significant area of the state that increased the number of clerical jobs for women.[69] She offers the example of Dundee, where 'by 1961 the council was the city's largest employer, of 7800 workers, of whom 38 per cent were women'.[70] The growth of local government had its roots in the late nineteenth century when the British state set the precedent of deciding that key public services should be delivered by local authorities rather than by central government.[71] This was a tendency which the Attlee government chose to continue when they expanded the welfare state and was maintained by the Conservative governments of the 1950s. The extension of local government infrastructure contributed to the ubiquity of the state in the daily lives of citizens in Britain during the 1950s and 1960s. Local government expansion particularly mattered to women of this generation because it provided interesting job opportunities that did not require qualifications.

The expanding service sector provided a pool of white-collar jobs for women to enter in the late 1950s and 1960s. These jobs were primarily in retail and clerical work and were available largely without qualifications or with skills in shorthand typing. After leaving grammar school with no clear sense of what she wanted to do, Cynthia took a short course in typing at the local commercial college.[72] She then took up a position as a secretary in the same steelworks where her father worked as an ambulance man. She proved good at this job and was soon poached by another firm. She explained: 'I just went with the flow'.[73] Linda went straight from school into an office job in an accountancy firm. Even though it was a more skilled job than she had originally been aiming for – 'in Woolworths' – she remembered the headmaster telling her he was a 'bit disappointed that you're not going for anything a bit better'.[74] She spent only a few months at the accountancy firm before moving to a similar role at an insurance company because they paid more. Linda noted that the job allowed her to pay board to her mother and still have money to socialize with friends, although she described feeling 'bored stiff' in these roles but without any idea of what else she could do.[75] While both Linda and Cynthia attended grammar schools, women who went to intermediate-type schools or were in the top stream of the secondary modern were also able to get white-collar jobs and move between them. Eileen (b.1945) left her technical school at sixteen in the early 1960s because she had 'switched off completely' and quickly found a job at a publishing house as an 'executive trainee' mainly doing proof-reading.[76] She said that they 'paid peanuts' and thought 'giving [me] a nice title made up for it', but she left after only six months when she found out how much more the girls in the typing pool were paid.[77] Similarly, Brenda (b.1938), who attended a central school, left her first job as a shorthand typist at an insurance company after only a year because she 'didn't find it interesting'.[78] The latter comment demonstrates that women of this generation felt they ought to find their paid work interesting. The buoyant job market meant that women could leave if they were not satisfied and try out other roles without much anxiety.

Administrative and support roles in the welfare state tended to have better terms and conditions than those in the private sector and, in some cases, more routes for promotion for women.[79] This is significant because although women were able to obtain good non-manual jobs out of school in the post-war decades, these jobs often lacked opportunities for advancement.[80] Barbara (b.1941) attended a central school and left at sixteen with a qualification in shorthand typing.[81] She started as a junior shorthand typist in the bursar's office at the university in her hometown. She was pleased that she was given specialist training in technology such as the 'Sumlock comptometer' and was moved into the accounts office. Barbara 'progressed' steadily within the accounts office and was promoted a number of times during the 1960s. She recalled that when she started she had thought she would just 'stick it out for a bit' but ended up deciding to make her career in university administration.[82] Ann (b.1939) left her grammar school at the age of fifteen, against the wishes of her father, who wanted her to stay on to at least gain her O-Levels. In contrast, her mother wanted Ann to work with her on the floor of the local sweet factory. Ann was not sure what to do and took a job in the office of the factory as a compromise and learned shorthand typing. At nineteen years of age, she went into hospital to have her appendix out and during this time realized what work she wanted to do:

> I decided I liked the hospital life. Then I went on my first holiday abroad with my friend to Italy, I enjoyed that. She left the office then, and she went to work with the hospital board. And I said I fancy working at the Northern General Hospital so she said: 'See what there is.' I went home, got *The Star* and there was this job as a medical secretary. I applied and got the job and stayed there for thirty-seven years. I liked it. It was me.[83]

Ann was given the responsibility of being the secretary to one of the top consultants soon after she started. She got on well with him and liked the fact that he tried to 'teach me things' and 'took me on ward rounds and to meet the heads of departments'.[84] This elevated the job above the routine and encouraged her to want to stay working for the hospital. Kathy, who started in further education administration a little later, in the early 1970s, also served a long tenure in her first position and was promoted within it rather than moving between jobs.[85] Women were inclined to stay put in white-collar welfare state jobs longer than in ostensibly similar roles in the private sector.

Working for the welfare state in white-collar roles could expand women's horizons. After rejecting the advice to become a teacher, Lois decided to apply to become a trainee shorthand typist in local government in the early 1960s.[86] Lois started in the public health offices but within a year had an interview to move to the arts department for a promotion to admin assistant. Working in the arts department engendered a lifelong passion in Lois: 'That interview was the beginning of it all,' she said. The department administered local art galleries and museums and her boss during the 1960s was a well-known curator who 'encouraged' Lois's interest in the arts.[87] Dawn went straight from school to a position in Sheffield central library which was run by the local authority. She explained that she had 'struck gold' with this role and quickly realized she wanted to become a librarian.[88] Dawn had been ready to leave school at sixteen but had always enjoyed reading and learning. The library offered her an opportunity to use and develop these skills. Bridget (b.1951) only spent a year working in the public library as an assistant after leaving grammar school in 1967. She had 'lost interest' in education and performed poorly in her O-Levels.[89] However, having access to the library resources 'inspired' Bridget to return to college and retake her exams.[90] Similarly, Kuhn wrote about the months she spent after leaving school as 'an assistant in an inner-city central public library', which she described as the start of her 'true education'.[91] She found this role very rewarding: '[A] storehouse of learning lay at my disposal; and during long commutes and between split shifts, I embarked on a programme of reading ... I happened upon books that fed my intellect and fired my imagination in entirely new ways.'[92] Kuhn was particularly influenced by Hoggart's *Uses of Literacy*. It was the first text she had read on social mobility and she explained how revelatory it was to discover that others shared her experience of 'belonging nowhere' even if it did not reflect the gendered nature of her experience.[93]

A new class of auxiliary jobs became available to female school-leavers, primarily in the health service, created as part of state expansion. However, the social status of these roles was ambiguous and their training requirements were in flux for much of the post-war period.[94] Joy started out after grammar school in a private sector clerical role before beginning to train as a dental nurse in the late 1950s.[95] She 'really enjoyed dental nursing' but 'gradually started going to art classes in the evenings'. The art teachers encouraged her to go to college, telling her, 'You're really talented.'[96] When a new requirement was brought in the early 1960s for dental nurses to sit an exam, Joy made the choice to apply for a foundation year at art college instead. This dilemma between a welfare role and studying art is illustrative of the generational nature of her experience. Maureen started on-the-job training for a role testing samples in a blood transfusion centre at the age of sixteen but moved into clerical work not long after.[97] She was starting to think about having children and explained that she had generally 'had enough' of education at that point in her life.[98] Angie and Wendy (b.1951), who both left school before sitting their O-Levels, began but did not complete training to become a pharmacist and dental nurse, respectively.[99] They both cited difficulties balancing the roles with familial responsibilities. Young women moved in and out of the newer public sector jobs during this period because the on-the-job training requirements and lack of flexibility could conflict with other priorities at this stage in the life cycle.

The supply of service jobs and the safety net of the welfare state allowed the space for an emerging trend of working-class women spending time travelling, either abroad or within Britain. Chrissie (b.1950) was one of the few interviewees who had attended a secondary modern school. She explained that, by the age of sixteen, she had started going out dancing most nights with her friends and was 'not doing very well' in school.[100] Chrissie decided to leave and took a clerical position in an office. She changed roles only a few months later when the opportunity arose for her to become a library assistant in the central library service. She described 'always wanting' to work in a library and 'really liking it'.[101] However, Chrissie also felt that a shortcoming of the clear promotional structure ('library assistant to senior library assistant to librarian') was that the library service was 'very hierarchical'. By the late 1960s she had become restless and spent the little money she had saved on a one-way ticket to Belgium, where she stayed for several months. While there she was employed as an au pair and a cleaner. Eileen had a similar trajectory, although she chose Switzerland instead of Belgium. Neither struggled to find work when they returned home – as Eileen stated, 'you could come back and walk into a job, there was none of this terrible thing where there aren't enough jobs'.[102] Another working-class interviewee, Rita, was prompted to leave her hometown to go travelling around the UK with two female friends after a huge row with her parents caused her to be thrown out of the family home at seventeen years of age.[103] She had upset her parents by leaving the clerical job she had started after leaving grammar school. Her mother had been pleased that she was working in an office and, unlike her older sister, Rita was taken specially to open a bank account as a kind of symbol of this social mobility. Rita stated that she felt able to leave her job and go travelling because 'I believed I wouldn't be in the gutter. That I wouldn't starve. That I wouldn't be homeless ... I think in a way [the welfare state] gave me more of a feeling of entitlement to take risks'.[104]

Continuing into education

During the late 1950s and 1960s, universities were highly gendered environments. At both Oxford and Cambridge, female students were only eligible to attend the handful of women's colleges until the 1970s. Dyhouse has emphasized that more rules governed women's behaviour, particularly with regard to sexuality, than at men's colleges.[105] Frances matriculated to a woman's college at Oxford in the late 1950s. She enjoyed her time there but did feel as though it was hard for female students because 'if you got pregnant you had to pack it in straight away; this only applied to girls'.[106] She was not able to access contraception until she became engaged to her long-term boyfriend in the final year of her degree. Diane (b.1946), who hailed from a middle-class family in Slough, explained that the situation improved for female students while she was studying for her degree in history at Oxford in the mid-1960s because of the increased availability of the pill. However, Diane felt restricted in other ways – for example, although she liked her college, she stated that if she had 'had the choice to go to Merton or Balliol, [she] might well have done', especially Balliol as it 'was the intellectual, left-wing college of the era'.[107] She was also frustrated that the history course was 'so narrow' and included 'no women's history' on the curriculum at all.[108] Celia Hughes has argued that it was not only the older elite universities which constituted a 'gendered landscape' but also the supposedly more progressive 'new universities' of the 1960s.[109] India's experience at the University of Warwick supports Hughes's arguments. She was the only university attendee in my sample to note that her most influential tutor was a woman – the lecturer Germaine Greer, who was later to write the seminal feminist text *The Female Eunuch.* Yet Greer led classes on male authors in the canon rather than on woman writers, and she was one of only two female lecturers that India could recall in the whole department.[110] Throughout the 1960s there was a seven-to-one ratio of male to female lecturers working in English universities.[111] Moreover, when India became pregnant to her boyfriend – 'a brilliant loser' – when they were both in the final year of their degree, his needs were prioritized over her own.[112] Medical professionals and the university put significant pressure on her to have an abortion because 'it would ruin his life having to have the responsibility of being a father at this stage'.[113]

As well as gender, social class inflected the university experience of working-class women and women on the cusp of the working and middle classes, as it had at grammar school. Penny (b.1948) was from a lower middle-class background and she noticed a class divide at her Oxford women's college. She described a group of women 'who were the upper echelons of society ... they didn't enter our orbit'.[114] Steedman did not write much about her time at the University of Sussex in the mid-1960s because her autobiography focused primarily on her childhood. She did note that, as a working-class grammar school girl, she felt like an exception: '[T]here were no other women to talk to like this, at least there were none that I met'.[115] Heron only dedicated a few sentences to her life after school, but she used these to describe her feelings of not fitting in at university, especially with the 'socially confident middle class who did less work but had better cultural camouflage to disguise their deficiencies'.[116] Diane Reay recalled finding university 'even more alienating than school … I was both the only female and the only student from a working-class background on the course'.[117] This alienation had concrete effects on her academic performance. She came top of her cohort in the first-year examinations but struggled with mental health issues and 'left university with a second-class degree and a strong sense of being bruised and battered by the whole experience'.[118]

In certain instances, working-class or lower middle-class women who made it to university decided once there that the potential future gains were not enough to justify further feelings of dislocation. Kathy, from a working-class family, performed well in her A-Levels and was encouraged to apply for a language degree by a young teacher at her grammar school. Her parents lived in Essex and she chose to take up a place at a local institution so that she could stay living at home. However, Kathy 'absolutely hated' the course and 'dropped out after the first term'.[119] She explained that she had never expected to go to university and that she felt her decision to go had 'a bit of guilt hanging over it' because she was constantly worrying her parents 'couldn't really afford it'.[120] This feeling of guilt was compounded by the fact that Kathy 'wasn't sure what [she] wanted to do' with the degree.[121] It is notable in light of the above discussion that after leaving she started a 'kind of fast track promotion scheme' with the Greater London Council, during which she had the chance to work for a variety of departments, including 'architects, housing and information'.[122] Likewise, Sadie (b.1943), who had a complicated mixed-class background, did not complete the general degree that she started at in Leicester. She became 'really depressed' during her first year and built up some debt.[123] She found it very difficult to study and this led to her failing some of her end-of-year exams. Sadie was keen to impress her father, and this had been one of her main motivations to go to university. Her father came to 'bail [her] out' and 'take [her] home' when she decided to leave the course instead of resit her exams.[124] Afterwards, Sadie pursued a teaching career, first working in a local authority primary school and then going on to teacher training college. She stated that she particularly wanted to work with children 'from poorer backgrounds' because she felt that she could 'relate' to their experience and help them negotiate education.[125] Their experience shows both the continued difficulties that women who were not fully middle class faced within educational institutions and the non-linear nature of many women's trajectories.

A far more common experience for women of this generation, especially for working-class women, was to attend a training college which prepared them for a semi-professional role in the welfare state. Jean retained the ambivalence about becoming a nurse that she had felt while at school:

> There was a high status to nurses in the sixties, as there was to teachers, within the population. People looked up to you when you were a nurse. But it was largely pretty boring routine, an awful lot of cleaning. I can remember going to a party and meeting this lad who was at university and thinking 'gosh, I wish I was at university' because it sounded so much better than what I was doing. It was hard work for little reward.[126]

Training colleges were widely held to be strict institutions offering a tough introduction to the world of work for their largely female student bodies. This was starting to change in the 1960s. Foster and Dale highlighted a shortage in nurses by the mid-1960s, due in part to the overweening influence of an older generation of matrons, who favoured a 'disciplinary regime'.[127] The Salmon Report of 1966 recommended that the management of nurses in the NHS become more diffuse rather than unitary control under the matrons.[128] The implementation of these recommendations occurred while Jean was undertaking training in the late 1960s. Jean noted that 'about a year into' training, 'we had complete freedom … things definitely changed'.[129] Sandra, who attended nursing college a few years prior to Jean, emphasized how much power the matrons had over the trainees.[130] Carol benefitted from the 1967 Plowden Report on primary education, which was concluded while she was at teacher training college. The report recommended more variety in the ways that children were taught and that teachers should have more autonomy to experiment.[131] Carol found her teaching placements tough as, unlike many graduate teachers, trainees at teaching colleges were sent to inner-city schools with large class sizes and lack of resources. Carol enjoyed the opportunity the placements gave her to exercise creative teaching methods such as using visual and aural aids. She noted that her more adventurous style 'went down quite well with the school' and led her to think 'right, I can be a bit off the wall'.[132] These shifts towards more autonomy in the practice of semi-professions were an early indication of changes that would attract more women of the welfare state generation to train in these roles during the 1970s.

The post-war period was a time of expansion in the arts with subsidies being invested in both arts premises and arts colleges as part of what was termed by the politician Roy Jenkins in 1959 as 'a modern, civilising cultural agenda'.[133] The creative impulse was evident in my interviews, with many women expressing a passion for art and a hope of developing this at art school. Yet this ambition was thwarted for more women in my sample than achieved. More men were able to participate in this creative cultural moment than women.[134] Carol wanted to go to art school but poor A-Level results and a lack of support from her school and her parents meant that her only choice was to go to teacher training college with a specialism in art. She struggled at training college and became entangled in a difficult relationship with a fellow student, describing herself as 'his possession'.[135] Carol contrasted the difficulties in her personal life with the achievements in the art element of her course, which was helping to build her confidence: 'I was really taking off with my art, I did an anti-war theme and I got a distinction in my exhibition.' In the iconic cultural text of the period written by a woman and with a young working-class female protagonist, *A Taste of Honey*, her talent at drawing and the possibility of attending art school is presented as the means of having a different kind of life to her mother.[136] However, in *A Taste of Honey* Jo decides not to apply to art school and ends up having vicarious contact with this world through her relationship with a male art student. Her experience encapsulates the complications and retrenchments that characterize many female journeys of this generation.

While a number of women wanted to go to art school, only Rose (b.1945) and Sylvia entered immediately after finishing their secondary education. Initially, Sylvia felt overawed by the middle-class students at the prestigious institution. She explained that, in the first year, she 'stayed in one night a week to try and do things with my hair and learn how to wear a headscarf like [the middle-class girls]'.[137] As Sylvia progressed through the course, she started to feel more confident, as though art school was elevating her into an 'elite' and making her realize that she did not need to emulate middle-class students to be successful: 'That was the great thing about art school. It offered you a bohemian route into culture, which was actually not to do with money or status – it was a lifestyle. You prided yourself on being a part of this elite.'[138] Once she had finished art school, however, Sylvia found it hard to maintain her career as an artist because the pay was low and the work was intermittent. She worked as a waitress for a while to support her art but, by the end of the 1960s, she was teaching art in a further education college.[139] Sylvia enjoyed this job, and it paved the way for a successful career in higher education. Rose also came from a working-class background, and, although her parents were sceptical of her decision to pursue art, they did support her to take a Pre-Dip course after leaving her secondary modern school. She then moved to Brighton for a DipAd course and did so well that she obtained a place at the Slade in London.[140] Her artwork received considerable plaudits during this time and she described being 'treated as the great hope of British painting'.[141] However, just like Sylvia, as a working-class woman with no family money and 'few contacts' she struggled to continue with painting once she had left the Slade. Rose poetically referred to herself as 'like a hothouse plant left out in the frost'. She soon needed to take a role teaching at a college of art. It is striking that both Sylvia's and Rose's post-art school careers hewed so closely to the broader trends of women teaching within a public sector educational institution.

Female university graduates were no exception to these career trends. However, a class hierarchy persisted, with middle-class graduates from professional backgrounds more able to find their way into the higher welfare professions or higher status areas of the semi-professions.[142] In 1961–1962, 48.7 per cent of female graduates in arts and social sciences took up employment in education, compared to 19.9 per cent of men.[143] Penny, India and Lesley all made the decision to undertake postgraduate qualifications in education after periods of time spent travelling abroad after graduation.[144] The period of time spent travelling between education and work is reminiscent of the emerging trend among school-leavers. Entering teaching was not necessarily a first choice. Lesley wanted to study to become a lawyer but was worried about how much this would cost her parents.[145] Penny wanted to work for the British Council as an English Language Officer so that she could travel. When she went to a recruitment meeting at her university, she was told, 'We put a lot of time and money into the training and they just go and get married and leave, so we don't employ females' in that role.[146] Elizabeth went on from her chemistry degree to undertake a Master's in 'clinical immunology' and subsequently a PhD in the same area.[147] She did her research in a 'lab called the institute of chest disease', which was attached to a London hospital, and became part of a team doing 'pioneering work on occupational diseases' for the health service.[148] Susannah opted to go on from her degree to a postgraduate medical degree at the University of London because she had been inspired by her opportunities at Cambridge to do medical research.[149] Margaret Cook (b.1944), who came from a similar professional middle-class background to Elizabeth and Susannah, undertook an undergraduate medical degree at the University of Edinburgh in the 1960s.[150] She explained that she was motivated to become a doctor by her belief in social democracy:

> I had a young person's sense of fairness, I felt that accidents of birth or income should not determine one's role and fate in life, that the best health service and educational opportunities should be available to all and that it was the government's job to set the scene for this to happen.[151]

Working for the welfare state had been normalized in society as a career path for women and, as Cook's quotation demonstrates, the choice could be further encouraged by a belief in the values of expansive state welfare provision.

Only two of the graduate interviewees took a route into the private sector after finishing their degrees, and close family advice or existing contacts were central to these decisions. Clara (b.1939) chose to study law because her mother was trained as a barrister prior to marriage.[152] When Clara finished her degree and needed to be articled, her mother contacted 'somebody who [she] had been at university with, somebody else who had read law, and he was working in central London, in a big firm. She phoned him up saying, "Will you take my little girl?" and he said, "Yes I will."'.[153] Diane's career choice required a significant number of external interventions and adaptations. Diane initially wanted to enter the civil service at graduate level but narrowly failed the entrance exam. Unsure what else she wanted to do, she enrolled on an International Relations Master's course at the London School of Economics (LSE) but soon realized that the course was not right for her. Feeling lost, she sought career advice from the mother of her closest university friend, who encouraged her to think about going into business. The mother of her friend was a German–Jewish refugee who had come over to England in the 1930s, and she felt that not enough British women considered a business career compared to women in Germany.[154] Diane said that this seemed 'true for [her] generation' – she could not think of any of her university friends who entered business and stated that 'most' of them went into the 'public sector'.[155] She said that this made her feel a bit of an 'outsider' in her university friendship group when she chose to try for the private sector. The mother of her friend suggested that Diane enter personnel management, which is often considered the most feminine aspect of business because it involves the well-being of staff.[156] Diane switched to the personnel management course at LSE and was lucky to meet a high-ranking female academic, who became her mentor. She noted that 'one of the things about my career is that there has been a quite large number of women who have given me really important pieces of advice at crucial stages'.[157] When she finished the course in the late 1960s, Diane's mentor helped her find a job in a company that was 'willing to give me the same training as they would have given a man'.[158] She explained that a high proportion of companies would only employ women in management roles that oversaw female clerical workers in the office. Diane stated that this was only the first instance of 'overt discrimination' she experienced in her business career.

Marriage and paid work

Despite the expanded opportunities, across classes women of this generation continued to expect that they would get married, and many did so in their early twenties. Marriage was an event they viewed as a natural part of growing up rather than a primary life goal. High rates of marriage at an earlier average age represented the new 'normality' constructed in British society in the wake of the Second World War.[159] Most of the women who married said that they had met their husbands by chance when out with friends or at work. Women who continued onto higher education also encountered their husbands in that environment. They tended to cite emotional rather than economic reasons for marrying. For instance, Maureen met her future husband at a dance hall when she was nineteen years old. She was excited when he asked her for a dance because she had 'liked the look of him' from 'afar', and their instant attraction meant that they carried on dancing together long after the customary three songs.[160] Their relationship grew from there and they married two years later in 1966. He came from a similar working-class background to Maureen and worked as a fitter at English Steel. Barbara also met her husband in her late teens and was married by the time she was twenty years old. He worked as a porter at the institution where she was employed in administration. Barbara explained that they decided to get married even though 'neither of us had any money'.[161] This chimes with Claire Langhamer's recent contention that there was an 'emotional revolution' in mid-century Britain, which saw love become 'an increasingly dominant requirement within spousal selection'.[162] Langhamer pointed to the 'backdrop of affluence and welfare state security' as central to the shifting 'balance between love and pragmatism'.[163]

Throughout the post-war decades, sociologists assumed – though not much detailed work was undertaken on the question – that marriage was the dominant mechanism for female social mobility and that women chose a partner with this aim in mind. In 1952, Ferdinand Zweig claimed that 'young girls expect or hope that they will be able to cross the borderline of their class by marriage' and that 'marriage, not work or study, is the main door of escape from class membership'.[164] This presumption informed many male sociologists' decisions not to consider women's mobility outside marriage until at least the 1970s. However, during this period, it was not common for women to achieve social mobility through marriage as most women married men of the same social class.[165] The Population Investigation Committee Marriage Survey of 1959–60 found that 48 per cent of marriages were between partners from manual occupational backgrounds. In a further 21 per cent, both partners came from a non-manual background.[166] This is reflected in my sample, with the majority of women marrying men of the same or very similar class backgrounds. For example, Sylvia met her husband at art school, yet they were from the same manual working-class background. Sylvia felt that her relationship with a fellow working-class student helped her negotiate the difficulties of being in such a middle-class environment.[167] Even in the few cases where there was a difference in class background, Zweig's assumption that women 'hope[d] or expect[ed]' to achieve upward mobility through marriage proves unhelpful. Joy, herself from a manual working-class family, married a man who was 'a bit more up the social scale than we were' as his father worked at a record company.[168] They met because his parents bought a house on the same street as her family home. He was studying chemistry at Brunel University when his parents moved in. Her future husband began dating another student at Joy's art college, but they started a relationship after she showed him the portrait she had done of him and he exclaimed, 'Oh that's much better than hers!'[169] They married a year or so later in 1963. Joy explained that, both in her work and love life, she was 'just winging it … I was never into planning my future. I didn't even specifically want to get married'.[170] There was limited opportunity to meet a partner of a higher social class. Yet it is also evident that women of the welfare state generation did not largely aim to achieve upward social mobility through marriage and did not seek a partner with this objective in mind.

It is important to note that some women felt compelled to marry for practical reasons. This was especially true for young women with children. Anita (b.1952) came from what she described as 'a first-generation lower middle-class' family.[171] In the final year of sixth form she secured a sought-after place at Bristol Art School, conditional on her achieving a good grade in art A-Level. However, she unexpectedly became pregnant by a 'bright, working-class' student headed to university. After finding out that she was pregnant, her parents 'threw' her out of the family home. The school let her partner continue as normal but insisted that if she wanted to sit her exams they had to get married. The pair married in 1969 so that she could complete her art A-Level, but the school would only let her 'in the areas she needed to access to finish'.[172] As Pat Thane and Tanya Evans have stated, post-war social studies 'demonstrated clearly that the 1960s did not look "permissive" to unmarried mothers in provincial towns who experienced as much stigma, shame and exclusion as their predecessors in earlier decades'.[173] Despite these difficulties, Anita managed to gain a prize for her final project and achieved the highest art A-Level mark in the county. Unfortunately, she was unable to take up her art school place because the state still did not provide universal childcare and she could not get a grant to cover the costs for her young child.[174]

The social security system made it very difficult for women to access certain aspects of state support outside the role of wife during the late 1950s and 1960s. Angie also became pregnant during her time at grammar school. She was fifteen years old and fell 'madly in lust' with a 'beautiful coal miner that all the girls were nuts about'.[175] When Angie found out she was pregnant over the summer holidays, she made the decision not to return to school and to get married instead: 'We thought we were in love and were going to be together forever.'[176] The relationship quickly soured and things only worsened between them when she became pregnant for a second time just a couple of years later. Her husband finally decided to leave her for his mistress while she was in hospital giving birth to their daughter. As a single mother with two young children, Angie had to give up the pharmacist training she had begun at age fifteen to look after them and struggled for money especially because

> [h]e refused to pay maintenance, even though he was supposed to, initially through divorce proceedings and then by court order … [A]nd because I had a maintenance order I wasn't entitled to any kind of benefits and social services were going to take my children into care because I said 'well I can't feed them'.[177]

These difficulties led Angie to remarry with a man she did not feel passionate about but thought that he would be a good provider for her children. Eileen married at twenty-one but said that after only a few weeks she knew the marriage had been a mistake. She described the relationship as 'mentally and physically abusive'.[178] Eileen did not have a child with this husband but the breadwinner model of state welfare limited her ability to get support when her husband used financial abuse as a way to control her. He would not let her find work but he also barely gave her enough money to buy food. These experiences demonstrate the ways in which the gender norms inherent in the structures of the welfare state continued to negatively impact women.

Although the majority of women born between the late 1930s and 1950s planned on marrying, they did not intend to give up paid work. The question, 'Did you give up work when you got married?', frequently provoked the emphatic response: 'No, that was my mother's generation.'[179] Only one woman in my sample did so: Frances. She married her university boyfriend the year they graduated from Oxford. Frances explained that they made a pact that he would forge his career first while she looked after the children and then when she turned thirty it would be her chance.[180] Notably, this decision arose in part because of her husband's class anxiety; he hailed from a working-class background, while she was middle class, and the unusual nature of this pairing made him want to ensure he had established himself. During the interwar period, women, particularly middle-class women, largely gave up work on marriage.[181] In 1931, only 10 per cent of married women were in paid work.[182] In some instances, this was a choice but, in certain occupations, including most public sector and clerical jobs, a marriage bar was in place, preventing women from continuing to work.[183] Patterns of married women's work were changing in the late 1940s and 1950s, and, by 1971, 49 per cent of married women went out to work. The emergence of new patterns of work and the lifting of the marriage bar in the public sector as a result of the increased requirement for welfare state workers in the wake of the Second World War made it increasingly possible for women to stay on at least until they had children.

Women outlined how memories of their mother's experience within marriage made them want to keep working, although the ways in which this influenced them depended on social class. Working-class women had often witnessed their mother return to employment once the children were in school.[184] For example, during much of Kathy's childhood, her mother was a housewife, but 'she hated it, being a housewife didn't really suit her at all. She was agoraphobic and depressed'.[185] Kathy said that her mother seemed 'much better, certainly' after making the decision to return to work part time in an accounts office when her younger brother started secondary school.[186] However, Kathy explained that she was influenced by her mother's earlier unhappiness: 'I thought "I don't really want that"'.[187] Jean's mother was a housewife during the early part of her childhood but went back to work as a part-time clerk once Jean started school in the mid-1950s. She stated that this helped alleviate her mother's intense feelings of 'loneliness'.[188] Her mother was required to give up work again only a couple of years later because Jean's paternal grandmother fell ill and moved into the family home. When her mother was not working, Jean found herself in a difficult go-between position in a way that her two elder brothers did not. She was asked by her mother to persuade her father to buy things that she needed because he 'was as mean as milk' to his wife but 'adored' his daughter, and she 'adored him'.[189] This experience influenced Jean's self-perception: she remembered thinking 'I can never do that! But what choice did my mum have?'[190] There are echoes here of the grammar school girl relating to the father and feeling in a privileged position compared to their mother. Paid work was an important way to retain the perceived elevated status.

In contrast, middle-class women were more likely to have witnessed their mothers occupy the role of housewives throughout their childhood. Women discussed this in terms of their mothers having skills that were being wasted and being determined not to repeat the pattern. Susannah's mother went to university and worked in a pathology laboratory prior to getting married. Susannah remembered that she thought that it was a 'waste' that her mother was now a housewife: 'She was clearly bright and had got a gold medal in medical school ... as a teenager I was particularly critical of the idea that she could not want to use all that education and ability.'[191] Similarly, Lesley recalled the influence on her career decisions of her mother's regret about not being able to make more use of her university education. She described a particularly vivid memory of the 'sad day' her mother dramatically decided to 'throw her book on Moliere into the bin ... saying to my father "what use is it to me now?" She craved intellectual stimulation.'[192] In 1957, Judith Hubback produced a study of married women with a university education, such as Lesley's and Susannah's mothers, in which she argued that, 'many find their minds are not fully engaged, not fully stretched.'[193] Hubback implored the government to introduce more part-time and flexible roles for women in the professions and semi-professions such as social work, nursing and medicine.[194] She presciently recognized that younger women would want to combine marriage and motherhood with professional occupations and that the state could play a key role in making this possible.

Conclusion

Examining the choices made by women born between the late 1930s and early 1950s as they left compulsory education has shown that the welfare state is a useful meta-framework to understand their lives beyond girlhood experience. The possibilities available to women, and the way that they experienced change in this moment of the life cycle, continued to be differentiated by both gender and social class. The welfare state semi-professions, primarily nursing and teaching, were presented to young women during school, and later by universities, as the most appropriate female occupations. Even if women did not go on to work in these professions, this encouragement normalized the idea that the best way for women, especially working-class women, to achieve a professional career was in gendered welfare occupations. In addition, there were burgeoning opportunities for women in administrative and support roles in the welfare state that were available without extensive qualifications. Including these jobs in the analysis allows us to fully understand the expansive impact of the welfare state on women's labour market opportunities. The 1950s and 1960s witnessed the creation of what Madeleine Arnot et al. have termed 'a feminised arm of the state', which I argue was to become fully entrenched over the course of the following decade.[195]

The increased economic and social security that the context of the welfare state provided had both tangible and unpredictable intangible effects on this generation's choices. Women found the expanded opportunities available to them simultaneously liberating and constraining, but they carved out small spaces for change in the cracks and dissonances between these conflicting experiences. Even if women still could not have everything they wanted, some aspects of the life that seemed mapped out for them could be refused. They felt more able than previous generations of women to consider their own desire for self-expression and to take more risks. This played out in a variety of ways and in different registers, including moving between jobs, marrying earlier, travelling and taking on creative endeavours.

The willingness to take more risks demonstrated by women of this generation has broader implications for public policy debate about the impact of welfare on citizens' actions. As a set of scholars led by Simon Szreter recently argued in the pages of *The Lancet*, historical research can challenge contemporary political rhetoric that suggests that state welfare leads to laziness and inertia among the general population.[196] They undertook a detailed analysis of welfare policy during the Industrial Revolution and found that the existence of a more advanced social safety net than in much of the rest of Europe was integral to Britain's social and economic dynamism. We need to conceptualize the expansive welfare state as not only offering practical possibilities, but also creating the conditions where experimentation can flourish.

The golden age of social mobility: Welfare expansion and adult education during the long 1970s

The long 1970s should be considered the 'golden age' of social mobility for women of the welfare state generation. The decade 1971–1981 was fundamental for women's social mobility as 'there was an increase in the numbers of women in higher socio-economic groups in Britain and a relative decline in their proportion in most of the lower socio-economic groups'.[1] Existing sociology contends that the 1950s and 1960s represented the 'golden age' of mobility, but this conclusion is largely premised on men's experiences. This chapter challenges the masculinized trope of attendance at grammar school followed directly by a university degree as the main instrument of social mobility in post-war Britain. The primary driver of women's mobility was the understudied second expansionary phase of the welfare state from the late 1960s onwards. This provided more opportunities for adult education and a diversified set of roles and hours in public sector employment. Women of the welfare state generation grasped the educational opportunities available, especially from the early 1970s and into the 1980s. These changes arose at a moment when women of this generation were re-evaluating what they wanted from life and what they thought was possible for them to achieve in their careers.

Historians have neglected the impact of the Wilson government's expansion of further education and creation of a new layer of public sector higher education in the mid-to-late 1960s – instead, a focus on the expansion of university for school-age students has predominated in historical study.[2] Carol Dyhouse has argued that the 1970s was a turning point for women's higher education participation from school as a result of 'changing expectations about the role of women in society, a widening of women's choice of subjects of study, and their anticipation of more favourable labour market opportunities'.[3] This chapter builds on Dyhouse's work, contending that these shifts were influential for women of the welfare state generation who made the decision to enter education as mature students. Returning to education led to many women achieving – albeit often short-range – occupational mobility into professional public sector jobs. Women who made use of the further education available and the new layer of the higher education system, achieving occupational mobility, largely moved upwards from National Statistics Socio-Economic Classification (NS-SEC) class 3 or 4 to NS-SEC class 2 – i.e. moving from routine non-manual occupations to lower professional occupations, such as from a clerical role to a nursing position.[4] Women's mobility was often short-range, between the middle classes of the NS-SEC occupational structure. While there may not have been 'room at the top' for women, there was 'room in the middle'. The short-range nature of women's mobility has contributed to the lack of research on women's social mobility – it is seen as less dramatic and worthy of study than the type of long-range 'scholarship boy' mobility or the model of the self-made man.[5]

It is no coincidence that a debate was ignited among British sociologists in the mid-1970s about how to define women's (especially married women's) social class – a debate not yet fully resolved. Conventionally, married women's class was assigned based on a head of household model in which the husband's occupation was considered sufficient to determine the class position of the whole family. Adult single women were barely even considered in this schema, framed as always potentially on the brink of marriage. It was also argued that neither married nor single women were highly attached to the labour market.[6] This model was vigorously defended in the 1970s and 1980s by sociologists such as John Goldthorpe and Clive Payne, even in the face of new research.[7] Anthony Heath and Nicky Britten contended that a new model for women's class positions was required in the wake of the educational and occupational expansion that occurred in Britain in the quarter of a century following the Second World War.[8] This chapter considers how women of the welfare state generation who experienced precisely this educational and occupational change defined their own social class.

Expanding educational opportunities

Unexpectedly and strikingly, in interview after interview, women stated that, although they left school with few qualifications and entered the labour market, they later made the decision to return to education. Once I began to understand the magnitude of this change, I found examples buried in collections of existing personal testimonies of women of the welfare state generation returning to education. The moment of returning to education and the subsequent life changes that followed represented a pivot point in many women's life stories. Yet historians have not explored this historically significant trend, in part because figures for further and higher education participation in the 1970s are not of very good quality and often exclude mature students.[9] It is also particularly difficult to access precise figures for the further education colleges or polytechnics that women were more likely to enter: these differing institutions were often subsumed under the broad umbrella of 'public sector institutions'.[10]

Fragments of quantitative data show the rise in older women in education, particularly in newer, less traditional institutions, during this period. Analysis of census data demonstrates that an increase took place in the numbers of women recorded as obtaining qualifications in the 1970s.[11] Between 1971 and 1981, the total number of the female population with post-compulsory qualifications increased by 50 per cent.[12] The census indicates that older women, particularly married women, gained more qualifications in this period. For example, the number of married women born between 1947 and 1951 to hold post-compulsory qualifications tripled in the decade from 1971 to 1981.[13] Sociologist of education A. H. Halsey stated:

> Women have gained on men but their advance has been disproportionately in the newer forms of higher education. It can be calculated that between 1970/71 and 1983/4 the number of women in full-time education rose by 34.8 per cent compared with 22 per cent for men. But the expansion of opportunities for women in higher education has been markedly in part-time studies where percentage growth over the same period was 354.6 for women and 47.9 for men.[14]

Research at the Polytechnic of North London conducted in the early to mid-1970s found a contemporaneous increase in mature students at their institution. A higher percentage of these students were working-class women than was the case in the wider student body.[15] By the later 1980s, feminist sociologists calculated that 'women accounted for 40 per cent of the [part-time] places in higher education, compared to 14 per cent in 1970/1. Of those women, 75 per cent were mature and over 25 years old'.[16]

During the 1960s, the two major political parties began to pay attention to the possible pent-up demand for education and training from women of non-schooling age. Women's policy groups were set up within both the Conservative and Labour parties, in part focusing on the specific issues surrounding women's (re-)entry to education. These groups have not received much historiographical attention. In their policy documents, both parties discussed women's participation in the job market over a much longer and more permanent time frame than was the case in equivalent documents in the immediate post-war period, which often presumed that female workers would complete only a short stint in the labour market.[17] The change in women's life cycle to a dual role and the continued expansion of the welfare state during the 1960s and into the mid-1970s meant that more attention had to be paid to educating and training older women. In 1962, the Conservative Party set up a 'Women's Policy Group', which produced reports on women's lives throughout the decade. One of these reports, in 1963, stated that 'many women today are interested in further education … [it is] important that facilities should continue to expand to satisfy this growing demand, [and] there is a need for schools, hospitals and industry' to provide more training and part-time work.[18] They reiterated this point more forcefully in a 1968 report from the Women's National Advisory Committee, arguing that 're-training older women, returning to work after some years of marriage' should be a priority for the party and that 'far too little is being done in this field, and more encouragement should be given'.[19] The Conservative Party framed this primarily in terms reminiscent of nineteenth-century campaigners for women's education, referencing the positive impact of female education on 'family' and 'nation'.[20] They also argued for encouraging 'married women' to return to teaching on the basis that they have 'a natural understanding of young people'.[21]

In 1968, the Labour Party followed suit, setting up a working group of their own to analyse women's position in society. Notably, the Labour Party was slower to set up a group dedicated to women's policy than the Conservative Party. This was a significant shift for the Labour Party – at least until 1966 they had largely neglected to create policy or rhetoric specifically directed at women.[22] Their reports in the late 1960s demonstrate that the Labour Party working group became much bolder than the Conservatives in articulating that women faced 'discrimination' in their efforts to return to education and training. They outlined the long association of post-secondary 'training' in British culture with industrial and technical apprenticeships (and day release) for men.[23] In a comprehensive report compiled in the early 1970s, the group emphasized:

> Women, especially women over twenty-one, have to rely on their own efforts. They do. Women are at least as willing, if not more willing, than men to use facilities of further and adult education as both the DES statistics and the evidence (which included evening institutes) of the National Institute of Adult Education to the Russell committee shows.[24]

The Labour Party group expressed a similar view to the Conservatives on a 'potential supply of female trainees' that could be a boost to the economy. They used the data from the survey of women's employment to show that 'over one-fifth of women and one-third of non-working women who would consider returning to work expressed a willingness to undertake some form of training, the majority for non-manual occupations. Three-fifths of potential trainees were aged 30 or over and half had children'.[25] However, they argued that more needed to be done to make it possible for women to return.

The overhaul that had long been required to make it possible for women to return to education as adults began to occur in the late 1960s and early 1970s. This was a time of experimentation in post-compulsory education. The educational expectations of the public had been rising since the end of the Second World War, with increasing demands for more further and higher education provision.[26] Employers also required more skilled workers. A quick expansion took place in places at and funding for further education colleges.[27] Fostering a rapid expansion of the university sector proved more difficult as universities had a liminal rather than direct relationship to the state.[28] Alongside expanding university places, the Labour government decided to create polytechnics – a new layer of higher education institutions assembled from existing technical, art and education colleges. The polytechnics were considered directly part of the 'public sector' and represented a key element of the Wilson government's intention to continue to pursue the welfare state agenda of the Attlee government.[29] These new institutions provided half of all places by the early 1970s.[30] Polytechnics could be situated in 'city centres near the target population, affording easier access by means of part-time study and sandwich courses'.[31] The Committee of Directors of Polytechnics stated that their remit was to have stronger links with the local area, as well as with business, industry and the professions, than other higher education institutions.[32] For example, Sheffield City Polytechnic had a central campus with connections to areas of the welfare state where women could train and work – notably two substantial teaching hospitals. This mattered because it meant that women could attend institutions nearby with relationships to their own local community and did not have to move or commute for higher education.

The Labour government set up the Open University (OU) in 1969, which was directly accountable to the Department of Education and Science. It was intended to be part of the 'developmental state', which aimed to revitalize the economy and provide opportunities for individual development.[33] Wilson placed one of the few women ministers – Jennie Lee – in charge of its implementation.

Although there was no entry requirements to its programmes, Lee was insistent from the beginning that this did not mean a lowering of standards: 'I am not interested in having the next best thing, a poor man's university of the air, which is the sort of thing one gets if nothing else is within reach.'[34] From the beginning, the OU had a mission to provide long-distance, often part-time, degree courses. If a whole degree course was too onerous, it was possible to take individual modules, a route which one lone mother in my sample decided to take.[35] The OU also brought students to the campus for short residential stays so that they could get to know the lecturers and focus on studying. Women mature students particularly appreciated this model: their percentage of the OU student body increased throughout the 1970s, and women 'achieved higher grades than men' once there.[36]

Worries about gaining places on further education or polytechnic courses were not routinely expressed. Rita stated that, when she entered further education in the 1970s, 'there were no fees to pay and no bar to entrance, it was a choice open to me almost without conditions'.[37] She mentioned that the institutions were often more flexible with her because they recognized that she was 'bright'.[38] The further education college let her sit her A-Levels in one year instead of two, she was allowed to join her degree course at a London polytechnic at the last minute, and, although she dropped out of the course, the Royal College of Art funded her to do an MA on the basis of her portfolio. Only Joy (b.1939) mentioned that she did not get straight onto a degree course at her polytechnic – she was asked to defer for a year in the early 1980s.[39] Maureen chose to take A-Levels through a correspondence course before starting her degree to boost her confidence in academic work. Places could be offered to mature students without A-Level qualifications, which was significant for women of the welfare state generation.[40] Entrance requirements could include an essay, interview or portfolio. Expanded further education colleges and polytechnics functioned in the 1970s as a second-chance safety net for women, meaning that, if they wanted to, women could return without being made to feel deviant for having left secondary school prior to or near the age of fifteen.

The material changes that made the cost of education more affordable really mattered to women's decisions to return to education. During the 1970s, course fees and living grants were paid for by the local authority. One Mass Observer, Hannah, born in the early 1950s, described this period as the 'good old days' because 'as a mature student I was entitled to a reasonable grant from my local education authority'.[41] Maureen (b.1944) explained that her living grant contributed to her household income and allowed her young family to retain a decent standard of living while she trained as a teacher.[42] Lois (b.1947) was encouraged by the local government department where she worked in the early 1970s to undertake a part-time degree to help with her promotion chances.[43] As a single working-class woman, Lois needed financial support to embark on her OU degree. She explained that 'the city council paid everything, all my costs, all the tuition fees, my set book costs, my fee for the summer schools. I was working but it would've been a very heavy strain on my resources to pay for it'.[44] It was harder for lone mothers such as Anita, who struggled financially without a full-time income when she returned to further education in 1979. However, it helped Anita that her son was then of school age, so she did not need to pay for full-time childcare. Women of this generation often contrasted their financial position while studying to that of students today, stating that they would not have gone back into further education if the cost was as high to attend as it is in the twenty-first century.[45]

Welfare roles

These shifts in education policy were a key aspect of the second expansionary era of the welfare state during the 1960s and early 1970s, which increased the need for trained state workers. Institutions such as schools, universities and hospitals benefitted from a significant rise in capital spending by the Labour government.[46] A report on patterns of UK public sector employment in 1980 showed that there was unprecedented growth in the sector during the 1960s and 1970s: '[A]fter 1966 public employment rose by 1.8 million in a decade, taking 30.5 per cent of the labour force in 1976 … as a percentage of persons in work it increased by 7.8 per cent.'[47] Moreover, the report showed that the percentage of women in the public sector workforce increased from 24 per cent in 1951 to 44 per cent in 1976, 'reflect[ing] decline in male-dominated nationalised industries and the growth in education and health, which employ over twice as many women as men'.[48] Notably, the majority of the jobs added in the public sector were part time. In local government (which included education and social services for much of this period), the number of female part-timers increased from 210,000 to 920,000 between 1952 and 1978.[49] This meant that more professional jobs that could be combined with familial responsibilities were available to women. In their research into women's employment in the late 1970s and early 1980s, Veronica Beechey and Tessa Perkins found that part-time roles in the public sector tended to be considered less prestigious.[50] Lesley's (b.1950) experience as a part-time teacher reflected this: 'I didn't like working part time because as a teacher your status as part time is not the same as full time whatever they say ... people are always saying "oh are you still here?" – as if your displays, and your marking, preparation, etc., will be done by magic because you're part time.'[51]

Women returning to gain qualifications in the 1970s continued to be concentrated in the subject groupings associated with the welfare state professions of health, education and social work. In the 1971 census, 381,000 women were studying under subjects classified as 'education', compared to only 140,000 men, and the picture was similar with 'health' subjects – 483,000 women to only 152,000 men.[52] By 1981, the comparable figures are 548,000 women to 212,000 men studying education subjects, and 631,000 women to 195,000 men for health.[53] As well as the gender comparison, however, the number of women in these subjects compared to others is also pertinent. Aside from health and education, in 1971 women only outstripped men in language studies (which included English) and music and visual arts courses. These comparisons held largely steady by 1981, but the biggest increase took place in the numbers of women studying subjects classified as social studies – these figures almost tripled.[54] Social studies disciplines included economics, psychology and sociology. Sociology and psychology were especially popular among my interviewees. Those who chose these social science subjects typically suggested that they offered a good balance between knowledge for its own sake and practical usage. Anita (b.1952) said that she had chosen 'applied social studies' as her degree because it allowed her to do social work placements and to learn more about 'society and community development'.[55]

A contradiction existed in the post-compulsory education reforms between the broad policy aim to 'expand educational opportunities' and the failure 'to pay any serious attention to the issue of gender inequalities in education'.[56] Feminist activists shone a spotlight on gendered inequality in education throughout the decade, campaigning for change.[57] The types of courses women attended during the 1970s began to expand but, throughout the decade, tiny numbers of women held qualifications in science and technology subjects compared to men – a tenacious trend both contemporaries and historians have highlighted.[58] In an article for the feminist magazine *Spare Rib* Liz Heron praised the new 'woman returner courses' and the provision of crèches at numerous institutions.[59] However, she lamented that these did not receive enough funding from the government and worried that this meant that married middle-class women were more able to take up the returner courses. Courses considered 'masculine' in nature slowly opened up to more female students. Angie (b.1945) recalled

A nurse is a girl like you.

"I soon got bored in an office job, doing the same things day in, day out from nine till five."

Like hundreds of other girls, Sue Murray wanted a more interesting working life. Now, training to become an SRN at St. George's Hospital, London, she's working in an atmosphere she really enjoys.

Constantly meeting new people, doing different things all the time.

And although it's often hard work, she has the reward of four weeks' holiday a year to relax in – five in her third year.

Plus the satisfaction that always comes with a really worthwhile job.

Nurses are girls like Sue Murray. Is nursing the job for a girl like you?

You can start training at 18 or over ($17\frac{1}{2}$ in Scotland).

Please tell me more about Nursing

To : The Chief Nursing Officer,
Department of Health and Social Security,
P.O. Box 177, MITCHAM, Surrey, CR4 3TN.
(In Scotland, write to : The Chief Nursing Officer,
St. Andrew's House, Edinburgh EH1 3DE.)

Name
(Miss or Mrs.)

Address

Age

GN/NI/GT/?

Move up to Nursing now. You'll get more out of life.

Figure 4.1 Magazine advertisement for recruitment of women into nursing from the Chief Nursing Officer, 1971. © Alamy images.

arguing with Ruskin, a trade union college, about wanting to take the course 'Labour Studies'. Tutors were initially reluctant because she would have been the first woman to study that subject at Ruskin.[60] By the 1970s, the polytechnics and further education colleges arguably decided their niches more clearly within the educational structure. A rise took place in numbers of women tutors to reflect the growing numbers of female students in these institutions. A report produced by women tutors at the Department of Adult Education at the University of Southampton in the late 1970s argued that women were more likely to be in part-time roles and in the 'lower status' areas of the 'adult education hierarchy'.[61] The authors also found that 'whilst a significant majority of the students are female, the organisation and provision of classes take very little account of the social, economic and political condition of being female in our society'.[62] They advocated for more such courses which would have analysed *why* women were clustered in educational areas associated with 'caring' and 'welfare'.

Returning to take these welfare-related qualifications in the context of the expanding state labour market did produce upward social movement for women of this generation. Prior to undertaking a teacher training course at Sheffield Polytechnic, Cynthia had worked as a secretary. Afterwards, she became a primary schoolteacher, and by 1980 she had been promoted to the head of department. Anita was a struggling single mother working in a print shop and not sure what direction to take before deciding to train as a social worker in 1979. After a few years working as a social worker, she then took her expertise into community development to work with the local and national government on care strategies. She hailed from a middle-class background, and going back into education functioned to stop her downward mobility and restore her middle-class status. Another interviewee left her administrative job when she got married at twenty-two but undertook a part-time OU degree in social sciences alongside bringing up her small children.[63] On completion, she became a residential social worker for the NHS. The trend of returning to education stretched beyond the women themselves in the testimonies and often included examples that showed some of the scars of the differences created by the eleven-plus exam partially beginning to heal. While only Rita and her brother passed the eleven-plus (both leaving grammar school early), her two elder sisters failed the exam and left school at fifteen to work in the local biscuit factory.[64] All three of her siblings returned to some form of higher education, while her two sisters qualified as a midwife and a nursery nurse by the mid-1970s. Sylvia (b.1945) and her twin had been on different paths since their differing school experiences. While Sylvia had attended grammar school and then higher education, her twin sister went to a secondary modern and left school at fifteen without qualifications. She lived at home for a few years and worked as a secretary before deciding to return to study nursing. She then took an MSc in health studies, which led to a career as a health visitor.[65] Birth cohort studies have found that women born in 1946 with either sub-degree tertiary qualifications or degrees had higher occupational earning returns to these qualifications than women born in 1958. Women in the later cohort had a 'unique[ly]' low return to their qualifications in a more difficult labour market.[66]

Women of this generation were also able to use the diversified education system to gain a foothold in post-compulsory education, offering them a possible route to career mobility. During the 1970s, women were still a 'beleaguered minority' in older university posts.[67] Some of the women who studied as adults in further education or the polytechnics went on to teach in these institutions. Joy took on teaching at a further education college after completing her part-time teacher training degree, as did Chrissie. Rita took a lecturing position at a polytechnic. The academic Janet Parr recalled the difficulties of starting her degree in social policy and sociology as a 'mature woman' from a working-class background with 'a husband and three children to care for and a home to run'.[68] After she finished this degree, she went on to teach in further education, using this as an important stepping stone to entering a career in higher education.[69] Others also went on to work in the sector – for example, by the end of the 1980s, India and Jean taught in further education colleges, Marion taught evening classes and Sylvia worked in a polytechnic.[70] Both Bridget and Barbara (b.1941) progressed in administrative careers in these institutions. Expansion afforded more women the opportunity to have careers in education that was not confined to school teaching.

Women's decisions to go back into education did not necessarily represent a social mobility strategy. Making the choice to do so was often presented as contingent and incremental. Chrissie's (b.1950) trajectory exemplifies this sense of chance over planning.[71] After leaving her secondary modern at fifteen years of age with no qualifications, Chrissie spent a few years doing menial jobs, interspersed with working abroad for short periods. In her early twenties, she got married and took a clerical job. Chrissie found this job 'boring', however, and by her mid-twenties she had decided to leave to 'start an O-Level course at night school then A-Levels'. While studying she explained that her teacher recommended a social work course to her 'which sounded really interesting so I applied to go on it'.[72] Chrissie became a social worker but later gave it up when she had her first child. However, she was soon asked by a neighbour to volunteer for an adult literacy scheme. Involvement in this scheme led to Chrissie being invited to teach evening classes at the local adult education college. She then embarked on an OU degree, followed by a teacher training course 'at some point' during the early 1980s. In the telling of her life story, one decision is presented as leading to another. Joy's interview is another example of narration that de-emphasizes planning, with her choice to give up her retail job and start a part-time teacher training degree at Sheffield Polytechnic in 1980 described simply as 'I just thought – I'm going to go'.[73] With each step, she explained, 'I didn't have career goals, you just think about the next little bit each time.' Similarly, Parr said that a 'casual discussion with a graduate friend' led her to enrol in evening sociology classes. She was frustrated after giving up her clerical work to have children and, when she returned to education, she was 'looking for something in my life which wasn't there, but I wasn't sure what it was. I had certainly had no "grand plan" at this stage … my goals were fairly short term … I gave little, if any, thought to a future career'.[74] This kind of language is common in the ways in which women (especially socially mobile women) talk about work and training – slippage was apparent in phrases such as 'things just happen', 'got the opportunity' and 'someone mentioned it to me'. Rita noted that going back to education was not necessarily about career plans but instead about 'wanting something different than the life that seemed mapped out for you'.[75]

Choosing change

Given that gender and education were always entangled for post-war women, it is notable that the catalyst for many women re-entering education was motherhood. This marked a big shift from women of their mothers' generation, who went into routine manual or non-manual jobs if they needed to go back to work after having children. Women with children often chose to retrain as semi-professionals such as primary schoolteachers, nurses or social workers. Women who went back into teaching drew the connection most closely with motherhood. Cynthia (b.1941) had worked in a secretarial position since leaving grammar school at fifteen years of age. She had her first child with her husband in the early 1970s and had always thought she would permanently give up work once she became a mother.[76] However, she soon found that staying at home 'wasn't as fulfilling as it might have been because I decided that I wanted to go back to work!'[77] She chose to study primary school teaching because she felt that she could bring her knowledge of having small children to the position. Maureen also gave up her secretarial job when she had children and presumed that she would largely be finished with paid employment. However, her sense of self shifted, and she started to think, 'I could be a teacher': 'Having children changes you. I had no ambitions when I left to have babies, it was only when I got the two boys that I was ambitious because I had a sense of the future.'[78] Both her husband and the teachers at her children's school encouraged this ambition. Maureen noted that other mothers of children at the school also went back to train as primary schoolteachers. This was possible because of the removal of the marriage bar. While teaching had always been associated with 'caring', actual mothers were barred from the job in the interwar period.[79] Laura Tisdall found that post-war female teachers 'often utilised the idea that experiencing parenting made them a better teacher'.[80] In contrast to policy-makers, women frame understanding of children as a form of learned expertise rather than 'natural'.

Even though returning to education increased women's workload, they still described it as a break from childcare and the monotonies of domestic labour. One interviewee felt pleased that she had 'something else on [her] plate other than housework and the home'.[81] Chrissie recalled that the OU recommended that students needed to dedicate at least twelve hours a week of study to the degree course. She framed this time as an 'escape':

> It was hard work because we'd got three children and my husband was working, I was working. And then you know, having to do this timetable twelve hours, I needed even more than that. But it was great for me because I escaped for that period of time. Poor old Peter had to look after the kids while I had my twelve hours.[82]

Angie (b.1945) took this sentiment the furthest, however, choosing to move to Oxford in term-time for her degree at Ruskin College and leaving her two daughters at home with their stepfather in London. She was forced to leave grammar school at the age of fifteen before sitting any exams because she was pregnant. Although she later trained as a nurse, she always regretted missing out on the intellectual stimulation of university. When her trade union sponsored her to go to university, she therefore wanted to make the most of it. She stated: 'I was challenged and invigorated at Ruskin, it was wonderful after eighteen years as a mum and a housewife to be able to say, "nobody come through" and not to be constantly asked, "Where's my socks?"'[83]

Despite men's vocalization of encouragement of their partners' ambitions in education and work, this did not necessarily translate into husbands taking on an equal share of domestic labour or childcare. Cynthia explained that her husband supported her return to study but only if it did not cause too much disruption to the family routine, and a relative was available to look after the children while she was in classes. In this case Cynthia's mother stepped in to help with the childcare. Maureen recalled doing her initial A-Level course through correspondence so that she could continue to look after the children. She 'used to work when the children were asleep'.[84] When she later started her teaching training degree, she would 'take the children in with me with an airfix model' in the school holidays.[85] Many marital relationships continued to operate under normative gender regimes even though things were slowly changing in the 1970s.[86] When Jean's husband went back to study in the 1970s, she was expected to work full time to support the family economically and also to continue to do all the housework and be responsible for childcare arrangements. She 'felt like a single mum' during that time.[87] This speaks to the fundamental importance for women of new institutions situated in local communities and offering part-time (or even correspondence) courses. These changes to education became feasible at a time when women were largely expected to negotiate their life choices around the needs of their husband and children.

The post-war decades were a time of early marriage. By the 1970s, though, some women of the welfare state generation were reconsidering their relationship status as their expectations changed. A rise in divorces took place during this decade, which was in part made possible by the 1969 divorce law reform.[88] As noted in the previous chapter, in her early twenties Eileen (b.1945) had been trapped in an abusive marriage.[89] Eileen managed to escape the relationship after two years but was unable to divorce her husband until this new law was introduced because he was making it exceptionally difficult for her. She explained that the new law allowed for a 'two-year separation or five-years if one party did not agree ... thank the lord for that or I might still be tied to him!'.[90] Another interviewee, Angie was particularly dissatisfied with her marriage prior to going away for her education, noting that 'it was ok, he was a kind man, but it wasn't turning me on'.[91] She continued that it was the 'golden age' of free education and that she knew afterwards she would be able to 'walk into a job'. Pursuing the degree gave her the confidence and the prospects to initiate divorce proceedings. Brenda explicitly used her return to education (at a polytechnic – she joked that the local university would not accept her recently obtained 'one A-Level at grade C!') as a mechanism to leave her husband in the early 1970s. She declared that, once she had secured a place, a grant and accommodation for herself and her children, 'at that point I left my husband'.[92] The changing education system provided space to women of this generation who wanted to leave their marriages but also provided opportunities to women such as Ruth and Lois, who decided that marriage was not right for them but came to need increased earning power. Lois recalled that, at the secondary modern, she was told that marriage was the main goal for women, 'but eventually I realised it was not going to happen for whatever reason, then you do think about [a career]'.[93]

As part of their schooling, women had been subject to contradictory discourses about girls' education. On the one hand, it was suggested to them that marriage should be their primary aim and that 'demonstrating intellect conflicted with being sexually attractive',[94] but an increase also took place in educational opportunities for girls as a result of the influential 1944 Education Act. Many young women found these contradictions hard to navigate and expressed regret about that time, although they often placed the blame on themselves rather than the context. Women emphasized that they felt that they gained more from education as mature students than they would have done if they had continued studying straight from school. Ruth (b.1949), who hailed from a working-class background, stated that 'it was better for me' to start an undergraduate degree in her mid-twenties because 'I had time to grow up'.[95] Those who described their childhood experience as on the cusp of working class and middle class outlined this feeling most intensely. They frequently compared their adult selves with their attitudes to learning as teenagers. Bridget (b.1951) recalled being at college as a teenager and 'wasting my time, took advantage of my mother honestly, [I] spent more time with my boyfriend, which was naughty'.[96] In contrast, when she returned to further education in the late 1970s, she described herself as much more focused 'rather than just pretending to be', even though she had a young family.[97] Hannah, who described her family as lower middle class, left school at sixteen years of age without sitting any exams because she suffered badly with anorexia.[98] She re-entered education a few years later, taking an evening course in A-Level sociology before gaining a place at the University of Reading in 1974. Hannah explained that 'at school, I hadn't been particularly academically able (largely I suspect because of lack of self-confidence!). Now I was studying through choice, I began to enjoy myself and gain confidence'.[99] As the decades progressed, it became harder, personally and economically, for women to let go of the idea of education and be satisfied with routine non-manual work.

Social class and credentials

During the 1970s, employers increasingly viewed qualifications as 'rough signals of labour market suitability',[100] thus making it more difficult to progress or feel confident without them. Dawn (b.1945) had left school at sixteen years of age to take up a position in a local public library because she had felt ready to leave education. She enjoyed the job and was able to progress up the ladder during the 1960s. However, she decided to take a sabbatical and return to do a degree in librarianship at her local polytechnic. This was not a necessity, but she felt 'inadequate' without one because, by the mid-1970s, librarianship 'had become a degree subject' and she also thought she would need a degree to have a chance of being promoted to regional level.[101] The phrase 'degree subject' is particularly notable here as it was government policy during the early 1970s to transform training for certain occupations into degree pathways. Teaching is the prime example of this, as training was moved from teacher training colleges into the polytechnics. One interviewee, Nancy (b.1940), was working as a deputy headteacher (before being promoted to headteacher) during the 1970s.[102] She had set up an educational policy research group with educational researchers and policy-makers and therefore they sought out her ideas in this period. Nancy advocated for a move to postgraduate training for teachers in universities:

> We wanted to close all the colleges of education which had been set up after the war under the forty-four act as mainly for women cut off from the rest of society … that the kind of social career division between teacher training colleges as they were then called before they were called colleges of education, teacher training colleges, that that sort of division should stop and that everybody going in to teacher training should do a degree of one kind or another and then do a postgraduate course.[103]

Nancy felt that this would 'make sure the quality of education for pupils was as good as possible in all cases and we were very much comprehensive school minded, and so teacher training was seen in that context'.[104] She connected this to her own experience of state education and the requirement for what she considered as better trained teachers.

This shift was particularly significant for women because they tended to lose out more than men in the labour market when they did not have educational credentials.[105] Men have more opportunities to achieve mobility through promotion within institutions or setting up businesses.[106] Geoff Payne and Pamela Abbott have argued that, although having educational credentials 'does not fully protect women from falling into a low status occupation', they need qualifications more than men do to move into social class I or II.[107] Gaining higher-level qualifications represents a concrete pathway for women to prove their abilities in circumstances such as recruitment processes, which may be stacked against them. In the mid- to late twentieth century, women were likely to earn 'occupational qualifications' with a 'universal validity' and 'transportable – both from employer to employer as well as geographically'.[108] This 'universal validity' made them more flexible and conducive to women's discontinuous career trajectories. Archetypal examples of roles that require occupational qualifications are those within the welfare state such as teacher, social worker and nursing positions. For example, Jacqui (b.1943) took a Master's degree in social work in the late 1960s after completing her undergraduate degree in psychology and zoology.[109] The postgraduate qualification that she earned allowed her to move around the country for her husband's career during the late 1960s and 1970s, finding employment as a social worker in various local authorities. In the 1970s, when both Maureen and her husband decided that they wanted to change jobs, it was Maureen who entered education to gain a teaching qualification.[110] In contrast, her husband, who had come to 'hate' his job as a fitter at British Steel, which he had held since leaving school, became a driving instructor rather than returning to study.

A recent study conducted by historians and anthropologists at the University of Oxford has interesting findings about the relationship between marriage and qualifications for women born in the 1940s. The study of social mobility analysed original data from the Oxford Biobank from three cohorts born in twentieth-century Britain. As might be expected, the comparison between men and women born mid-century showed a significant proportion of husbands with university degrees whose wives were less qualified.[111] However, more surprising considering assumptions made about marital mobility during this period, the comparison also revealed a high proportion of women who were more qualified than their spouses. Relationships where the man had few qualifications demonstrated this most clearly. This reiterates the significance of women needing to gain qualifications – men can achieve in their career without them. Of the fifty women married to husbands with no qualifications or with only pre-A-Level qualifications, 52 per cent were either as qualified as, or more qualified than, their husbands. Notably, the study also found that, of the ninety women in the cohort sample, half obtained their highest qualifications as mature students. This suggests that a number of women, like Maureen, had a similar lack of qualifications as their spouses when they met, but in order to move up in their careers they obtained qualifications, while their husbands did not need to.

Contributing to the contemporary debate on defining women's social class, sociologists Pamela Abbott and Roger Sapsford suggested that women's qualifications need to be included in any measure of married women's class.[112] Particularly pertinent here is that they identified the number of years spent in post-compulsory education as one of the best predictors of class: '[E]ven displacing husband's occupation, it can be very useful assigning housewives' class position … as well as correcting the false impression of own class which may be given by current occupation because of the distorted nature of the labour market and career pattern for women.'[113] This can be linked to an important sense for women that educational achievement cannot be taken away – unlike career progression or marital status. This sentiment is apparent in Theresa's (b.1941) interview. She failed the eleven-plus exam and left secondary school at fifteen years of age, before sitting any exams. She then worked as a chef but left her job after getting married. However, following her divorce in the 1980s, Theresa decided to undertake a degree at Ruskin College in Oxford. Despite the fact that the qualification did not lead to significant occupational mobility, it was central in Theresa's discussion of her own social class: 'The education I've had – no can take that off me. Once you've had that it's yours forever.'[114] Jean, who also experienced social mobility, echoed these feelings, stating: 'See, you are never going to take away the confidence that education, that experience has given me.'[115] Women's lives are often volatile, and status such as occupation and relationship can change, but these women indicate that qualifications are permanent. This point is vital for understanding women's conceptions of their own social class in contemporary history.

Women who chose to go back into education before moving into professional jobs described this process and their own endeavours as central to their experiences of upward mobility. Ruth worked in a clerical job prior to returning to study and beginning a career as a social worker in the 1970s. She came from a working-class background and did not marry. Speaking of her social mobility, Ruth explained that she had 'done it on her own'.[116] Harriet (b.1940) hailed from a working-class family in Lancashire and attended a secondary modern school after failing the eleven-plus.[117] She left school at fifteen years of age 'without any qualifications' and went straight into employment. However, Harriet explained to Mass Observation that she ended her career as a librarian and adult education teacher after returning to education in the late 1970s: 'I feel that I have progressed upwards from being working class to a middle-class semi-professional.'[118] She elaborated that 'my husband and myself had to get all our Qualifications [*sic*] after we left school and during a long working life. We feel that through our own efforts we have raised ourselves into a totally different class'.[119] Similarly, Cynthia referred to her 'higher education' as one of the key reasons that meant she had 'gone up' from her working-class parents in social terms. Another interviewee, Chrissie, outlined that a 'professional job' is a hallmark of middle-class identity: 'I think by [the] process of Open University and teaching, then I guess I am middle class.'[120] These women were clear that they had experienced upwards social movement as a result of, as Maureen (who became a teacher in the 1970s) summed up, 'education and work … I do a middle class job, I have middle class qualifications and education'.[121]

When women of this generation discussed their social class or mobility journey, they repeatedly invoked their educational and employment experiences but also their family and upbringing. Socially mobile women tend to retain a strong sense of their working-class origins even when their class positioning has changed.[122] Maureen and Chrissie both referred to their working-class 'roots': Chrissie felt that these roots 'never leave you', and Maureen explained that she still saw herself as working class in some ways because 'that's where my roots are'.[123] Kathy (b.1950) described herself as 'uncomfortably socially mobile' because although she felt that she was 'probably middle class now' she 'despised' certain aspects of the middle class.[124] She poetically stated, 'I'm a kind of working class girl through and through. You know, I've got it through me like a rock. Working-class politics, working-class ethos, working-class everything.'[125] Angie also ascribed value to being working class, saying that, although her lifestyle and income level were middle class, 'aspirationally I was never middle class'.[126] She did not view being middle class as something to aspire to, instead explaining that she 'shared my parents' values and we shared their aspirations for working-class people. My dad's mantra was always "nothing stupid for the workers"'.[127] Women of this post-war generation are au fait with the language of class. They feel ambiguous about simply wanting to become middle class and they do not believe that only the middle classes should have access to interesting jobs and education. Their own history matters to them and their class attachment is not easily shifted.

Women held their own lineage and experience so strongly that, even in examples where they experienced long-range social mobility and started families with men from middle-class backgrounds, they still felt a chasm between their class and their partner's class. Carol met her long-term partner in the early 1970s while she was working as a teacher, and he was studying at the University of Oxford. He came from a middle-class family, and she spoke about how he had the opportunity to fail in a way that she never had: he did not even pass the eleven-plus exam but was sent to private school by his parents, where he was 'primed' for Oxford.[128] They went on to have careers of similar status within the public sector. Carol described herself as 'definitely middle class now' because of her professional career, but stated that 'my background will never leave me and I'll never have the same confidence or feeling of entitlement as some people I see, that doesn't go – it can be ameliorated a bit'. Her inability to bridge the gap between herself and her partner was illustrated most forcefully when she recalled: 'My partner told me that when he was a boy growing up his mother said he wasn't to talk to certain people, like working-class kids, and I said, "Oh you mean like me?" We'd been living with each other for about 25 years.' Rita expressed a similar sentiment about her relationship with the middle-class father of her children, who she met in the late 1970s but never married, when they were both beginning careers teaching in post-compulsory education. She recalled the first time she visited his parents' house: 'It was so awkward, like one of those tense dinner party scenes from French movies. In the evening, I sat and listened to his mother as she fretted about her son's possible fall down the class ladder. I felt like the attentive maid.'[129] Their differing upbringings continued to influence their relationship throughout the decades they were together. Rita stated that she had 'followed blithely into a relationship of economic chaos, not really aware that our lifestyle was predicated on his deep-rooted belief that he would always be bailed out. When we broke up, his family bought him a house. I had to start from scratch with our three kids.'[130]

It is remarkable how rare it is for women of the welfare state generation to demonstrate a shared sense of class with their partners. Very little emerges of a joint sense of class with their husbands, even from women who married men of similar class backgrounds. Whether married or single, women scarcely used 'we' to discuss social class. 'I' or 'my' were much more commonly used, and 'we' was mostly used about husbands and wives as a *team* rather than solely being defined by his experiences. Barbara's husband was more central in her interview than many others and even she used the term 'I', stating: 'I would – I mean I still would like to think of myself and obviously Fred would as well – as working class.'[131] Cynthia defined her class and mobility journey within her multi-generational lineage, referencing not only her parents, but also her grandparents and her sons, but she did not mention her husband once.[132] Social class – and women's achievements – is not subsumed by their relationships or handed over to their husbands.

Conclusion

The material presented here offers a fresh way to understand the mobility processes at work in women's lives in this period. The reconfiguration of further and higher education led to fewer barriers to entry and more varied routes through the education system for mature students. This change was itself part of the structural expansion of the welfare state, which required trained workers to fill new positions in areas such as health, education and social work. These wider shifts in the public sector occurred at a time in the life cycle of this generation when they were experiencing big changes in their own personal lives – such as new motherhood or divorce – and were re-evaluating their priorities in life. The moment of flexibility in education coupled with expansion in the job market created an environment of possibility for women of the welfare state generation. Rather than having plans or particular destinations in mind, women grasped these opportunities with both hands, driven not by career goals as such, but more by feelings of restlessness and desire for change.

An interrelationship exists between the social and the individual in social mobility journeys, which deserves particular attention when studying the more volatile female life course. Mandler has argued that historians are uniquely positioned to bring analysis of these 'dense complex of mechanisms' to the study of social mobility.[133] Not only did the immediate moment of structural and social change matter here, but the longer-term experiences of women of the welfare state generation who, as we have seen, grew up feeling more able to adapt and take more risks, with higher expectations of education and work. Instead of defining their mobility through relationships, women's social mobility was achieved through their own endeavours in the public sphere. This is related to the broader finding that women of this generation own their social class and frame it through first-person possessive pronouns and their own experiences. Even decades-long marriages and lives spent together do not necessarily produce 'we' framings in the discussion of social class. Women of the welfare state generation have agency in determining their own class positioning.

Agents of change: Women transforming the welfare state

Women of this generation were fundamental in reshaping the welfare state during the 1970s and early 1980s, especially as employees of the state. During these decades, women workers could have a real influence on welfare provision because state structures were run in a decentralized manner, with local government having significant responsibility for the implementation of social policy. Previous historiography has underestimated the vitality of the welfare state in this period, preferring to focus on the post-1945 expansion. Partly because of this, historians have not fully grasped the numerical and political strength of women working in the state during the 1970s. More women were working in both the professional and administrative strata of the welfare state, and a higher proportion came from working-class backgrounds.[1] This chapter takes seriously this new aspect of the workforce as an important and understudied intervention in the space of the state. The state was recognized as the centre of politics and a key instrument of opportunity for women. Women working within the welfare state directed political energy to effecting change in the way that they carried out their duties. In particular, women of this generation continued to be affected by their own experience of state education, and as educators, they sought to approach teaching and talent in more complex ways than they had experienced as pupils.

Focusing on women's lives shows that, rather than being predominantly a period of crisis, the long 1970s was a time of flux, which opened up space for new ideas and agitating for change. Indeed, severe macroeconomic difficulties faced Britain, contributing to the fracturing of social democracy. By the mid-1970s, inflation was hitting record levels, unemployment was increasing rapidly, and the minority Labour government needed to take out a $3.9 billion loan from the International Monetary Fund.[2] Yet women's employment was surprisingly resilient during the recessions of the mid-1970s and early 1980s because of its concentration in the state, the service sector more broadly, and within part-time roles.[3] Women's trade union membership grew substantially during the 1970s. By 1975, their participation rate had reached 40 per cent of those in the workforce, rising particularly rapidly among white-collar and public sector workers.[4] Women of the welfare state generation increasingly asserted themselves *as workers* in this period, and their experience has to be understood differently to that of male industrial workers.

Scholarship on women's lives during the 1970s tends to focus on the Women's Liberation Movement (WLM) and feminist activism.[5] The women in my sample were not chosen for their involvement in second-wave feminist activism, and their relationships to the movement were varied and complex: activism weaved in and out of women's lives at different moments: some women were engaged but never active while others supported gender equality but were uncomfortable calling themselves 'feminist'. This reflects the long history of women's 'complicated' attitudes to formal feminist movements.[6] However, this chapter contributes to new forms of historiography, which seek to engage with the significance of feminism for understanding women's experience in this period but also to complicate and move beyond analyses of WLM activism. Recent research by Emily Robinson, Camilla Schofield, Florence Sutcliffe-Braithwaite and Natalie Thomlinson demonstrates an innovative approach to feminism, imploring historians to 'critically interrogate the extent to which we can read social changes as simply the product of feminism; such a link needs to be analysed rather than assumed. Certainly, shifts in the economic base, part of a wider shift of developed economies towards the service sector, is also a crucial part of the story'.[7] Put simply: more analysis is needed of the ways in which the WLM was itself the product of a particular social, political and economic context, and how this context was instrumental in changing women's lives and values.

A major argument of this chapter is that the WLM emerged from, and manifested itself in a particular way, as a result of the welfare state and was led by the generation of women shaped by the post-war settlement. This insight emerged from analysis of the oral history interviews and is enhanced by examining the interviews alongside key writings by feminist activists of the 1970s and early 1980s. The chapter conceptualizes the feminist scholarship as writing by women of the welfare state generation and examines it through that lens: this demonstrates the similarities and blurred lines between the attitudes, experiences and relationships with the state of feminist activists and women of the welfare state generation more broadly.

Feminist writing on the welfare state

In the mid-1970s feminist writers began to produce a body of literature on gender and the welfare state, which altered the ways in which the state was conceptualized by scholars. Prior to this, scholarship on the welfare state was primarily 'gender-blind', with little sense of gender 'as a major organising principle of the [welfare] system'.[8] Research on the welfare state in the immediate post-war period was written primarily by male social policy experts who placed the emphasis instead on 'income and class inequalities'.[9] Even where writers such as Richard Titmuss made reference to gender in the 1950s and 1960s, they tended to be overly optimistic about women's position in society and their satisfaction with their gender role.[10] Helen McCarthy has highlighted the small number of women working in social science departments at British universities in the post-war decades who did pioneering research into women's paid work, particularly that carried out by married women.[11] She argued that 'the personal and professional experiences of the individual researchers' – many of whom were married middle-class women – 'were integral to this opening up of new intellectual problems'.[12] Notably, McCarthy counter-posed the research on women's work with that being done on the welfare state by their male colleagues, suggesting that they were competing intellectual endeavours. Women's lives and the welfare state were conceived of separately by researchers in the immediate post-war period, and contemporaneous women scholars did not see the welfare state as central to their personal and professional experience.

The wave of scholarship on the welfare state that began in the mid-1970s emerged from women born between the late 1930s and early 1950s. The 1970s was the decade when women of the welfare state generation entered employment in further and higher education institutions in large numbers. Unlike earlier female scholars, they felt that analysing the welfare state was central to understanding women's experiences and that reforming state structures was key to improving their lives. This was influenced by their childhood growing up within the welfare state but also the ways in which it continued to shape their adult experience. These women were the 'children of Beveridge and Keynes'[13] and, while they were often critical of aspects of the welfare state, they often sought to make changes within the overarching framework of the state. The social and economic context in which feminism emerged is crucial to understanding its priorities and the primary frameworks in which the movement chose to situate female experience.

Feminists writing in the 1970s aimed to render visible the tangible and intangible ways in which the welfare state governed gender roles in the public and private sphere. The writers made use of Marxist critiques of the state but incorporated the domestic arena into their analysis. In her path-breaking 1977 book, titled *Women and the Welfare State*, Elizabeth Wilson argued that 'the welfare state is not just a set of services, it is also a set of ideas about society, about the family, and – not least important – about women who have a centrally important role within the family as lynchpin'.[14] Hilary Land wrote a series of articles on a similar theme during the 1970s, positing that 'social policies are implicit family policies, because most, if not all, of them are based on certain assumptions about the pattern of "normal" relationships between the sexes and the generations within families'.[15] Wilson argued that the ideology of the welfare state impeded women 'imagin[ing] a different kind of lives for themselves'.[16]

In feminist texts, the Beveridge Report of 1942 became a symbol of the ways in which gendered norms were enshrined in the structures of the post-war welfare state. Wilson argued that the Beveridge Report 'located women firmly within the home' and thus was 'given a warm welcome' by men who were not happy with the 'increased independence of their wives' during the war.[17] Land also posited that Beveridge's 'assumptions about the economic dependency of married women led him to disregard the importance of their financial contribution to the family. He therefore helped to perpetuate a social security system which failed to meet the needs of many women'.[18] Sheila Blackburn critiqued the feminist approach to the Beveridge Report and argued that Beveridge's views on women in the social security system were more complicated than first appears.[19] For example, Beveridge explicitly stated that certain existing features of the system were 'indefensible':

> The census includes women who do not work for money outside their home among unoccupied persons. The unemployment insurance scheme recognises such women as adult dependants on their husbands, in respect of whom the benefit of the husband is increased if he is unemployed. The health insurance scheme does not recognise such women at all, except at the moment of maternity.[20]

To ameliorate these issues, in his plan for future arrangements, Beveridge proposed 'treat[ing] married women as a special insurance class of occupied persons' and decided to 'treat man and wife as a team … each of whose partners is equally essential, and give benefits as for the team'.[21] Yet Beveridge did continue to believe that social policy should prioritize the majority of women, who were financially dependent on their husbands.[22] This argument demonstrates the different ways in which Beveridge and later feminists conceptualized the role of the report: he chose to work within the existing bounds of economic arrangements, whereas they believed that the foundational text of welfare expansion could have been used as an instrument for creating fundamental change in gender relations.

While feminists critiqued the ways in which the welfare state was set up, they also contended that, by the late 1970s, an increasing contradiction existed between women's experience and the gendered structure of state policy. Women were expected to provide care in the home but also to participate in the labour market. Land argued that 'the model of the family based on one breadwinner is one to which the majority of men and women did not conform for most of their working lives'.[23] However, welfare policies remained largely premised on the assumption that there would be one wage earner in a family and women were likely to be economic dependants.[24] Land offered the recent example of the 1975 Social Security Act, which excluded married women from an 'incapacity to work' benefit because 'they would not normally be in employment'.[25] Feminist writers did note that some important legislative changes improved women's position in the workplace, including the 1970 Equal Pay Act and the 1975 Sex Discrimination Act. They agreed that even more needed to be done to help women's economic position. Mary McIntosh highlighted that part-time jobs did not have equal pro rata benefits to full-time jobs and advocated increased protection for women in these roles.[26] Feminist writers made it clear that women were finding it increasingly difficult to negotiate the competing demands of the public and private sphere, meaning that more wide-ranging action needed to be taken.

Much writing on the welfare state in this period came from the perspective of socialist feminists, who believed that participation in trade unionism was one of the best means through which to improve the socio-economic position of women. Feminist writers acknowledged that, historically, trade unions privileged retaining higher wages and protections for male breadwinners but argued that women should not be excluded from 'the main agent for change in workplace practices'.[27] Wilson praised the increase in union membership among women in the 1970s. She pointed in particular to the 'accelerated rise' in female membership of white-collar and public sector unions, such as the National Union of Public Employees (NUPE).[28] In 1980, McIntosh described an alliance between feminists and the Trades Union Congress (TUC) on campaigning to extend protective legislation to men so that they might be able to request shorter hours for child-rearing.[29] However, other feminist writers such as Carole

Pateman argued that debates in the labour movement continued to be premised on male life cycles and that women should engage with unions but also find supplementary strategies to enact change in the workplace.[30]

In this vein, some feminist writers made the astute observation that women workers employed by the state were attempting to 'chang[e] the welfare state from within'.[31] This insight has been overlooked by later scholarship which has engaged with feminist theories of the welfare state.[32] McIntosh noted that women became not only the main users but also the main providers of welfare services. She argued that this allowed feminists to move beyond 'purely anti-statist positions' towards aiming for 'the development and provision of feminist services'.[33] McIntosh stated that it was difficult for feminists to sustain anti-statism as this was a 'dream' reserved 'for men who can envisage a world of self-supporting able-bodied people'.[34] Similarly, Pateman suggested that women being 'involved in the welfare state on a large scale as employees' meant that 'the possibilities for political action by women now look rather different than in the past'.[35] Notably, Pateman emphasized that not only 'activists' sought to 'transform the welfare state', but also female employees who could base their desire for change on being 'the people on whom the daily operation of the welfare state to a large extent depends'.[36] We should understand that this was not necessarily an explicitly radical or feminist approach but rather emerged as a result of shifting power dynamics within the state.

Welfare state workers had particular experiences, which shaped contemporary political culture in the 1970s. A pamphlet titled *In and Against the State* was published in 1979 by a working group of the Conference of Socialist Economists. The research was led by the feminist researcher Cynthia Cockburn and outlined the strategy of changing the state from within in significant detail.[37] They argued that, as a consequence of welfare state expansion, the definition of what was political concomitantly expanded:

> Many people have started talking about such institutions as schools, hospitals, local councils and local Magistrates courts as 'the state'. Yet just a few years ago it would have seemed quite out of place to most people to use such a hard political term about such familiar everyday things … more and more of us in more and more ways are closely tied up with the state's institutions … about one-third of all people in jobs today are employees of the state.[38]

Thus, they suggested that working for the state had an influence on their politics but also that working for the state was in itself political. They argued that workers had particular power in existing state structures because they were often local and decentralized.

The authors of the pamphlet were self-identified socialists although the main perspective from which they wrote was as a 'group of people who work for the state or for organisations which receive money from the state'.[39] The pamphlet made a distinction between different class positions of workers within the state: 'Many public sector manual and clerical workers are the lowest paid of all employed people. For others it is equally obvious: they are highly paid management staff, top civil servants, and directors of nationalised industries. But what about nurses, teachers, social workers? Their position seems ambiguous'.[40] The eight co-authors of the pamphlet belonged to this latter group: 'a middle group of workers, who are often termed "professional". We are social/community/advice/research workers'.[41] They argued that the impact of working for the state was especially powerful and contradictory for employees in these semi-professional roles, where women predominated, because they were often at the sharp end of the provision of state services and frequently 'given impossible problems to solve arising from poverty or from the powerlessness of our clients'.[42] This predicament intensified during the 1970s as the economic crisis hit and public resources started to become scarcer. In these roles, workers' choices were part of constructing the welfare state, although workers were often constrained in their actions and reliant on the state for their own social status.

Gender and work

Women of the welfare state generation expressed strong support for the idea of gender equality, if not necessarily the organized women's movement. Jacqui (b.1943) stated that she had 'always hesitated to call myself a feminist. I do believe in equality for each; and I think men have things to wrestle with, too. So, I've never called myself feminist. I've never been directly involved in anything'.[43] Sylvia (b.1945) also chose not to identify as a feminist because she did not 'hate men', although she did believe that 'patriarchy sort of maintains the status quo that women are the chattel and men are in the position of authority'.[44] Working-class women's experiences of class divides within the women's movement could affect their views on feminism. Chrissie (b.1950) explained that she was 'all for women's rights' but she was not feminist 'in the sense that [the WLM] were'.[45] This disconnect was in part because she felt that the 'middle-class' feminists she met in her educational workplace 'talked down' to the working-class women they taught.[46] Rose (b.1945) was not involved in activism but did hold feminist beliefs, which she specifically stated 'arose from my personal situation' as both the main 'breadwinner' and the 'dogsbody' in terms of housework:

> I'm out and out feminine. But I can't still see why in an equal situation, I've got to be the dogsbody in the house? I mean, it's as simple as that. And why should women get less money and things like this?[47]

This quotation points to the growing interrelationship between women's experiences of employment and work–life balance, and their feelings about inequality.

By the 1970s, women born between the late 1930s and early 1950s saw themselves as both paid workers in the public sphere and unpaid carers in the private sphere. Although women, especially working-class women, had always worked, a notable rise took place in the numbers of married women working in the post-war decades, and women increasingly spent more years in employment. Rather than properly adapting to women's new life course, though, society expected women to be 'superwoman' figures, who dealt with new challenges presented to them largely on their own.[48] In my interviews, it was striking how many women spoke at length about the dilemmas that they faced between family and work life, their analyses chiming frequently with the writings of declared feminists on the welfare state. Women often described feeling expected to perform both these roles as a hallmark of their generation. Jean (b.1950), who was employed as a nurse during this period, stated that 'my mum was of a generation where women were held back. I think I probably was in the generation – the worst of both worlds – with a career and still looking after the house and children … at times I felt like a single mum'.[49] Jean wanted to work and returned to nursing only a few months after her first child was born in 1975: 'I was going up the wall … I enjoyed having children, but I enjoyed it better when I worked and had children.'[50] Another interviewee, Susannah (b.1940), who came from an upper middle-class background and studied medicine at Cambridge, stated: 'I was determined I was going to work and I wanted to have children, but I always wanted to have it all, to do both. I thought I'd have to make opportunities myself, I didn't think it would all fall into my lap.'[51] She had two children in the 1970s, and she took on primary responsibility for childcare alongside trying to arrange for her employers to keep her on an upward career trajectory while reducing her hours. Susannah also noted that her friends working in universities mitigated against the lack of formal part-time roles by working 'the maximum part-time hours that still allowed a salary [rather than hourly wages] … almost full time' – with full-time responsibilities, they could continue in their chosen careers and carve out time to look after their children while their (male) colleagues did research and were promoted.[52] Women had no right enshrined in law to request flexible working until the late 1990s. Women of this generation were caught in a nexus of contradictions that only intensified: the expanded welfare state largely maintained existing gender norms but also provided increased educational and occupational opportunities. The structure of the state was changing during the 1970s, but women still felt that they had to negotiate the contradictions and complications themselves.

Women who worked in senior roles frequently described facing hostility and having to work harder to prove their commitment to and suitability for their chosen career path. There were still few part-time roles in the upper echelons of the private sector and no expansion in part-time jobs in the higher strata of the welfare professions took place, despite an increase in the semi-professions. In her autobiography, Margaret Cook (b.1944) recalled experiencing a 'strong feeling of guilt' about going back to work soon after having her first son in 1973, but her aim to become a consultant meant that she could not take a long maternity leave.[53] She explained that, on her return to the hospital, she 'knew there would be no flexibility on the part of my colleagues, who took the view that I was being paid the same as them so my contribution should be exactly equivalent'.[54] Cook

Figure 5.1 Teacher with schoolchildren in a primary school classroom, Cambridgeshire, UK, 1978. © Alamy images.

was shocked that she had been rostered to work her first two weekends back but decided not to complain about it in case she was seen as difficult. Both Susannah and Cook stated that, in the medical profession, women 'had to be extra good to be credited as equal to men' but, even then, they constantly witnessed 'less qualified men being promoted above [them]'.[55] Diane (b.1946) continued to build her career as a personnel manager in business after finishing university and progressed well in her career.[56] In the mid-1970s she was pleased to receive an unexpected promotion as a result of the sudden departure of her boss, but she pinpointed the timing of this promotion as the reason for her decision not to have children. Diane said that 'employment rights' for women were 'only just starting to come in properly' and she was 'the first and only woman on the executive committee'.[57] She was sure that the company 'would not have made any concessions' for her.[58] Diane described generally feeling that her employers were willing to give her 'responsibility' but not the 'status' that this responsibility should have conferred, whereas with male colleagues the reverse was arguably true. However, she was wary of being labelled 'too emotional', so she did not mention her frustrations. In 1981, Clara (b.1939) made the decision to leave the law firm where she worked to strike out on her own.[59] She was paid less than the men at the firm, and this was still justified using the argument that she had a husband so did not need as high compensation. Clara said that 'they were quite probably quite relieved actually [when she left], because they didn't have a woman partner again for years'.[60] She enjoyed setting up her own firm because it meant that she 'got [her] own way all the time. Which maybe is what it was about really, to be honest'.

Despite these experiences, women in senior roles were well placed to try to improve working conditions for themselves and their female colleagues. Susannah and another interviewee, Elizabeth (b.1939), had female mentors early in their professional careers, who gave them individualized advice and represented role models in how to navigate a male-dominated career. In turn, they consciously took on the role of mentors for more junior women in their organizations. During the 1970s and early 1980s, Elizabeth had two young sons and worked part-time hours ('with full-time responsibilities') running a research project at a laboratory.[61] Like Susannah, Elizabeth had to negotiate this contract with her employer. This was not run on a properly pro rata basis. More prestigious aspects of the job were squeezed, meaning that Elizabeth often did not receive recognition in proportion to her intellectual input. She produced research ideas in collaborative research, but her male colleagues would 'go off to lectures and meetings' in her place.[62] Nonetheless, she still always made sure of the presence of a female scientist on the project and found time to be their mentor. Susannah was central in a strategy among female staff at the hospital where she worked in the late 1970s to 'ge[t] involved within the organisation and ge[t] ourselves elected into positions on the council and tr[y] to change it by being within the structure, having influence, making decisions'.[63] Calls were also made to set up a women's caucus but Susannah was ambivalent about this because she thought that it would mean 'separating ourselves off' from where decisions were made.[64] Diane's approach to improving conditions was the most self-consciously 'feminist'. She used her position in personnel management to 'generate data' on the experience of women working within her organization, with the aim of 'developing policies to remove structural barriers' for women.[65] Diane also recalled being 'involved in various bits of collective action … in the seventies there was the equal pay and opportunities campaign and I was very much part of that'.[66] Women felt empowered to enact change within the established structures of their professions and often deployed more individualist approaches, such as mentoring, to achieve this.

A growing number of women chose to use collective action to effect change in the workplace, primarily through the mechanism of trade unions. This could be a contradictory experience for women, both rewarding and frustrating, because unions were 'slow' to acknowledge the 'importance of women in the labour force'.[67] In the mid-1970s, Anita (b.1952) had recently completed a short course in printing and wanted a position in a print shop in Leeds. She explained that 'the printing industry was a closed shop, you joined the union and they had to place you with a job'.[68] They found her a position, but the shifts started at 6 a.m., which was very difficult for her as a single parent because no childcare was available so early in the morning. In the late 1960s the printing unions were among the biggest opponents of flexible shifts for women,[69] so she was especially pleased when they agreed to let her begin working at 7.30 a.m. However, the men she worked with were not happy with the arrangement and she felt that the union retaliated against her a few months after she started: 'They hired an unskilled guy … and they put him on the machine next to me and he didn't know how to print so I had to show him what to do. His wages were far higher than mine. I didn't last long after that.'[70] The poor treatment led Anita to leave the position, but she did choose to get 'involved in the trades council and help to unionize women in different companies' to try to change the gendered power imbalance.[71]

As Sarah Boston has highlighted, during the 1970s 'women were still absent from or grossly under-represented in the top official and lay positions of trade unions and the TUC' but these organizations were starting 'to realise women's demands could not be ignored'.[72] Angie (b.1945), a trained nurse, was sponsored by her trade union to attend Ruskin College. Angie was working as a nurse and was already a shop steward but wanted to go further in the movement. She was inspired by her father, who was a high-up official in the National Union of Mineworkers during her childhood.[73] After graduating from Ruskin, Angie described her experience as a female official:

> I didn't have a strategy about where I was going. There were so few women trade union officials and I was asked to go into work in a couple of places, and there we had a situation where there was a promotion opportunity. The criteria stated you had to have been a full-time official for at least seven years before you could apply. And there were only a half a dozen of us women, but we said 'that's discriminatory' – because none of us have been employed for seven years so we couldn't apply for this promotional post; it was only men that could apply. So the union agreed and of course we had to do all the stuff about equal rights and equal pay – so we had to challenge it within our own union. Well then one of us had to apply having won the battle and none of us wanted to. I was working in Newcastle at the time, I loved the job, I really enjoyed my colleagues. And this was in Oxford, this promotion. I put in for it – somebody had to do it.[74]

Angie was awarded the promotion even though she had not expected it. One of the key actions she chose to take in her role was to establish women's committees and to unionize women, particularly women working in precarious, lower-status jobs in the public sector, such as positions in 'school cleaning or school meals'.[75] Theresa (b.1941), who was a trade union rep in local government during this period, also made unionizing women a top priority.[76] Women of this generation aimed to produce a critical mass of women within unions.

The welfare state had particularly high rates of union membership during the 1970s. Membership of public sector unions rose from 3,420,000 in 1951 to 5,700,000 by 1976.[77] Parry suggests that a 'new public sector' was emerging in the 1970s, which was 'increasingly female, qualified and unionised'.[78] This was reflected in my sample: welfare workers were all members of a union during this period, and they were largely positive about the union movement, often making a link between their own membership and their fathers, whom they fondly described as 'union men'.[79] However, women expressed ambivalence about certain union tactics, especially suspension of their labour through striking. Jean stated that she had been an active member of the union throughout the 1970s but left in 1979 because she disagreed with the decision to strike.[80] Similarly, Barbara (b.1941), who worked in university administration, chose to leave her union because she felt pressured by her union rep to join the picket line of a strike.[81] Taking part in strikes could be a particular problem for welfare state workers because they were often concerned about the effects on their clients and likely demonization from the public.[82] Cook, who was a junior doctor in a hospital and a Labour Party member, found that this attitude was prevalent among her colleagues at this time: 'At work I was discovering that many medical colleagues were natural conservatives … there was a strong antipathy to trade unions and any strike action raised unbounded fury, with highly charged phrases such as "holding the country to ransom" being cast in my direction.'[83] Nevertheless, the high rates of unionization did contribute to improved occupational conditions for women: with regard to women's rights 'the public sector [was] far in advance of the private sector.'[84] Rita's experience demonstrates the slow but significant progress of women working within public sector unions. In the 1980s, she was employed on two part-time contracts at different further educational institutions to make up full-time hours.[85] Rita explained:

> The days I worked would be organized termly. I was often asked to work more hours than originally agreed and received no holiday or sick pay. I had quite a lot of responsibility as I was the only tutor there teaching script writing and directing. Part-time work in this way meant that I didn't have any down time at all, whereas the people I worked with at that time had one day a week allocated for research, my time was almost 100 per cent contact time or meetings.[86]

Rita was eventually able to 'work with [the] union to get a proper two-and-half-day week contract by demonstrating the consistency of my employment'. This made a real difference to her working conditions, but she described the process to get there as 'quite a battle'.[87]

Women who worked in the welfare semi-professions during this period were less likely to feel that they had experienced overt discrimination. Lesley (b.1950), a primary schoolteacher, stated that having a career allowed her to 'vie[w] myself as an equal … maybe not all women were equal, but I was treated equally at work, I had my own opinions and I could express them'.[88] Cynthia (b.1941) moved from clerical work to primary teaching. She was soon promoted to head of a department. She made it clear that women's activism held little interest for her because she did not feel that she needed it: 'This is going to sound very conceited, people do take notice of me and ask my advice. If you asked people, I know they'd say I was forceful and opinionated! I never was a headteacher but people would come into school and assume I was the headteacher.'[89] Cynthia said she never applied to be a headteacher simply 'because I didn't want to be one' and that she had 'never come across any discrimination at work – I would've done something about it if I had but I really honestly don't think I did'.[90] In her research into the cohort of women born in 1947 at 30 years of age, Mary Ingham found a similar sense of personal power among some of her teaching friends, which led them to reject organized feminism:

> Those of my school year who went into teaching continued blithely, retaining an innate sense of equality which they brought to their relationship with men, but did not need to test in their professional relationships because for various reasons they did not climb high enough on the ladder to feel the cold draught of male prejudice. Because this was their choice, they did not see ways in which they would have been restricted from climbing higher.[91]

Women working in different semi-professions in the 1970s demonstrated similar attitudes. Dawn (b.1945), who was a librarian in a local government-run library, explained that she was 'not very sympathetic to women's lib' and 'thought it was silly' because 'I didn't feel inferior and I was happy, I was quite senior [at work] and I thought I'd done quite well'.[92] She had no truck with her colleagues 'feeling there was a glass ceiling ... because of the local government salary grading our salaries were the same, there was no difference between men and women's salaries'.[93] Daniel Walkowitz's research into women social workers in America supports the conclusion that the status achieved through this type of occupation could be enough to satisfy the female worker without provoking male hostility.[94] This chapter now considers how women welfare workers mobilized this sense of personal autonomy in the workplace.

Politics of working for the welfare state

Working for the welfare state allowed women to make a politicized intervention in society. This could be an avenue chosen by established activists but, in addition, simply being a state worker could give women the impetus to want to enact change in this manner. Women emphasized the ways in which employment and political action intertwined for state workers. They did not primarily agitate for a change in their own conditions but instead focused on the political impact of the work itself. For instance, during our interview, Chrissie became a little frustrated with me for asking her separate questions about 'work' and 'politics' as if they were two discrete areas of her life history.[95] She was not an activist but referred to her desire to become a social worker in the early 1970s as 'emotionally political' and motivated by a kind of gut feeling about 'what's right and wrong and what's equal and justice and all that kind of stuff that's in your face – you can't ignore it really'.[96] Chrissie left social work later in the decade after she had her two children but returned to the workplace a couple of years later to teach in further education. Notably, she repeated a similar sentiment about the political nature of her approach to work, stating: 'I used to think that teaching adult literacy was quite political. Because it was about equality and about giving people the tools to have a voice, really. So that was my political anthem at that time'.[97] Frances (b.1939) hailed from a more middle-class background than Chrissie, and after attending the University of Oxford, she spent time as a housewife.[98] She described the envy that she felt that, while she was at home with the children, her husband was able to 'do [his] politics through [his] work' as an adult education tutor in an extra-mural university department.[99] Frances wanted to have the opportunity to operate in the same way as her husband in the public sphere and, during the 1970s, she made the decision to start working as a teacher. She went on to use this knowledge to become the education policy spokesperson for her local Labour Party. Her concept of 'doing politics through work' is a useful prism through which to think about the political engagement of women working within the welfare state.

It is also important to consider the gendered aspect of 'doing politics through work'. Repeated allusions were made to lacking time to engage in direct political action because of familial responsibility. Motherhood could be a hurdle to direct political involvement for women of this generation.[100] Frances made this connection, as did Sylvia, who mentioned the hours she spent looking after her children and preparing for work in explaining that her 'political commitment was to education'.[101] Likewise, Carol explained that she had reduced her political activism in favour of 'doing politics through work', primarily because she became a mother for the first time in the early 1980s. She stated that 'up until I had Jess I'd been very politically involved all the time and then when I had her I couldn't be, it just wasn't going to work ... we tried to get somebody to mind Jess when she was asleep but she just woke up, it was uncanny'.[102] Nancy (b.1940) decided not to marry or have children because she felt that having a family would be a hindrance to her career progression. Interestingly, she still chose to step back from her direct political activism once she was promoted from teacher to deputy-head level (and beyond). Instead, she enacted her politics through her work in education and her focus on educational reform:

> You know, if you do this kind of schoolwork it takes up a lot of time and I was very friendly with a Professor and we set up a special group, and then we set

up another group, to do with reforming and improving secondary education. So those informal kind of think-tank sorts of groups I was involved in, so I spent quite a bit of time beyond the school that I was in or schools with that kind of networking, of like-minded people who wanted to see developments and innovations, first in teacher training and then in secondary education generally.[103]

With women in higher-level positions under so much scrutiny about their levels of commitment, and facing hostility from male colleagues, it might have been a valuable strategy to do politics *through* work – especially as employees of the welfare state with scope to make change during this period.

It is significant that women of this generation used the language of 'politics' rather than 'citizenship' to explain their actions at work. In the immediate post-war decades, there was an expectation that young women would make their choices based on ideas of service and citizenship. In her 1957 book *Wives Who Went to College*, the sociologist Judith Hubback argued that women should be encouraged into the semi-professions to 'devote at least part of her energy and ability to socially valuable work', using the terminology of 'civic responsibility'.[104] However, women of the welfare state generation rarely deployed the terminology of citizenship. Stephanie Spencer similarly found that, despite successive post-war governments' concern with defining female citizenship, it was not a concept that arose in her discussions with women who attended secondary school in 1950s Britain.[105] She noted that her interviewees 'gave the impression that that they did not need the notion of citizenship to justify their actions'.[106] Historians have directly connected the rise of the welfare state to a dearth of theorizing among intellectuals during the 1950s and 1960s because they believed that the question of what made a good citizen was now 'redundant'.[107] The welfare state brought what had been social questions into the realm of the political. A political belief in egalitarianism was characteristic of women of the post-war generation.[108] These women believed that people were entitled to comprehensive and fair public services as a right.

Not only was the state considered a more political entity in this period, but it also functioned in a more local and decentralized manner, which provided women with the opportunity to have individual influence. As noted in Chapter 2, the Attlee government chose to keep the structures of the state diffused, and the Labour governments of the 1960s continued to increase the autonomy of welfare workers through initiatives such as the Plowden Report of 1967. By the mid-1970s, local governments were still responsible for delivery of education, housing and social work services (although the Heath government removed health services from their control, a move that presaged the direction of travel in the 1980s).[109] Brenda (b.1938) took on a series of clerical jobs after leaving school but, by the 1970s, she was working with local government.[110] Her position involved liaising with local families in poverty, and she ran a weekend club for children whose parents did shift work. As a single mother with a school-age son, Brenda explained that she struggled for money and could empathize with the experience of the families with whom she worked.[111] Likewise, after Anita returned to education to study social studies, she worked briefly as a social worker but then took on a role in a community project working with local (and later national) government to 'help give people a voice, and getting people involved in organising and decision-making around public services'.[112] Anita linked her belief in producing change for the 'collective' good to growing up during a 'unique time ... after the Second World War and beginning of [the] welfare state'.[113]

In welfare roles where women workers came into close contact with vulnerable clients, they sought to take actions with awareness of the power differential and structural social injustices. Chrissie used the phrase 'emotionally political' to describe the way in which she approached social work. Likewise, Ruth (b.1949), who also came from a working-class background and was employed as a social worker in the late 1970s, explained that 'I always felt social work was political ... I knew there was a power imbalance and I didn't want to exploit it'.[114] Notably, both Chrissie and Ruth spent at least part of their childhood brought up by lone mothers so had a more personal sense of what it felt like to be the target of social concern. Ruth explicitly drew a connection between her discomfort at the 'middle-class social worker' coming to visit her mother and the way she aimed to 'show respect not judgement' to her own clients.[115] Todd has argued that, in the post-war period, social workers became more professionalized and urged the government to take responsibility for alleviating poverty rather than blaming individual 'problem families'.[116] Carol (b.1948) spent much of the 1970s as a campaigner for women's rights and helped set up one of the first women's refuges in the country in Oxford.[117] When she returned to education to train as a social worker in the early 1980s, she chose to make use of the knowledge she had gained and specialized in antenatal care, working with vulnerable expectant mothers. Carol viewed this as an extension of her politics, which were about 'protecting the underdog'.[118] Social workers increasingly tried to use their positions to challenge social policy rather than policing the behaviour of women and families.

Working to broaden access to, and improve experiences of, education was a key aim of women of this generation. Anita pointed to her female friends who 'went to the Institute of Education, which is quite a radicalizing place and then they've gone into education ... and they were committed to bringing working-class girls to universities and [similar] stuff, so that's where their interest politically has been working to get more access to people who are less privileged than they are'.[119] Many women were keenly aware that they had themselves benefitted (albeit often in contradictory ways) from the post-war drive to increase educational provision, and they wanted to extend the advantage. Nancy had a chaotic childhood, and she felt that she had only passed the eleven-plus by the skin of her teeth. She kept returning to the idea of luck or different sliding-door moments at each instance in her education that changed the course of her life. What she perceived as the unfair element of chance, particularly in the selective exam, motivated her interest in educational reform:

> Well ... I think I was very conscious of my own experiences of how slight was the difference, in any objective sense, between those of us who passed the eleven-plus and those who didn't. I mean, it was a huge, traumatic split in people's lives. It was quite extraordinary. So that always hit me and, you know, I was very conscious that, as I may have said, the girl next to me, Jenny, in primary school, was who I was leaning on most of the time 'cause I couldn't understand quite a lot of what we were doing, but she didn't pass and I did.[120]

As a result, Nancy was a strong proponent of comprehensivization in secondary education. Sylvia (b.1945) came from a manual working-class background and became a fine art lecturer in a polytechnic during the 1970s. She described, powerfully, that 'it was through gaining qualifications and working in education that I gained both access to a much better economic standard of living than that of my parents and to the cultural activities of the dominant class'.[121] She was not involved in political activism, but she described her choice of work as political: 'I wasn't politicized at all really, but I was in my commitment to education.' She explained: 'I had young children and I was reading up for work, writing lectures that sort of thing ... So I suppose my political commitment was to education. I believe education is a political act because of its transformative powers.'[122] Sylvia was concerned with increasing access to higher education for working-class students and ensuring that these students could be educated in a way that was not simply functional: 'in other words "training", which I think is too narrow'.[123] She continued that 'it is through the processes and practices of education that the dominant ideological, sociological and historical constructs are inculcated'.[124] Thus, it is important to challenge these constructs in teaching and to give students the 'skills for critical thinking'.[125]

Similarly, Rita's (b.1952) approach to education was informed by her own experience of selective secondary schooling. She left grammar school with few qualifications but made the decision to return to education during her twenties, graduating from art school in 1979. She explained that 'one thing I learnt at college was that intake is fundamental to the quality and outcomes of the educational experience. The possibility of comprehensive grant funding did make a real difference to the cultural and therefore intellectual mix of the student body'.[126] As one of the few working-class students at her grammar school, she was made to feel as though she did not have much to contribute, whereas here she was reframing the argument to suggest that attending a course with a wider mix of students had added to her educational experience. After graduating, Rita began working as a visiting lecturer, first at the London College of Printing before moving to Newcastle in the mid-1980s, to take on a similar and more long-term role. At both these institutions Rita said that she learnt even more about the 'crucial importance of admissions' and worked with others to ensure a diverse intake.[127] She stated that she was keen to 'avoid replicating the divisions of the 1944 Education Act', which placed the majority of working-class students into 'second-class' vocational training and saw middle-class students as the 'academics' or 'theorizers'.[128] Like Sylvia, Rita indicates that 'training' has classed undertones. Tertiary education institutions were centres of political change in this period, especially further education colleges and polytechnics.

Women working in primary and secondary school teaching had the autonomy in their own classrooms to take a politicized approach to their teaching. They felt that the long 1970s was when they had the most flexibility to influence curriculum content and teaching practice. Lesley and Maureen (b.1944) were typical in describing their aim in this environment as to provide more individualized and creative lessons for their primary school students rather than aiming for conformity.[129] Sociologists identified a strain of 'educational feminism' in 1970s and early 1980s British schooling, which was 'closely tied to … the decentralised form of the school system which allowed teachers an "active role in the expansion of equality of opportunity"'.[130] In particular, the huge increase in female teachers created by the expansion of the state meant they could act as 'internal reformers'.[131] This could take different forms. For example, explicit educational feminism advocated by writers such as the authors of *Learning to Lose*, who offered specific 'feminist practices' to undertake in the classroom.[132] It is striking that the starting point in this text was 'recollections' of their gendered experience of attending grammar school in the post-war decades.[133] Educational feminism could also be more implicit, for instance in an increase in female teachers making a specific effort to treat girls (and non-white students) more equally, encouraging them to go into a more diverse range of professions.[134] Jane Martin has argued that female educators working largely through local Labour councils in this period aimed to 'offer support to teachers to develop classroom strategies and produce their own curriculum materials to change rather than reproduce the values of patriarchy and androcentricity'.[135]

Conclusion

This chapter has emphasized the centrality of the welfare state in women's political thought during the 1970s. Feminists wrote extensively about the welfare state and permanently altered the way in which it is conceived. Rather than a narrow conception of the welfare state as solely a set of institutions, they defined it as a gendered ideology, which organized economic relationships in post-war Britain. Feminists emphasized that by the 1970s women were struggling to make sense of their lives within the nexus of contradictions the welfare state society produced. Changing economic opportunities for women, in large part driven by welfare state expansion, had not yet provoked a wholesale shift in welfare ideology. Feminists argued for fundamental changes in policy, but they also saw the value in working through trade unions to improve women's conditions in the workplace (as well as economic relations more broadly). As women of the welfare state generation themselves, they intimately understood the competing demands of paid work and unpaid care in the private sphere.

The feminist analysis of women's position in society resonates with the ways in which women born between the late 1930s and the early 1950s spoke about their own dilemmas during the 1970s. This was the period when women acted against the gendered discrimination they experienced in the workplace, either through trade unions or other forms of collective and individual action. Working for the public sector offered more opportunities for women to push the boundaries of what was possible and to negotiate a different type of working week – even if that often saw women still losing out on prestige or promotional pathways. However, not all women of this generation identified with the collective label of 'feminist' even if they believed in gender equality, and it is difficult to say whether their actions were influenced by feminist theories of the welfare state. Two examples from this chapter challenge the assumed process of progressive values diffusing outwards from the WLM: first, the way in which welfare state workers claim 'equality' on the basis of their professional role rather than as a recourse to feminist activism and, second, the fact that, in their writing on the welfare state, feminists identify a trend of political action by women on the basis of their employment within the state – they do not claim that this originated with the WLM. Women of this generation shared a common experience of gendered living under the auspices of the welfare state. This commonality could be a fruitful starting point for better understanding why second-wave feminism arose at this historical moment and why the WLM chose particular priorities.

Both non-activist and activist women working within the welfare state directed political energy to effecting change in the way that they carried out their duties. The insight that women saw their state roles as inherently political should broaden how we conceive of political action and the relationship between work and politics in this period. Women of this generation believed that their individual actions could make a real difference to the lives of their clients, patients and students. The impetus for this can be linked to their collective biography: they mobilized a sense of personal entitlement and value, held a shared belief in equality, and also referenced their own experiences of and relationships to the state. Women acted as agents of change within the welfare state during this period, redefining its meaning and reshaping how it functioned in practice.

A clash of experiences: The process of de-professionalization from Thatcher to Blair

The opportunities and living standards of women born mid-century were profoundly affected by political reforms to the welfare state from the late 1980s onwards. The changes to the welfare state enacted by successive Conservative governments onwards constituted 'de-professionalization' for women workers. I define this process of 'de-professionalization' in the welfare state and show that it was characterized by three elements: the devaluation of professional expertise, the rise of managerialism and a loss of autonomy for state workers. Women lost status and power in the workplace – and society more broadly – because of the process of de-professionalization. Many found themselves unexpectedly downwardly mobile at a crucial stage of their career, through a decline in conditions, moving roles or losing a job as a result of reorganization or redundancy.

The third election victory in 1987 of the Conservative government, led by Margaret Thatcher, empowered her government to enact a sweeping programme of welfare state reform, which was previously feared too radical. While public support for the principle of a welfare state remained high, the government was able to harness a growing sense of dissatisfaction with the dominance of the professional voice in state services which some felt gave scant regard to the choice or views of the user.[1] Particularly important for the purposes of this chapter was the 1988 Education Reform Act, which historians agree was the most substantial change since the 1944 Education Act, and the 1990 National Health Service and Community Care Act, which constituted the first phase of the largest review of the NHS since its inception (and also affected all welfare professions that came into contact with the health service).[2] Further significant welfare state reforms also took place during John Major's government, which social policy scholars often bracket with the late Thatcher era.[3] These included the 1992 Further and Higher Education Reform Act, an ambitious piece of legislation ending the binary phase of universities and polytechnics in higher education policy.[4]

This wave of reform sought to introduce neoliberal principles into the welfare state. The political philosopher Wendy Brown argues that a fundamental aspect of neoliberalism is the '"economization" of heretofore noneconomic spheres and practices, a process of remaking the knowledge, form, content and conduct appropriate to these spheres and practices'.[5] The logic of the market was now intended to govern the functioning of welfare institutions. The *Working for Patients* white paper published in 1989, for example, stated that 'health authorities [should] become more business-like in their provision of services and the uses of resources at their disposal'.[6] The impact of these policy changes has thus far largely been considered from the perspective of users of these services,[7] but here the perspective has been reoriented to focus on workers and the gendered nature of the changes. As we have seen, women's employment was increasing in the public sector workforce during the 1970s and overtook men's employment in the 1980s (women constituted 63 per cent of public sector workers by 1997).[8] This trend intersected with the onset of neoliberal policies. It is notable that, post-1987, 'the education and medical professions were a prime and deliberate focus for public displays of government contempt'.[9] Already, by the early 1990s, sociologists were recognizing that the power of welfare state professions dominated by female workers had been eroded further than those dominated by men.[10] The so-called 'semi-professions' where women had gained a foothold experienced the brunt of the changes during the early period of reform.

There is a complicated interrelationship between neoliberalism, the welfare state and gendered roles in late-twentieth-century Britain with which historians have not yet fully engaged. Shifts in how welfare provision is provided influence women's experience both within and outside the workplace. Brown has argued that 'gender subordination is both intensified and fundamentally altered' by neoliberalism.[11] She emphasizes that 'when public provisions are eliminated or privatized, the work and/or the cost of supplying them is returned to individuals, disproportionately to women. Put another way, "responsibilization" in the context of privatizing public goods uniquely penalizes women'.[12] One of the aims of decreasing public services in the late 1980s was to reinvigorate civil society and family life. Ewen Green highlighted that Thatcherite politicians believed that caring should be the responsibility of women but largely (and ideally) in a domestic or voluntary setting rather than under the remit of the state.[13] Ben Jackson has recently made a significant contribution to the debate about the relationship between gender and neoliberalism, arguing that market liberals aimed to defend the male breadwinner model in the 1980s and 1990s and sought to limit the role of the state in supporting women in the labour market.[14] In contemporary writing, women sought to mitigate criticism of the welfare state during this period because they feared that cuts to provision would be used to justify precisely this movement of caring responsibility from the public to private sphere. This moment also prompted reflections on the part of women of the welfare state generation about the significance of the welfare state in their own trajectories and social-class positioning.

This chapter focuses primarily on women with (semi-)professional welfare jobs but also uses the testimonies of the clerical workers to show that de-professionalization produced a ripple effect in the public sector, which altered the conditions of administrative staff. The material circumstances of women of the welfare state generation, and their identity, were deeply affected by the decline in conditions. Lynn Abrams has argued that women born in mid-twentieth-century Britain grew up during a period of social change that 'rewarded achievement and self-development through education and work rather than marriage and motherhood'.[15] She concluded that, as a result of these changes, women experienced a 'liberation' of the female self and a progressive journey away from 'a model of womanhood represented by the service and self-sacrifice of their mother's generation'.[16] This chapter complicates the narrative by focusing on the experiences of women of the welfare state generation in the later twentieth century.

The early 1980s

The welfare state was wounded by the economic crises of the mid-1970s and was vulnerable to sustained ideological assault. Inspired by the writings of monetarist economists such as Friedrich Hayek and Milton Friedman, Thatcher's government took a 'neoliberal, pro-capital stance', which centred upon the individual rather than the state.[17] This had implications for their approach to provision of social services in the long term, although they had to take public support for the welfare state into consideration. Thatcher strategically emphasized her government's support for the NHS, insisting that it was 'safe in our hands'.[18] One interviewee, Eileen (b.1945), stated that she was worried about the economic situation in Britain by the late 1970s but was only able to vote Conservative in 1979 because 'Mrs Thatcher said the NHS is safe with me ... on that alone I voted Conservative, the one and only time'.[19] During Thatcher's first two terms, the welfare state was not altered significantly and she chose to proceed cautiously with unpopular public sector spending cuts.[20] The

Conservative government spent their early political capital on macro-economic policy and confrontation with the unions. The economic environment during their first term in office deteriorated rapidly. Between 1979 and 1981, 'industrial output and GDP fell respectively by 16 per cent and 5 per cent, whilst inflation peaked at 22 per cent and unemployment rose inexorably towards 3 million'.[21] This economic situation made more of the population dependent on welfare state provision.[22]

During the early 1980s, two lone mothers in my sample, Eileen and Bridget (b.1951), were on social security benefits. Unsurprisingly, they both stated that this was a particularly difficult time to need state support. Although changes to welfare provision were proceeding slowly, the Thatcher government made cutting social security a priority because they believed that benefits had created 'dependency' and 'undermined Victorian virtues'.[23] In 1980, the government abolished the earnings-related supplement for unemployment benefit, also making it more complex for women to claim maternity leave and to return to work after having a baby.[24] State benefits had been Eileen's primary income since giving birth to her daughter in 1975. She outlined that it was tough to survive solely on benefits, but her finances became even more constrained in the 1980s. Eileen recalled having to 'make an art form of living on sod all' and noted that when her daughter was of school age she encouraged her to become a 'vegetarian' because she could not afford meat.[25] Another interviewee, Bridget, spent much of the 1970s as a housewife looking after her two children full time.[26] When her children started school, Bridget returned to education to study for a degree in history and politics. However, after graduating in the early 1980s, Bridget experienced a difficult time in her life: her husband had recently asked for a divorce, and she struggled to find employment (she blamed graduating into a poor economic environment). Bridget explained that if 'you were on a low wage or benefits, and you were a single parent or a woman on your own, you were just not as respected by society as a married woman'.[27] In her view, 'it would not have been quite so bad [to be on benefits] under a Labour government' because she felt that the Conservatives 'lacked empathy' for the contingencies that could lead to citizens needing state benefits.[28] Hilary Land has argued that cuts to benefits were the start of a move towards what Richard Titmuss termed 'a residual welfare state', in which access to welfare was 'no longer an unqualified right'.[29]

Ray Pahl found that the recession of the early 1980s hit male employment especially hard. In his contemporaneous study of the Isle of Sheppey, Pahl analysed the experience of a married couple, Linda and Jim. Jim had been made redundant and, although Linda was still working part time as a cleaner, the period was stressful for both of them. This was exacerbated by the ways in which the state continued to define the division of labour.[30] As Linda (b.1944) explained:

> It's silly really because if Jim took a low-paid job he would be able to get all the benefits and get all the money made up, but if I take a low-paid job I don't get it. And you're still doing it for your family, so you're not depending on social services. So, it must be cheaper for them in the long run and yet they stop you doing it.[31]

Not much discussion of male unemployment took place in my interviews, but one significant example demonstrated how difficult this could be for women even if they were still working. Jean's (b.1950) husband decided to leave his job in the building trade in the late 1970s so that he could study for a degree.[32] She recalled that when he finished, 'Thatcher had just come in and he couldn't get a job … there were offers around that there might be work, it was like a carrot being dangled, but there was no work'.[33] Jean was close to tears discussing a 'dreadful interview' he had the week before Christmas for a further education tutor position where he was told he 'didn't stand a chance of getting a job like this'. She described this as 'rock bottom' – the couple had built up a lot of debt while her husband was a student and now felt as though it had all been for nothing.[34]

Women with teenagers were preoccupied with concerns for their children's economic prospects in Thatcher's Britain. Maureen's (b.1944) eldest child left school in the mid-1980s and spent a year on the Youth Training Scheme (YTS) (the Conservative replacement for unemployment benefit for young people) before being able to find a job.[35] Although Theresa's (b.1941) son was a couple of years younger, he too was on the YTS for many months prior to finding work.[36] She described this as a 'demoralizing' experience for him. Chrissie (b.1950) stated: 'I think [Thatcher] was negative on kids' attitudes and unemployment, I think she had a huge impact on [my children's] generation, in a bad way'.[37] She continued that this 'bad way' was a reverence for 'capitalism' and a degree of 'selfishness'.[38]

By the mid-1980s, women were beginning to experience changes within their own workplaces. Lois (b.1947) recalled the 'large redundancies' across Sheffield city council owing to the rate-capping policy.[39] She believed that the council 'suffered very badly from rate-capping' because the Conservative government chose to 'hit the Labour councils very hard'.[40] Likewise, cuts to local government funding led to Theresa's position teaching unemployed youths being merged with another role, and both women had to competitively reapply for the one job. Theresa was unsuccessful and instead took up an administrative role in the same department. Her experience is emblematic of the broader process of de-professionalization in the welfare state that was to begin in earnest after the Conservative government's third electoral victory in 1987. This General Election was particularly significant for women because it was the culmination of their move away from the Conservative Party since the 1970s and reversed the gender gap in British voting patterns.[41] Stephen Lee has suggested that this shift was a result of 'women's fear[s] that possible inroads into welfare provision would affect them more fundamentally than men'.[42] From the late 1980s, a shared experience of worsening conditions in the welfare workplace emerged organically in the interviews among women born in the long 1940s.

Defining de-professionalization: Expertise

The process of de-professionalization, which can be identified from the interviews, involved the devaluation of professional expertise by politicians, the introduction of a culture of managerialism (with an attendant shift in priorities for resource allocation), and a loss of autonomy in the workplace. These interrelated changes undermine the features of a professional career outlined by Harold Perkin in his work on the rise of professional society: 'specialised occupations, selected by merit and based on trained expertise', 'salaried with benefits' (hence more scope to decide how their time was spent) and 'secure'.[43] Perkin observed that professional society was always an 'ideal' that never functioned perfectly but was at its zenith in Britain during the post-war years.[44] This was connected to the 'occupational transition' discussed in Chapter 3, which provided more professional roles in the welfare state for women. Just as Perkin has argued that professionalization is not an autonomous process but driven by changes in social and political culture, we should understand de-professionalization as a consequence of successive Conservative governments' efforts to reshape the welfare state. Through centring women's experience, it is possible to view changes to the welfare state and their impact holistically rather than as disparate occurrences in various aspects of the sector.

The first aspect of de-professionalization in the late 1980s was a shift away from political elites valuing the expertise of welfare state professionals. The Conservative government sought to review and restructure the health and education systems but chose not to seek the views of welfare professionals in doing so. They expressed not only distaste for an expansive welfare state but also a distrust of the professionals who worked for it. Thatcher found these professionals insufficiently 'cost-conscious' and slow to respond to market forces.[45] Rodney Lowe has explained that 'any claim [professionals] had to expertise or altruism … was thrust aside. Doctors and teachers alike were excluded from the major reviews of health and education … so too was academia, which was denied its accustomed privileged access via royal commissions to policy-making'.[46] Women working in these areas of the welfare state certainly felt that big changes in the structure of their professions were being imposed by the state without much consultation. Elizabeth (b.1939), who worked in medical research, exemplified these sentiments when asked her views on politics: 'I just feel politics is interference. I think if you're a professional especially in the medical world it's just crazy. They downward manage teaching and medicine.'[47] Sandra's (b.1946) thoughts on the reorganization of the NHS in the late 1980s and early 1990s demonstrate workers' frustrations. Having trained as a nurse in the late 1960s, by the 1980s Sandra had worked her way up to a position she enjoyed in a regional health authority. She described this coming to an end when 'Thatcher and her cohort decided they didn't want as many regional health authorities and made us all redundant'.[48]

Despite the fact Sandra did not agree with the decision to get rid of regional health authorities, she did believe that significant scope for change existed in the system. This pattern was reflected in other interviews – the women did not disagree with change per se – 'we needed to shake things up'[49] – but specifically with the choices made by the government. Sandra offered a detailed alternative to the choices made in the reorganization and also noted that she had tried to raise concerns at the time but was made to feel 'naughty'.[50] Nancy (b.1940) worked in education in London at this time and believed that a big shake-up needed to happen.[51] She felt that the Inner London Education Authority (ILEA) was too powerful and that not enough priority was given to the schooling of sixteen- to eighteen-year-olds.[52] As outlined in the previous chapter, women of this generation offered some of the most detailed critiques of the way that the welfare state operated, but the way the state was reorganized in this period was not the way they had envisaged or desired that this would happen.

The majority of interviewees shared a sense that interference by the state was poorly thought through and ultimately more concerned with political priorities than public service provision. One woman referenced the 'inappropriate short termism' of the changes,[53] and others noted that the Thatcher era settled little but instead ushered in a period of almost continual reform in the welfare state.[54] The Labour Party was potentially amenable to some of the changes and we can see this in the policy writing of Labour figures in the mid- to late 1980s.[55] However, the 'grossly improvised nature of much policy, above all the 1988 Education Act' increased their opposition to the reforms.[56] Personal testimonies collected by the social research organization Mass Observation echo these views. Alice (b.1950), a secondary schoolteacher, wrote that 'every education initiative since the days of Thatcher seems to have been introduced without any thought about its ultimate effect'.[57] The Conservative government wanted 'preparation for working life' to be the principal aim of the education system,[58] but teachers do not agree that this can be a workable end in itself. Alice elaborated:

> If I had any say in the matter (which of course I don't because the government never consults teachers except those who have left the profession often because they couldn't do the job in the first place), I'd try to revive the principle of education for education's sake … the government talks about its great achievements in 'improving education' through targets but it's complete nonsense. All that's happened is that teachers have learned to adapt their methods in order to fit the targets and test.[59]

This exclusion of welfare professionals from decision-making was in stark contrast with the mid-century, when 'faith in the beneficent, public-minded expert underlay the creation of the modern welfare state'.[60] As Paul Wilding has noted, a 'welfare state is a professional state' and requires professionals' knowledge to function well.[61] Throughout the post-war years there was an increasing cachet to expertise and professionalism in the public sphere and in construction of personal identities.[62] Obtaining professional standing had been particularly difficult for female welfare workers, and only during the 1970s were they really able to make use of political flux to leverage the value of their expertise. Thatcher's government was certainly concerned about welfare professionals as a 'site of political resistance'.[63] It was likely frustrating for women of this generation (many of whom came from working-class backgrounds) that, just as they had gained professional status and expertise through working for the welfare state, these characteristics began to be devalued by politicians.

Politicians came to value new kinds of knowledge during the 1980s, which were developed in the private sector but that they wanted to import into the welfare state. This knowledge built on the technocratic expertise that had developed in the post-war decades, associated with new careers and specialisms – largely in corporate industry – and lower to middle-class masculinity.[64] Frank Mort's father trained as an accountant after the Second World War, and he suggested that his father's role was 'to advise, to warn, to regulate by the sheer weight of numerical detail'.[65] The qualities that were expected from these 'organisation men' were 'complete neutrality in decision making ... and the ability to act, as Max Weber put it, without regard to persons'.[66] The type of expert who could make supposedly rational, not emotional, decisions chimed far more with the neoliberal, Thatcherite world view.[67] Moreover, during this decade, this form of expertise developed in the private sector was becoming more generalized and dynamic and was increasingly perceived as transferable.[68] As a consequence, 'masculine' technocratic expertise was actively brought into the welfare state by Conservative governments. An example of this is the decision to ask the newly founded Audit Commission (note the terminology of accounting and finance) to audit the NHS, and the government expressed this explicitly in terms of the commission having the 'expertise [to] look at the professional aspects of the [health] service'.[69] In addition, the *Better Schools* white paper, which laid the foundations for the 1988 Education Act, proclaimed the value of 'prospective teachers having had previous employment ... it is particularly helpful for teachers to gain some experience in industry or commerce'.[70]

Managerialism

The introduction of a culture of managerialism into welfare state institutions was central to the reorganizations and hence to the process of de-professionalization. Managers were considered an important mechanism for ensuring the dissemination of technocratic expertise and staff compliance with the reform agenda. 'Strengthening management' in welfare institutions was outlined as one of the government's key reform principles. They wanted both more layers of management and certain positions – such as that of head teacher – to be reconceptualized as management.[71] Margaret Cook (b.1944), a hospital consultant, noted in her autobiography that 'the number of managers, and the cost of managing, rose exponentially'.[72] Managerialism illustrates that the state did not straightforwardly shrink, but instead priorities altered. In fact, overall social expenditure increased year on year in real terms almost every financial year between 1987 and 1996.[73] The government openly declared that 'the salaries for [new chief executive posts] will be set significantly higher' than existing posts in the NHS 'so as to be attractive to good quality managers from both inside and outside'.[74] Thus, unlike in previous years, this new wave of managers were not all promoted from within the profession.[75] This distinction was noted by Lois in her description of her new manager in the local government arts department: 'She was a new breed – a young administrator not your traditional curator type'.[76] She felt that being interviewed by this manager when she was forced to reapply for her own during restructuring exacerbated her feeling of humiliation.

Managers across the welfare state were tasked with allocating front-line resources in a manner which would exact more from workers for less. Employees felt that 'it was perfectly clear what the new priority was amongst the hierarchy of general managers: money and savings'.[77] Barbara (b.1941), who had worked as an administrator at various tertiary education institutions throughout her career, echoed this point. She recalled that 'in 1989 higher education was changing'. From then onwards university management 'didn't always recognize that you needed more hands, it was quite stressful sometimes, in that I might have to take work home or I would stay on and work in my lunchtime'. Barbara continued that management 'were always looking to where they could save money ... we weren't getting things churned out quickly enough for them, we didn't have the person power'.[78] My interviewees frequently mentioned an increase in workload, sufficient to interfere with the separation between work and home life, and between work time and break time.[79] Technological innovation from the mid-1980s onwards meant that managers expected increased productivity from administrative staff.[80] Barbara initially enjoyed aspects of computerization in the workplace but found that this soon became quite overwhelming.[81] During the 1980s, Marion (b.1942) took a position as a liaison officer in local government.[82] She explained that the role was initially quite flexible and she could request time off if she needed it 'for a sports day, say'. Marion stated that, over time, owing to 'government policy ... finances got tighter and tighter' and 'the number of liaison officers decreased'. She recalled that her 'managers were much fussier about things'.[83]

Increased pressures led many women to fear for the continued provision of 'a humane service'.[84] Doctors at Cook's hospital were instructed to see more patients, while spending less time with each. Carol (b.1948), a social worker, experienced similar demands in the early 1990s. Carol worked in the child protection side of social work, doing pre-birth risk assessments in hospitals. This was difficult and stressful because 'a lot of it was drug related and domestic violence' and there was a great deal of responsibility involved.[85] Carol did not get on very well with her manager, who saw no issue with repeatedly increasing her caseload:

> My manager hadn't given me a supervision for three months and she told me to take another case and I said I can't I've got too much work already and she said, 'Oh it'll only take a week,' and it turned into a really nasty case ... and I thought

I can't do this anymore. I was going around crying all the time. I had terrible headaches and I wasn't sleeping so I did go off with stress, and I was very angry with my manager because she didn't protect me.[86]

Although she was signed off with stress for three months, Carol returned to work within a month because she felt a lot of guilt about being away from her casework. Cook also noted that health workers retained 'good will' towards the NHS and therefore 'bore the burden of trying to maintain standards in the face of constant erosion of support and finance'.[87] The cover image of this book is taken from an article published in *The Sunday Times* magazine in 1989 titled 'Doctors in Distress' which was written to expose readers to the reality of hospital working conditions.[88] One source stated: '[M]ore patients are passing through many less beds, without more staff, inevitably increases the workload of all doctors working in NHS hospitals'.[89] The main protagonist of the piece was a paediatrician – Dr Janet McConaghy – who had risked her career to be named in the article. The reporter included a tick-tock of one of her tough overnight shifts. But it was a different female doctor featured in the photographs because Dr McConaghy's superior had been 'severely reprimanded' for letting the press into the hospital to witness the increasing difficulties faced by staff.[90]

Managerialism created an especially difficult environment for female workers. Social policy scholars argued in the early 1990s that the introduction of managerialism by Conservative governments into the welfare state should be viewed as 'a new set of male power relations located within a performance-oriented culture'.[91] In her research on social work, Mary Langan noted that the changes to the profession in the late twentieth century produced a 'growing feminisation of welfare', which had 'been accompanied by the further masculinisation of the social services hierarchy'.[92] Mike Savage provocatively suggested that, because female welfare professionals were moving away from the Tories, it was beneficial for the party to create new layers of management that as a group were more likely to vote Conservative.[93] The *Working for Patients* white paper outlined a system whereby consultants were encouraged to have a role in their own management, and to self-manage as far as possible, but this was not recommended for the overwhelmingly female nursing staff.[94] In 1992 only 37 per cent of managers in the public sector were women despite being in the majority of all workers.[95] Jean stated that she 'was always discriminated against – it's never fair in nursing. It seemed like 95 per cent of nurses were female and only about 5 per cent of nurse managers were women'.[96] Women were less likely to benefit from managerialism, enabling men to get promotion more easily and devaluing the practical experience of working with clients or patients.

Women who became managers in public sector institutions during this period could find it a difficult experience. Nancy recalled that, in the late 1980s, 'there were very few women in senior positions in education administration outside of the ILEA'.[97] When she took up her position as chief education officer in Warwickshire, 'there was a different world outside the ILEA from the point of view of being a woman ... it was old-fashioned'. Nancy stated that a few more women were being appointed in senior positions but that her role was difficult to navigate especially at such a politically charged moment for education: 'I had to learn a lot about knowing when to keep quiet and when to give advice and, you know, when things were possible and were not.'[98] In 1989, an assistant director of social services argued that 'any women manager will be relatively isolated and will have considerable problems with her male colleagues'.[99] Two of my interviewees, Rita (b.1952) and Sylvia (b.1945), were promoted to management positions in academia around the mid-1990s. Rita had a difficult experience. She was given only a temporary contract and felt that she was often ignored or talked over in meetings, with male peers given different treatment even if voicing similar issues.[100] She was also under a lot of pressure to recruit international students to bring revenue to the institution even if they did not meet entry requirements, and her professional decisions were often overridden by more senior managers. Sylvia had a better experience as a manager, but she also expressed frustration at the creep of economization and the expectations from above that students be treated as 'consumers'.[101] White papers produced at this time began to describe students as 'customers'.

Autonomy

The impact of large public sector reorganizations and the introduction of new layers of management filtered down to the regulation of the day-to-day activities of women working in the welfare state: political change was experienced on a personal level. Paradoxically, therefore, although Thatcherite rhetoric was framed around freedom from state intervention, successive Conservative governments' dislike of an expansive welfare state meant that, in practice, many women experienced a steep increase in intervention from the late 1980s onwards. Land argued that, during this period, it was 'of particular significance to women' that 'those involved in the production of the social wage [had] a weaker voice'.[102] The pioneering Labour minister Barbara Castle had defined the 'social wage' in 1981 as 'the standard of publicly provided services which mean so much to famil[ies]- health, education, housing and a good environment'.[103] This loss of autonomy was fundamental to the process of de-professionalization and made it harder for women to make the kinds of politicized intervention through welfare roles outlined in the previous chapter. Women of this generation described this in detail in their interviews because they had often worked in the welfare state before, during and (sometimes) after the policy shifts.

Some women, who had divorced and were now single or married to new partners, experienced positive moments in their personal lives during this decade. This feeling of more agency in their personal lives could contrast with increasing loss of autonomy in the workplace. After marrying young, many women of this generation indicated that they felt happier living on their own or found their new relationships more compatible than their first marriages. India (b.1947) and Clara (b.1939) both emphasized that they knew themselves a little better by early middle age and felt more relaxed in their second marriages. Theresa (b.1941) and Jacqui (b.1943) were relieved to be separated from the husbands; they had long thought it had been a mistake to marry. After her divorce, and with a young daughter, Jacqui made the decision to leave social work because it was becoming very stressful and took an entry-level position at a publishing house.[104] She described 'missing the sense of professional self terribly' and occasionally decided to put an application in for a social work role but ultimately resolved that 'it was all retrograde, there was no way it was going to work'.[105]

Women articulated that having a degree of freedom to exercise their own judgement in their work was very important to them. They believed that there had previously been faith in their ability, and they were often left alone to carry out their duties. Jean expressed these sentiments about her nursing role during the 1970s: 'When I was a district nurse back before I had my children, you'd use your common sense you know – you went in to see somebody, and you'd decide well do they really need a bath or did they need breakfast? You'd use your skills and make a decision.'[106] Women employed in other welfare professions shared similar experiences. Rita described her time in an early academic job: 'I could do things and I could really make a difference.'[107] Ruth (b.1949) stated that she used to feel a sense of 'control' over her engagements with clients as a social worker and that she believed that she could make a 'real difference' to people's lives but that this had changed by the late 1980s.[108] Langan noted that 'by the close of the 1980s … the social work profession was in shock'.[109] She pointed to the 'optimism' of the profession in the late 1960s, which evaporated in the face of the 'ideological attack on social work … which was becoming increasingly virulent'.[110] Teachers in both primary and secondary schooling noted that they had previously enjoyed the autonomy that was given to them to 'decide what you wanted to do in the classroom' and to be 'creative' in adapting their teaching to the needs of different pupils.[111] During the 1970s there was an increasing emphasis on the subjective judgement of the teacher and the centring of personal experience. We have seen the ways in which women of this generation used their roles within the welfare state to effect change from within. This was in part possible because of the decentralized structure of the welfare state, with much of it under local government control. Conservative reforms thus sought to shift control to the central Department of Education: '[L]ocal government lost control over polytechnics, other higher education colleges and opted out schools in 1988, and over further education and sixth form colleges in 1991.'[112] One of the aims of the reforms was to marginalize the subjective in the way that the welfare state functioned.

The focus on results and performance across the welfare state led women to feel as though the centrality of the patient, the student or the citizen was being forgotten and replaced by abstractions. Cynthia (b.1941) decided to leave primary teaching in the late 1980s because she was 'becoming disenchanted with teaching; like all professions it's become too obsessed with results'.[113] When she returned to work in the mid-1990s, 'in the hospital as a secretary and the same happened there, it was statistics, you know, you had to prove your worth, so you had to bring all these stats – never mind the clients!'.[114] Ann (b.1939) also felt uncomfortable with having to spend time producing stats and making cost calculations about healthcare provision in her role as PA to a hospital consultant. She felt that this violated her belief in healthcare according to need: 'I think if you're urgent, you're urgent.'[115] Similarly, Maureen stated that teaching should be about the 'whole person' not just 'the maths and … the records'.[116] The performance of the welfare state had always been measured and assessed, but measurements had not always been statistical, and outcomes were expected over a longer period of time. This is striking when the 1985 white paper *Better Schools* is compared with the 1968 survey of the education system, *All Our Future*. The latter features voices of students, and the meaning of 'results' is problematized rather than taken as objective truth of ability (of either pupils or teachers).[117] One Mass Observation respondent summed up the shift as follows: '[I]n my view since the early 1980s up until today there has been an increasing and progressive tendency for governments to treat individuals in society as customers and not as human beings, each with their own individual rights needs and rights. This had a negative influence on welfare services.'[118]

In 1982, Ursula Huws (a contributor to the *Truth, Dare or Promise* collection) wrote a book outlining how she thought technology would affect women's work in the 1980s.[119] In the chapter on the 'caring professions', she argued that, because the majority work for the state, they are particularly vulnerable to changes in government policy. Huws elaborated that technology could be introduced into these professions in such a way as to aid the political outcome of 'making work for many professionals more routine and removing responsibility … the same processes could also lower the quality of the service for clients … leading to errors … that could be avoided by the exercise of an individual worker's common sense and professional judgement'.[120] Examples offered of this included the possible introduction of computerized records, which require standardized forms for welfare professionals to fill out about their clients. These can distort information because of the need to adhere to 'pre-existing categories'.[121] Huws did not idealize state workers, arguing that individuals could make poor judgements, but argued that this did not justify taking away responsibility from all care professionals.

Welfare professionals stated that they had lost some of the autonomy to exercise their judgement in their working lives. Jean was forthright in her opinion that reorganization of the NHS in the late 1980s had 'deskilled' nurses. She explained that it became: 'formulaic about what you had to do, how many patients you were seeing and for how long'.[122] She did not think that this was good for patients because nurses often had to 'cut corners like mad' to get everything done and produce all the paperwork to prove that they had stuck to the given timetable.[123] The terminology of 'deskilling' and 'box-ticking' also emerged in interviews with female further education lecturers in the mid-1990s.[124] The interviewer argued that this was because 'control over the conception and design of academic work is increasingly being taken away, by management, from practitioners responsible for its delivery in the classroom'.[125] Kathy (b.1950) found, for example, that cuts to further education largely affected 'what most people who believed in further education saw to be their bread and butter: English as a foreign language, basic literacy, courses for women returners'.[126] Stella Dadzie (b.1952), an academic who had been a key figure in the black feminist movement, had chosen to use teaching in further education as one way to direct her political energies but decided to leave in the late 1980s. She recently said that she 'stopped working in FE once I felt that I was losing my autonomy. It was around the time when legislation was being passed that was taking power away from the local authorities … at that point I decided I could be more effective from the outside'.[127] Further and adult education was relatively protected until the later 1980s, but things began to shift, and a significant amount of restructuring and redundancies took place in the wake of the 1992 Further and Higher Education Act.

Reflections on changes in school teaching after the 1988 Education Act demonstrate the kind of 'formulaic' shifts described occurring in the NHS and further education. Teachers found that the successive introduction of the national curriculum and SATs was increasingly restrictive – one interviewee described it as 'literally a different job'.[128] Alice stated that 'the testing system means everyone has to do exactly the same thing'.[129] Similarly, Maureen noted, 'It got to the point where you had a booklet for maths, week one, day one you do this – some children didn't understand it – "sorry we're moving on". And you have to write it up, all these sheets to fill in.'[130] Rita described academia as becoming increasingly like a 'piece meal' job.[131] This encapsulates a central theme of de-professionalization – the idea that the welfare worker should not be allowed to make judgements on a case-by-case basis but actions should instead conform to a standardized knowable and measurable regime, with each moment accounted for.

There was a marked increase in inspections and observations in schools, linked to the broader culture of managerialism, which was especially stressful for teachers and further reduced their autonomy. Teachers had been highlighted by the Thatcher government as a group of particular concern, and the *Better Schools* white paper noted that 'a significant number of teachers are performing at a standard below that required to reach the new objectives'.[132] The government therefore advocated a 'regular and formal appraisal of the performance of all teachers', which could lead to 'early retirement or dismissal' if unsatisfactory.[133] The Major government strengthened these provisions by creating OFSTED in 1992, then introducing the Schools Inspection Act in 1996. Maureen recalled 1996 as an especially difficult year because it was the first inspection she experienced under the new regime. She and her colleagues found the whole process overwhelming:

> People started having nervous breakdowns … we had to write policies for every area because we didn't know what we were going to be tested on … a lot of people were off sick with stress, early retirement, even relationship problems, you know, full-time teaching plus stressful meetings and demands to write policies – all your spare time.[134]

Teaching staff were controlled through exposure, or possible exposure, to the gaze of the observer at all times. This worked literally though the inspection system in schools and through the exponential increase in management figures across the sector, but also more figuratively through the standardization of tasks. De-professionalization was an important element of the Conservative governments' nascent 'regulatory state', which constituted 'a more complex pattern of government activity ... more inspection and regulation – even if less public provision'.[135]

When New Labour came to power in 1997 they slowed down, but did not reverse, key aspects of these trends. The government was committed to an expansive welfare state and increased welfare spending (especially following their pledge to stick to Conservative spending plans, which came to an end in 1999). They also enacted policies to narrow the gender pay gap in the public sector workforce.[136] Yet, as Martin Powell has suggested, their overarching aim to 'modernise' the welfare state led New Labour to try to 'assert control over organizations that were seen as variously too bureaucratic, too professionally dominated and, in some cases, self-interested and self-serving'.[137] Adrian Barton has posited that the government 'embraced and, moreover, enhanced the use of the audit and evaluation processes constructed by their Conservative predecessors ... to ensure that professionals adhere to policy by undermining, or at the very least curbing, professional autonomy'.[138] As we will see below, the testimony of women born between the late 1930s and early 1950s demonstrates that the personal cost of de-professionalization primarily took place under successive Conservative governments, but also offers examples of how the cumulative effects of the process could build up with consequences into the new millennium.

Downward mobility

Women's career trajectories were altered by the process of de-professionalization. The changes resulting from this process could be compulsory or voluntary but often led to downward occupational mobility. Growth in health and education employment had slowed in the 1980s and the early to mid-1990s witnessed an overall contraction in the number of state workers.[139] An increase also took place in contracting out services to the private sector, undermining some of the efforts to improve pay for women workers in the public sector. This was occurring at the same time as paid work had become increasingly central to the lives of women of the welfare state generation. Loss of occupational status could have a significant negative impact on women's life experience in profound ways, just as historians argue that de-industrialization has affected male workers.[140] In a 1987

Fabian pamphlet, the feminist researcher Cynthia Cockburn underscored this, writing that 'women's attachment to paid labour has increased, more women are in paid work for more of their lives. For this reason, unemployment when it occurs has become more significant for women too'.[141]

The importance of this type of work to women's lives and the space it provided them to do things that they found both personally and socially fulfilling led many to extend their time in the public sector. Some women even chose to move into different areas of the sector, making this decision in the face of the stress and precarity caused by increased workload, more monitoring and fewer resources. This reduction in conditions can be viewed as a form of downward occupational mobility even for women who stayed in the same employment. In turn, this meant that the risk of moving jobs often felt worth taking. Job status does not remain static over time and downward mobility can be experienced as a drift rather than a sudden shock. India (b.1947) moved from secondary school teaching to the extra-mural department of a university in the late 1980s. Initially, she had a lot of flexibility to create her own courses, which she chose to make interdisciplinary and 'woman-centred'.[142] However, she noted that the department 'became obsessed by accreditation in the nineties, I had to fit into a module system to degree level'.[143] This meant that much of her course content was marginalized and deemed inappropriate for progression to degree-level study. Feeling that what she had to offer was no longer of value to the department, India left in the mid-1990s to pursue freelance teaching, placing her in a fairly precarious financial situation.[144] Jean decided to leave nursing around this time because she felt that it had become untenable. She had already been a representative on a committee about stress among NHS staff because 'they wanted my opinion about why they were losing so many nurses through stress'.[145] She went on to teach nursing in a further education college, which she found 'fulfilling', although she later took early retirement to avoid redundancy as part of a restructuring process. Similarly, Ruth was made redundant from her role as a social worker and began working as a social work tutor before leaving in a restructuring process.[146]

Penny's (b.1948) experience of working abroad illuminates the changes that were taking place in the welfare professions in Britain and how they affected women's careers. She had moved to central Europe to teach at various international schools in the early 1980s. She had been enjoying working at the school she had chosen to settle down at in the 1990s – until the school employed a new director 'who came from Britain, and who hadn't been in an international school before'.[147] She explained that the school environment 'became quite masculine and toxic' and her promotion was blocked by a restructuring 'stitch-up'.[148] What is remarkable is that she framed this in terms of the school 'going on the route that Britain had gone along, which we were, for a long time, spared in international schools. And that is you have to spend so long proving you're doing a good job, you don't have time to do a good job'.[149] These changes to the school environment led her to make the 'hard' decision to retire much earlier than she had planned, and she returned to the UK in the early to mid-2000s.

The necessity of altering their career path left many women taking positions of a lower social status or that they found less fulfilling than their previous roles. This could be especially difficult for women who had grown up working class. After Sandra was made redundant from her position in the regional health authority, she took a role 'in the health service, rehousing the mentally ill from a big psychiatric hospital'. However, this was another consequence of NHS reorganization that she did 'not approve of – it was the idea of mov[ing] people to the community, which meant you could hide them'.[150] Sandra was so uncomfortable with the approach that she decided to leave the sector to start a cafe with her husband in the mid-1990s. She lamented that, as an older woman, she had to spend hours on her feet every day doing fairly menial labour and worrying about finances, especially through autumn and winter.[151] Sandra was not happy that she ended her career in a non-professional job.[152] Other interviewees from working-class backgrounds echoed this sentiment. Ruth stated that being made redundant 'felt like a horrible inevitability, that you can't really escape your background', and Rita explained that 'it fe[lt] like being put back in my box'.[153]

In her research on women and social mobility in the early 1990s, Steph Lawler found that many of the upwardly mobile women from working-class backgrounds she interviewed, the majority of whom worked for the welfare state in health or 'education and training', had recently experienced upheaval in their working lives.[154] Lynne (b.1950) worked in the health service for much of her career but, because of deteriorating conditions, returned to university study.[155] Frances (b.1945) was unemployed after leaving her job as a lecturer. Lawler described this as a 'crisis, which brought home to [Frances her] outsider status' in class terms.[156] In her narrative, Frances 'represents her working-class subjectivity as forgotten but returning'.[157] Frances had to sell her house, a 'large Victorian villa', and downsize to 'an inter-war semi-detached house'. This move 'induced shame' and was 'filled with anxiety' because it had been the most 'visible class marker' of her upward mobility.[158] Material possession in this case is a symbol for the broader sense of loss that Frances, and other women of working-class origin, experienced when faced with declining access to meaningful work and slippage in the once enabling character of an expansive welfare state.

Women from middle-class backgrounds also struggled with the changes caused by de-professionalization, although they had more social and economic capital to mitigate downward movement. During our interview, Susannah experienced a moment of what Penny Summerfield has called 'discomposure',[159] when our discussion of the main body of her working life came to an end and she became almost literally lost for words. She asked if we could wrap up the interview, stating: 'I don't know whether, I'm not sure sort of where we should go now, because we've covered my work in the 1980s and 1990s.'[160] This suggests that new cultural narratives are in the process of being constructed for women where work is central rather than periphery. Susannah's career was so important to her understanding of herself that it had structured her life story in the interview. Born in 1940 to what she described as 'an upper middle-class family', Susannah had always expected to go to university and have a career. She gained a 'first-class' degree in medicine at Cambridge and afterwards went to London to train as a psychiatrist. At the turn of the millennium, Susannah's professional life was at a crossroads and she was encouraged to retire. Her prestigious job as a director in a hospital was 'coming to an end' because the hospital was being restructured and she had recently turned sixty years old.[161] After a break in the interview, Susannah came back and explained to me that her desire to keep working led her to apply to the position of principal of an Oxbridge college, which she got and held until she was in her late sixties. Even now though she has retired, she continues to have associations with the college and the wider university.

Women in my sample working in the private sector recounted more positive experiences of this period. Diane's (b.1946) career as a personnel manager continued to go from strength to strength during the late 1980s and 1990s. She moved companies in order to obtain a full board position, which came with an impressive package of bonuses and share options.[162] It is important to note that Diane encountered resistance from other board members to her appointment as the first female member of the board.[163] Another interviewee, Linda (b.1954), began the 1980s as a public sector employee but, by the end of the decade, was working for a large accounting firm in the City of London.[164] She had started as 'the lowest clerical assistant' in the civil service in the mid-1970s and managed to achieve steady promotions despite her lack of many formal qualifications.[165] Linda decided to leave her position as 'executive officer' after 'Thatcher got in and she stopped all promotions for three years', meaning that she was stuck at that grade 'for years'.[166] She was able to make use of her specialism in the accounting firm and received a substantial pay increase. A couple of years later she was headhunted by another 'big ten' firm to set up a new department for them. It is significant that one of my interviewees born just outside the temporal limits of the welfare state generation managed to make a successful move from the public to private sector. Both Diane and Linda benefitted from the Thatcher government's pro-business and finance policies, but they were in the minority as these sectors remained dominated by men, especially at the highest levels.[167] Women within the private sector continued to suffer sex discrimination but (particularly in the upper echelons) had the advantages of economic security and autonomy, both of which were reduced for public sector workers.

Although many women of the welfare state generation disagreed with the changes and suffered in their careers as a result of them, they frequently blamed themselves for not being adaptable enough. Despite Maureen's feelings that the process of de-professionalization had 'undermined teachers' authority', she took the position in her interview that teachers themselves need to take responsibility if they cannot handle the increased pressure: 'You either do it, you have a breakdown, or you think "I'm going". And you get out because you know you can't do what is demanded.'[168] Like many of my interviewees, Maureen found herself in the latter position, feeling that she was just no longer up for the job, and she took early retirement as soon as she was able to in the early 2000s. Anita (b.1952), who was made redundant from her public sector job because of funding cuts, expressed this self-blame even more emphatically. Her statement in the closing moments of the interview, when we discussed her continued search for work, is particularly poignant: 'I want to be out getting on, I want to make change happen. It's hard to know how to do it, so I'm trying to change myself rather than the outside world, but that's not easy.'[169] This feeling is very much in line with the neoliberal worker, who 'is totally responsible for their own destiny, and so techniques and technologies of regulation focus on the self-management of citizens to produce themselves as having the skills and qualities necessary to succeed in the new economy'.[170] Women of this generation hold the sense of neoliberal individual responsibility alongside, rather than in place of, a continued macro commitment to social democracy.

Reflections on the political moment

The increasing fragility of the welfare state and the rise of these new political discourses of self-management and aspiration were jarring for women of the welfare state generation, prompting moments of acute reflection about their own life experience, particularly among women who had been socially mobile. The resulting writing and scholarship constituted a new 'field', which analysed women's experience of social mobility in post-war Britain and made an important intervention in masculinized understandings of class, gender and mobility. The 'field' that we can identify is fractured, as women used their own autobiography in different ways and approached their life stories from differing disciplinary angles (including history, film studies, sociology, psychology and education). Nonetheless, it is clear that a network of citation and discussion of certain works written by socially mobile women born in the mid-twentieth century emerged between the mid-1980s and 1990s. Liz Heron's edited collection *Truth, Dare or Promise*, which was published in 1985, followed by Carolyn Steedman's *Landscape for a Good Woman*, published in 1986, should be considered the foundational texts.[171] This is the first body of sustained and analytical knowledge that we have about the experience of women's social mobility through education. The women set out a more complex understanding of gender, class and mobility, drawing from a range of disciplines and modes of thought, and, in doing so, emphasized the profoundly deep-rooted and historically situated formation of social class.

The context of the 1980s (and its interrelationship with the 1950s) is key to understanding how and why the 'field' of writing on women's experiences of social mobility developed. Heron reflected that the *Truth, Dare or Promise* collection was 'prompted by the end of an era, when a hope for progress and increasing social justice foundered in the wake of the 1979 general election'.[172] In her introduction, she stated that women writers had 'had confidence in the future – a confidence that has been severely shaken since the end of the seventies. Britain's economic recession and the ravages of a right-wing government on the foundations of the very welfare state that had nurtured us, were, until then, unthinkable'.[173] This did not signify an uncomplicated nostalgia for the past and, in her opening remarks on the welfare state, Heron set the tone by asserting that, alongside its benefits for the post-war generation, 'there was the resonance of late nineteenth-century philanthropy in welfare rhetoric (like the need to educate the working class for parenthood – working-class girls, that is)'.[174] The rapidly changing historical context and the fragility of aspects of society that had been taken for granted led Heron to ask the contributors, as Steedman recalled, to 'place their personal narratives of the 1950s within socio-political time'.[175] She explained that the later decades of the twentieth century 'witnessed much academic and journalistic re-evaluation of the first post-war Labour government, and, looking to the 1950s attempts to understand "what had gone wrong"'.[176]

Women who experienced social mobility saw their life histories as products of the post-war moment. The sociologist Valerie Hey, who was herself socially mobile in this period, explained that she was one of 'the late 1940s and 1950s generation of working-class girls who grew into adulthood through a particular set of political, cultural and economic circumstances. We were raised as "welfare subjects", products of a more generous settlement between capital and labour'.[177] However, as she stated, these women began to write about their life histories at a moment when class was not being discussed by politicians: '[W]e are the ones who, now finding ourselves in this world of incessant aspiration bear the marks of an earlier makeover; mobility achieved through a different set of ideological and material circumstances in which there existed (unlike now) a public discourse of class, class action and class representations.'[178] During the later decades of the twentieth century, a move took place away from a discourse of social class. The ideology of neoliberalism was more concerned with the language of the individual, the family and the market to explain social positioning and support networks. As Jon Lawrence and Florence Sutcliffe-Braithwaite have argued, 'during the 1980s, Thatcherites wielded the power of office to weaken bastions of class discourse. One institution which came under attack was the discipline of sociology. The budget of the research council responsible for social science was cut by half'.[179] This was compounded by the contemporaneous rise of post-modernist modes of analysis in the academy, which led to a decline in research into personal experience and social class. Valerie Walkerdine stated in the mid-1990s that 'class is no longer a fashionable subject'.[180] It is notable that women were provided with some breathing space to theorize class and their own mobility during a moment when the mainstream academy was not focused on class analysis. Todd has emphasized that the discourse of a 'classless society' was a construct and that disparities in class power and social hierarchy remained, but the language used to discuss this was largely obscured, to the detriment of those in the working class.[181]

In contrast, socially mobile women of the post-war generation actually experienced an *intensification* of class relations in the 1980s and 1990s. As they grew older and entered the professions (especially academia), they actually felt class dislocation and disjuncture more deeply. Hey, for example, only began teaching in higher education in the 1980s and wrote that she had 'come to feel [herself] more, not less, "working-class" through the prevailing conditions in academic life'.[182] This strength of feeling and motivation to write was outlined in detail by the co-editors of the 1997 book *Class Matters: 'Working-Class' Women's Perspectives on Social Class*, Pat Mahony and Christine Zmroczek, two socially mobile women of this generation:

As we began talking about these issues in the mid-1980s we discovered that we shared a massive sense of confusion about where we fit in if anywhere and as we talked more we were relieved to learn that we tend to have similar reactions of outrage to the subtle reminders of our difference, sometimes ascribed as inferiority.[183]

The editors found that this social positioning had consequences for how socially mobile women acted in the workplace. They highlighted conflicted feelings of intellectual excitement and 'anger and guilt' found in the contributions, with an abiding sense of 'insecurity' and a 'fear that one day the "fraud" will be exposed'.[184] This produced a tendency to 'overwork' in order to prove that 'we are worthy of our places in the academy'.[185] As resources became scarcer and institutions of higher education were reorganized, these feelings of insecurity intensified.

The writings of the women attest to the significance of the entrance of more working-class women into the academy for new types of knowledge to be created. Walkerdine wrote in the mid-1990s that

we are witnessing a ground swell in academia, one brought about by the much delayed entry of a relatively small number of women from the working class into the academy … Indeed, rather than talking about a defunct topic from their childhoods, the new feminist writers on class open up new possibilities for inquiry – new ways of understanding of a topic which has been played out in the academy and in politics.[186]

This quotation from Walkerdine is particularly important because it lays claim to socially mobile women making imaginative interventions in their understanding of social class. They draw on different modes of thought to make sense of their own obscured histories and to argue for the significance of social class for women's identity and experience. Yet this knowledge developed from a historical moment where the structures this generation perceived as permanent were revealed to be ephemeral.

Conclusion

Women's testimonies reveal that between the mid- to late 1980s and the late 1990s, a rapid process of de-professionalization was engendered in the welfare state by successive Conservative governments. The process involved a devaluation of professional expertise, the introduction of a culture of managerialism and a loss of autonomy for workers. The changes were slowed by the New Labour government elected in 1997 but not wholly reversed. Unlike de-industrialization, which has impacted male workers, the process of de-professionalization identified here has disproportionately affected women because of their majority position in the public sector and has specifically had ramifications for the semi-professions within health, welfare and education. The lack of focus on this process raises significant questions about how women's labour is valued and defined in contemporary Britain. Linda McDowell has highlighted 'implicit masculinist bias' in overarching narratives of post-1945 employment, which she argues 'ignore women's different labour market histories'.[187] Analysis of de-professionalization, and its gendered implications, represents an important corrective to this tendency.

Analysing later life stages can complicate myths about the collective experience of a generation. Focusing on the childhood and early adulthood of women born between the late 1930s and early 1950s offers a portrait of progress and expanding possibilities for women. Nonetheless, it was precisely the women who benefitted from welfare state expansion who struggled when it was reshaped and welfare provision reduced during the late twentieth century. The clash between their experiences as 'daughters of the state' and the impact of neoliberal policy on their later lives prompted a wave of writing from socially mobile women of the welfare state generation, as they navigated the changing conceptions of social class, aspiration and welfare. Many women experienced a form of downward mobility through the deterioration in conditions and devaluing of their occupations. This chapter thus poses a challenge to sociological research on social mobility, which tends to measure change in social class at two static points in time. Social mobility is a relational process with moments of upward and downward movement across the life course.

Generational divides? Older age and the politics of welfare

Women of the welfare state generation have had a fundamentally different experience of older age than women of previous generations. The expansion of the welfare state changed the life course of many women, offering them a different experience of work and education, changing their understanding of femininity, and raising expectations. This is nowhere more vivid than in retirement, with women finding it difficult to give up paid work and the social and political citizenship which this provided. Women expressed discontent with the role of carer that is frequently prescribed for them in older age. This chapter is the first study of women of the welfare state generation in older age and makes a significant intervention in the existing historiographical consensus that women find retirement easier and less disruptive than their male counterparts.

The welfare state generation are at the centre of contemporary political debates in a way that previous generations have not been. They have reached older age at an historical moment when questions of intergenerational fairness and distribution of resources are at the forefront of the public imagination. Since the financial crisis of 2007–2008 and the onset of austerity, a political discourse has emerged that frames the post-war generation as having benefitted disproportionately from the welfare state to the detriment of future generations.[1] Yet, as this book reveals, women of the welfare state generation were keen to transmit the benefits to younger generations. In the private sphere, they aim to help younger relatives and have a keen awareness of class differences. In the public sphere, they continue to value social provision of services and seek to use their expertise to fill gaps in welfare as the state contracts. For these women, the welfare state remains pivotal to both their conception of politics and their choices in retirement.

We know comparatively little about older women's lives in recent history. As Paul Thompson has stated, 'the social history of ageing has barely begun'.[2]

There is a historiographical tendency to take a top-down approach to ageing, which focuses on the priorities of professionals and expert discourses rather than centring the experiences and narratives of older people.[3] This neglect of the social history of ageing is compounded by a wider methodological issue – even those making use of personal testimony source material are usually researching youth. Thompson identified a dual problem – that sociologists often prefer to interview young people – and oral historians are often concerned that their work be defined as 'history', primarily focusing on 'the past'. Wendy Webster expressed similar concerns when she took issue with the 'ageism' inherent in the practice of oral history, which often takes older people as its subject but then focuses on memories of earlier life.[4] I contend that, for a fuller understanding of the influence of historical change on individuals, it is important for historians to analyse later in the life cycle and to examine the dialectic between early and later experiences. Women's experiences of older age are influenced by their childhood – in this case as 'daughters of the state' – but are also affected by changes over time and the ways in which their lives have intersected with broader trends across their life course. The social and political context of their older age must be taken into consideration alongside a longer view. Generations are not frozen in time but rather adapt to differing circumstances, despite often being strongly informed by early experience.

Pat Thane has pioneered the historiography of women's older age in modern Britain.[5] She has emphasized that researching recent experiences of old age is vital because not until the second half of the twentieth century was it the case that 'for the first time in history it became normal to grow old'. This has unsettled the notion of 'what it means to be old'.[6] In 1951, British women who reached sixty-five years of age could expect on average to live another thirteen years, but by 2001 this had increased to nineteen years.[7] People were not only living longer but remaining healthy into older age. Thane's work differentiates between male and female experiences of retirement in mid- to late-twentieth-century Britain, noting that 'women were less likely than men to experience retirement from paid employment as a seriously disruptive break in the life-course, partly because their places in the labour market were less secure than those of men, partly because they had stronger family and social ties'.[8]

Her influential arguments relating to gender were about a specific moment in time but are often cited by historians who do not necessarily primarily research older age as an enduring truth about the different experiences of retirement.[9] As we have seen throughout the book, women of the welfare state generation identified less with their domestic role, and employment became increasingly central to their sense of self. From analysis of their personal testimonies a generation of women emerges who found it much more difficult to transition to retirement than previous scholars have understood. Their experience increasingly has more in common with established male apprehension about retirement and possible loss of public standing. This insight in turn helps us to better understand twenty-first-century Britain.

Welfare and pensions

The New Labour government that took office in 1997 made social policy and welfare reform one of its highest priorities. Their agenda was focused on welfare through work, and the slogan 'work for those who can, security for those who cannot' encapsulated this sentiment.[10] Aspects of Labour's social policy were explicitly gendered and, 'working women were some of the biggest winners under New Labour's policies'.[11] Bridget (b.1951), a single woman who worked in a succession of low-paid service and clerical jobs, stated that her financial situation noticeably improved under the Labour government.[12] She noted the introduction of the minimum wage and, later, working tax credits, which together helped her finally begin to pay off the debts she had accrued as a single mother during the 1980s and early 1990s. These policy changes, alongside increased state provision of childcare, were particularly helpful for lone mothers who 'were previously excluded from the labour market because of childcare duties'.[13] Only one woman in my sample was a single parent with school-age children during this period. Rita (b.1952) lost her job as a lecturer in a post-1992 university during the mid-2000s when two of her three children were still attending secondary school. Rita explained that hailing from a working-class background and being largely estranged from her extended family meant that this professional job was central to her financial security.[14] Without it, she said, 'it would not have been possible' for her to leave her partner in the late 1990s. Unable to get another full-time professional job, she maintains that her redundancy occurring under the Labour government just about allowed her to keep her head above water and not lose her house. This resulted from the working-tax credit she received because of the supply teaching she took on, but also from improved levels of child tax credit and means-tested educational maintenance allowance for her children. Rita shuddered at the thought of what would have happened if her redundancy had occurred in the 2010s and compared her experience to that of younger friends who had reduced access to state support under the Conservative-led coalition government.

Pension reform was the change to welfare with the greatest impact on the lives of women in the early twenty-first century. The majority of women in my sample turned sixty years old under the New Labour administration. Pensions were a key aspect of the welfare state to be expanded by the New Labour government, although change was slow and patchy.[15] Under the Conservative governments of the late twentieth century, pensions had dropped to their lowest value in real terms since the end of the Second World War.[16] As Thane has argued, persistently low pensions in Britain were linked to a 'widely held commitment to an essentially liberal view of provision of social welfare: that the role of the state should be confined to providing the minimum that is desirable and acceptable, supplemented by private effort'.[17] Women have always been in a weaker financial position than men in retirement. Many women were unable to collect a full state pension because they had not paid enough National Insurance (NI) contributions. The threshold for number of years worked was very high (at its height it reached forty-nine years) and did not include any allowance for childbearing. Moreover, in terms of occupational pensions, women were more likely to take on part-time contracts, which, for much of the post-war period, were 'not, or [were] inadequately, pensioned'.[18] These issues were exacerbated by the acceleration in divorce rates during the 1980s and 1990s. Not until the turn of the millennium were women given the right to claim a portion of their former spouses' pension.[19]

The Labour government did not fully take on the question of women's pensions until the mid-2000s. In 2005, only 13 per cent of women were entitled to a full state pension, compared with 92 per cent of men.[20] One of my interviewees was directly involved in the effort to expand women's eligibility for state pensions. Frances (b.1939) was elected as a local councillor in the early 1980s, and her success in this role led to her selection to stand as the Labour candidate for a parliamentary seat during the 1992 General Election.[21] She chose to focus on women's issues as soon as she got to parliament and campaigned to get all-women shortlists passed in the Parliamentary Labour Party. This stepped up a gear once Labour were elected into government in 1997 – Frances described herself as 'getting stuck into the women's pension business'.[22] She also helped to set up the Pensions Commission in 2004, which was led by Lord Adair Turner with Baroness Jeannie Drake – 'a good feminist and economist'[23] – playing a significant role in redressing the gender imbalance. The commission addressed the need for reduction in the number of years paying NI contributions required for full state pension and the need to make allowances for childbearing. This choice to make specific changes for women 'brought a couple of million women into the state pension bracket'.[24] A primary aim of the commission was to change the underlying assumption in social policy that women would gain a pension through their husband and instead ensure that 'the vast majority of women accrue pension entitlements, both state and private, in their own right'.[25] In order to pay for the changes to pensions, the report recommended incrementally increasing the pensionable age for men and women. Women in my sample were able to benefit from the positive changes to state pensions but were only marginally affected by the increase in pensionable age. It is important to note that women were still more likely to be in poverty in retirement than men, and Frances actually decided to step down at the 2005 election because she felt that the reforms had not gone far enough – a decision she later regretted because she felt that she left parliament before she was ready.[26] Poverty among older women was not eradicated, but the situation was relatively improved for female pensioners from a low base in the late twentieth century.

State pensions are often excluded or marginalized in discussions of social security and the welfare state. They are viewed as 'reward for past work'[27] and therefore more legitimate than other types of state benefit. This is reflected in the fact that there was no shame expressed by women in claiming the state pension. Diane (b.1946), who hailed from a middle-class professional family, explained that she felt state pensions to be one of the main benefits the middle class receive from the welfare state (alongside free schooling and the NHS) and that this needed to be emphasized when defining the welfare state.[28] She argued that a narrow conception of the welfare state functions to position the working class as the sole beneficiaries of its services and therefore weakens support for its continuation among the middle class.

Working within the welfare state also improved pension provision for women of this generation. Public sector pension schemes often had better terms and conditions than private sector schemes in gender-segregated sectors. In the early 2000s, 18 per cent of workers were public sector employees but they 'accounted for 36 per cent of all pension rights and funds'.[29] The Pensions Commission noted that the greater concentration of women than men in the public sector was one of the few employment trends beneficial to female retirees.[30] Women respondents to Mass Observation praised 'public sector pensions' for helping them have a more comfortable retirement than they expected.[31] Cynthia (b.1941), who worked as a primary school teacher for much of her career, highlighted 'decent pensions' as one of the key reasons why she felt 'women of my age are so fortunate'.[32] Kathy (b.1950) was especially pleased that her years of paying into a final salary pension scheme while working in a further education college and the increase in the state pension meant that her 'income did not go down at all' when she retired.[33] However, Kathy's experience reflected not only improved pension provision but also the low wages she received as an administrator in the public sector. The relative financial improvement experienced by this generation of women contributed strongly to creating a space where women could remain active after retirement. A more defined sense of worth, both professionally and personally, led women to a deeper consideration of how to continue to contribute to society in ways that they found rewarding.

Retirement: Power and agency

The demographer Peter Laslett articulated his theory of the 'third age' in his 1989 monograph *A Fresh Map of Life*.[34] He observed that a new life stage was emerging in Britain in the late twentieth century because of rapid demographic and social change in the post-war period: a stage between the familial and work responsibilities of middle age and the health and mobility issues associated with later old age. This life stage did not have a clearly defined age range because much depended on individual experience, but it broadly covered the period from the mid-50s to the mid-70s and was alternatively termed 'recent retirement'. Laslett argued that this life stage had the potential to be an 'era of self-fulfilment', although it all too often felt like being in 'limbo' – particularly in the early stages. He claimed that, in a market society, it is difficult to gain 'social recognition' for voluntary or familial tasks.[35] Laslett posited that the rising life expectancy of women in the late twentieth century and the growing numbers of women in employment made the issues associated with the 'third age' increasingly relevant for women. Women of the welfare state generation found it difficult to adjust to retirement. They wanted to retain a voice in the public sphere and to continue utilizing the knowledge that they had built up across the course of their lives as a result of their education and paid work.

By the early twenty-first century, there was a growing social and political awareness that older people were living longer, healthier lives and that this would have life-cycle implications. A rise took place in activist groups of older people, such as the Campaign Against Age Discrimination in Employment (CAADE) and the Third Age Employment Network, who 'were angry at their inability to work for a living, even when they were highly skilled, experienced and active'.[36] Activists argued that people should be treated more as individuals and that 'flexible pension and retirement ages are preferable, as Beveridge once recommended'.[37] Offering people increased opportunity to work was central to New Labour's welfare strategy, and they chose to do the same for older citizens, although Thane noted that the government proceeded cautiously because they wanted to maintain a balance between older people making use of their skills and having leisure time.[38] In 2004, the government extended the New Deal programme, which originally targeted helping the young unemployed into work, to people over fifty.[39] In 2006, the Employment Equality (Age) Regulations were introduced in the UK to tackle age discrimination in the workplace. This was a significant shift, which allowed people to request to stay on after they turned sixty-five years old, but employers could refuse without giving a reason. It is important to note that cultural attitudes did not keep pace with legislative changes in this period and many people continued to report age discrimination in employment.[40]

The strategies of the New Labour government to extend employment chimed with the increasing centrality of work to the identity of women of this generation. Professional women born in the 1940s did not aspire to traditional retirement in the same way as previous cohorts and wanted to work well into their sixties.[41] Lois (b.1947) put off retiring from her local government arts department role as long as she could, feeling such strong emotion about leaving that she cried discussing it during our interview.[42] After retiring, she returned to take up a voluntary position at her old workplace and chose to be interviewed in this venue rather than her own home. Lois seemed pleased to be able to demonstrate her authority to take me beyond areas that the public can access and introduced staff to me as her 'colleagues'.[43] Similarly, a woman of this generation who worked as a psychiatrist described being forced to take early retirement as 'like experiencing a death'. The sense of not feeling valued as a non-worker was evident in the concerns women expressed about loss of status in retirement.

An illustrative example of this centrality of work to women's sense of self is Angie's (b.1945) trajectory. Angie was a high-ranking official in her union by the time of her retirement in late 2009. The last few years of her career were tough: she was widely tipped to be the first female head of health in her union, but machinations on the part of male officials made it logistically impossible for her to apply for the role when it came up in the mid-2000s. This setback made her even more acutely aware of the importance of work to her selfhood. She explained: 'I would meet people in my role and say, "tell me about yourself", and they would reply "I'm a paramedic" or "I'm a nurse" – and they defined themselves by their job. Take that away from people and who are they?'[44] Instead of retiring at the age of sixty, she was led by this realization to stay at work to campaign to change the way in which the unions represented members struck off at work, because she thought too many people were losing their livelihoods for making small mistakes. She argued that the union had to fight for people's jobs on the basis that the erosion of their working conditions meant that many health workers were often placed in unsafe situations. She offered this example of a nurse:

> I would get her to hold her hands up and say, 'I made a mistake,' but then we'd go in and mitigate it. I would say, 'There should have been eight qualified nurses on duty and there were three; she should have had a break – she was on duty for eight hours and had no break; the doctor was supposed to sign this and they didn't come.' You explain why the mistake happened.[45]

Angie pioneered this shift in approach, which brought huge success. She gained the nickname the 'Caution Queen' because of the increased numbers of workers being cautioned rather than struck off. She did not want to leave her position and explained: 'Work was important to me, I worked right up to the wire … my last day of employment was the 31st December and on the 30th December I was in my office and on the 23rd December I was in Belfast representing someone.'[46] Angie mentioned these concerns: 'I know too many people who have just stopped and they've dropped dead, or they become depressed.'[47]

Many women of this generation looked to retirement with apprehension, but for others it was a desirable prospect, particularly if they were working in jobs that were no longer fulfilling or increasingly difficult to manage. However, women shared concerns about unstructured time, less income and a desire to continue contributing and participating in life outside the home. Jean (b.1950) found her last few years working as a tutor in a further education college difficult and, as noted in the previous chapter, took early retirement to avoid the stress of having to reapply for her own job.[48] She explained that she had 'built up' that retirement was 'going to be quite wonderful' and was 'quite shocked' how hard it was to adjust.[49] Jean grew up in a working-class family and experienced a degree of social mobility through working in the welfare state. She stated that, when she first retired, she spent a few months volunteering at a local historical site because she thought that was 'the thing middle-class women do when they retire … I got a voluntary post one afternoon a week. Talk about boring. I used to sit there thinking "I'd rather sit and watch paint dry than this"'.[50] Jean and her daughter-in-law made up a game that she would invent one fake historical fact about the site each week to tell visitors to see if they would believe it. She explained that she now thought of retirement as 'almost like a third career', which required planning.[51] Likewise, Maureen (b.1944) retired because of changing conditions in primary school teaching, but found it 'scary':

> From being a full-time teacher, and working hard in the evenings, it's a life, it takes over your whole life teaching. But from that to suddenly retire it's like a completely empty week … because I'm somebody who's got to be doing things. My worst fear is sitting in my dressing gown and watching daytime TV. You hate yourself, it's self-loathing.[52]

Maureen tried different types of volunteering, using her teaching skills in various forms to support women refugees learning English and secondary school students who were behind with their reading level.[53] Chrissie (b.1950) echoed the sentiments expressed by Jean and Maureen, stating that she found it difficult to fill her time in retirement because she wanted to do things that were 'worthwhile'.[54]

If they are going to perform voluntary roles, women of this generation would rather do so in a way that allows them to use their expertise and have a measure of influence in public life. Rita, who was a university lecturer, exemplifies this desire. In the wake of her redundancy, she felt that, 'after doing something that allowed you to gain expertise and be a player out there in the world, most of what's expected of you and available to you now is just to do caring way below your skillset without power or status'.[55] It is important to note that women from middle-class families with successful careers were more able to follow this model of more prestigious voluntarism. For example, both Diane and Susannah (b.1940) continued to be involved in the university where they were principals and also had advisory roles on boards in the sectors in which they worked prior to education.[56] Thane adeptly outlined the relationship between gender, voluntarism and status in Britain, noting that a 'reservoir' of middle- and upper-class women in the late nineteenth and early twentieth century was 'effectively socially prohibited from paid work, many able, energetic women [who] wanted to make a contribution outside the home … very many of them were highly committed to what they regarded as serious work, despite the lack of payment, and increasingly they were trained'.[57] Thane stated that after the war this 'reservoir of voluntary labour dwindled' because more middle-class married women were entering the labour force, primarily in the 'new and expanded public and non-governmental services'.[58] It is significant that, in retirement, women of the welfare state generation are once again taking up the mantle of more highly skilled voluntarism, resembling work, as they sought to find meaningful and valued ways to spend their time. However, this also represents a cruel paradox: the restructuring of the public sector that led to the process of de-professionalization and redundancy for many women of this generation was also the reason behind more opportunities to undertake the type of volunteering that women found more fulfilling.

The New Labour government intended for 'public–private partnerships and voluntary organisations [to] have an increasingly important role in delivering welfare. And welfare was not just about benefits but about services and community support'.[59] The government were keen to encourage participatory citizenship and, in 2001, introduced the biennial citizenship survey, which measured rates of voluntary activity.[60] The 2009–10 survey found that 29 per cent of people aged between sixty-five and seventy-four regularly participated in formal volunteering (which included areas of health and education) and that this figure increased by 2 per cent over the decade.[61] The survey reports consistently stated that key indicators of a citizen likely to take part in 'formal volunteering' included being a woman in her sixties with a professional background.[62] Anita's (b.1952) experience demonstrates the contradiction between there being fewer paid roles in these sectors during this period, but more possibility of returning to prestigious voluntary roles. After being made redundant, Anita became involved with the National Association of Voluntary and Community Action, which describes itself as 'a vital bridge between local groups and national government, funders and decision makers'.[63] This involvement was closely related to her earlier paid role as an advisor on care strategies to local and national government. Similarly, as soon as Angie retired, she took an unpaid yet prestigious position on the board of a complementary health regulator which she had recently been instrumental in setting up and was quickly elected chair of the board. She referred to this role as 'work' in our discussions. Angie liaised with the Department of Health to obtain their support, and they funded the initiative. This is in the vein of similar types of 'third sector' organizations that were set up under New Labour and aimed for 'strategic unity' between the state and voluntary organizations.[64] These organizations provided an opportunity for women to make use of the expertise they had gained through education or working in the public sector during their career, rather than undertake more hands-on caring roles.

In many cases, women of this generation were involved in non-state organizations in order to protect or encourage state service provision. This was especially necessary in the wake of funding cuts and further restructuring of public services during the period of coalition government.[65] Ann (b.1939), who was employed as a medical secretary for much of her career, volunteered her expertise in the hospital department where she had last worked. As a consequence of shrinking budgets, which placed more pressure on staff time, Ann stepped into an unpaid charity role to help patients prepare for surgery and answer any questions they might have about their upcoming procedures.[66] Sandra (b.1946) took a position on the board of a housing association after she gave up work in the 2000s because of her deep-seated belief in social housing and her frustration that it was being made deviant and separate from the rest of society. In this position, Sandra worked to protect the rights of those living in social housing and lobbied the local council to build more housing.[67] Despite his focus on the 'Big Society' during the 2010 General Election campaign,[68] David Cameron chose to end the citizenship survey when he took office because of the cost of conducting the research. This made it more difficult to measure rates and types of volunteering in the 2010s. However, as Thane has argued, the scope of voluntary action tends to adapt to fill where the gaps are in welfare provision.[69]

Theresa (b.1941) took up an unpaid position as the 'chair and director' of the Healthwatch Board in her local area, which brings together 'stakeholders' in health and social care provision.[70] In the late 1990s, Theresa studied for a degree at Ruskin College, finally getting the educational opportunity she had always wanted but had little access to as a working-class child who failed her eleven-plus.[71] After her degree, Theresa could not easily obtain satisfying paid work. She then suffered with breast cancer. She was involved in socialist action throughout her adult life and was well known to politicians in her locality, who encouraged her to apply for a seat on the board. Theresa was proud of this position. She tellingly encouraged me to 'go Google' her and styled this as 'work', even though she does not get paid for it:

> So, I now go and work and negotiate and am on the health and wellbeing board
> – I go to the quality surveillance group – also I do a lot of work as Chair to keep
> the NHS the way it is! It's not a campaign group – it's a statutory group made
> by the government – every area has one. Since 2012 we have had the Clinical
> Commissioning Groups – so we keep those to account as well. I thought to
> myself I've taken early retirement, I was ill, I had a battle, and I thought 'now
> I've got this education, what do I do with it?' – so for the community I live in, so
> that's why I do what I do. So, my social mobility has given me that choice – and
> I sit there with doctors, professors, managing directors, whatever – faze me not
> at all. In fact, they're frightened of me.[72]

The power to influence welfare services was increasingly stripped away from the state and local government in the twenty-first century.[73] New structures provided openings for women to undertake what they could conceive of as unpaid work rather than volunteering.

In line with the idea that the third age can feel like being in 'limbo', there is a noticeable trend emerging among women born at the younger end of the sample of classifying themselves as not yet officially retired despite receiving a pension. Instead they often classified themselves as 'self-employed' – i.e. perpetually in a liminal state of 'looking for work' – and therefore 'may work' in the future. India (b.1947) discussed retirement as 'terrifying' to her and outlined her aim 'never to retire'.[74] Nearing seventy years old at the time of our interview, India continued to undertake freelance teaching with no plan to stop doing so. Rita also described herself as self-employed despite not currently working. She acknowledged that this was largely a performative gesture as her upcoming sixty-fifth birthday was leading her to give up hope that she would find any interesting work in the future. During our interview, Rita answered the phone to an insurance company and, asked her work status, described herself as 'self-employed'. After the call, she explained that she just could not bear to refer to herself as 'retired' to strangers because of the 'loss of status' she felt it would confer on her. Anita resented the Conservative rhetoric of 'hard-working families' because it excluded her even though she wanted to work and was actively seeking work.[75] Mass Observers were also in the workforce despite claiming a pension. For example, soon-to-turn sixty-five years old, Wendy (b.1951) remains self-employed as a homeopath and counsellor.[76] A significant rise in self-employment has taken place in Britain since the late 1980s as a result of neoliberal economic policies.[77] Notably, Nigel Meager and Peter Bates observed that the highest rates of self-employment can be found among 'people older than the normal state retirement age' and can be used as a tool to continue flexibly working into retirement.[78] They also suggest that the women most likely to become self-employed are those with a measure of pre-existing professional expertise or higher educational qualifications.

Connected with this trend towards liminality between employment and retirement was the number of women choosing to return to education during this period.[79] For some of these women, this represents another way of conceiving of their self as a possible future paid worker. Linda (b.1954) was one of the few interviewees to achieve social mobility through promotion in the civil service rather than tertiary education, but conditions in the civil service became so bad in the 2000s that she decided to leave and try to gain her degree. She was in the final year of her part-time degree in social studies when we met for her interview and on course for a first-class degree.[80] Her intention was to look for work after finishing this degree. Rita undertook a Master's degree after losing her job in the mid-2000s, which she hoped would help enhance her professional skills. Rita and India had both completed counselling diplomas in order to channel their welfare expertise into differing but related career paths better suited to self-employment.

The importance of education in retirement for women born between the late 1930s and early 1950s emphasizes the significance of education for women of this generation across their life course and how their earlier experience continued to shape their retirement. The 1944 Education Act was one of the most significant pieces of legislation of the twentieth century. It enhanced opportunities for the select few through the system of grammar schools, and the later development of further education for many more redefined the aspirations of a generation. The divisive and complicated nature of the eleven-plus system continues to resonate, impacting on sibling relationships to this day, with some of my interviewees still nursing the old wounds inflicted by a system that defined success or failure at such a young age. Sylvia (b.1945) passed the eleven-plus exam but her twin sister failed, and the potency of feeling about this moment persisted throughout their lives.[81] Sylvia stated that, although her sister later returned to education and became a welfare professional, her relationship with her twin never fully recovered. At her twin's recent seventieth birthday celebration, a familiar argument erupted about Sylvia's sister's feelings of exclusion and failure when her sister went off to grammar school. Nevertheless, education provided both women with a route to social mobility and a strong sense of active participation in society outside the domestic sphere that continued to influence them in older age.

Post-war women understood the transformative value and power of education. Both Jean and Lois (b.1947) credited joining the University of the Third Age (U3A) with improving their retirement.[82] The U3A was founded by Laslett and Michael Young to provide an educational space for older people to learn and to teach others about their areas of expertise. Angie was considering going back to education to do a PhD on industrial relations. She had a possible female supervisor lined up, whom she had met during her time working in the trade union.[83] Nancy (b.1940) worked in secondary education throughout her career, although, like many women born in the mid-twentieth century, this was not initially the career that she wanted. She explained:

> I enjoy carrying on learning and going to lectures ... I do quite a lot of art history and European history courses at the Department of Continuing Education. I think doing one's own learning is wonderful. I mean there would be something wrong with me if I'd done all these years in education and I wasn't actually interested in my own learning.[84]

Nancy had only fully retired recently and had tapered her hours down in various roles over many years so that the shift to retirement was a process rather than an acute change. She continues to make use of her expertise in education, gained over her career, particularly for the age range of fourteen to nineteen, which she thinks is considered narrowly by policy-makers. Nancy sits as the deputy chair of the New Visions Education Group, based at the Institute of Education, and they submit policy proposals to the government and to political parties.

Women of the welfare state generation found that engaging in politics in retirement was an important way to maintain a voice in public life. More of my interviewees stated that they had been more involved in party politics since retiring than at any other life stage. Ruth (b.1949), for example, had recently been made redundant from her job as a social worker and was now retired.[85] She explained that she had been shocked at the impact the change had had on her sense of self because she 'had been not prepared for' – in her terms – 'not being anyone'. Ruth felt that this was exacerbated by the fact that she came from a working-class background and had achieved social mobility through her career. She noted that she had always been 'underestimated' because of class, but she had had institutional power through her job. Now, she felt 'invisible and unrecognised'.[86] Ruth became involved in local politics to try to reclaim 'a sense of power in society' and found it 'enjoyable'. Through her previous paid roles, Anita had been involved in politics and remained a local activist after being made redundant. At the time of our interview she explained that she had a dilemma about which party to support in the upcoming 2015 General Election as she usually voted Labour but had been personally asked by the Green Party candidate to throw her weight behind her campaign.

The political actions of women of the welfare state generation have taken on more of a sense of urgency since the onset of austerity policies, driven by their belief in the social benefits of state-run services. Women in my sample with differing political allegiances took action to protect welfare provision. This is reflected in a recent British social attitudes survey, which found that trends in attitudes towards welfare have been converging between older voters from across the political spectrum.[87] A nurse for much of her career, Jean chose to direct much of her political activity towards protecting the NHS by running petitions and campaigns to try and stop the closure of the local accident and emergency unit. Sylvia (b.1945) and Lesley (b.1950) both stated that they had not had time when they were working to get involved in politics but had recently taken part in anti-austerity marches. Cynthia leaned Conservative in her politics. However, around the time of our interview in late 2014, she was directing her efforts

Figure 7.1 Pensioners protesting cuts to the welfare state and low state pensions, London, UK, 2010. © Alamy images.

towards trying to stop recent severe cuts to her local library.[88] She had been asked to volunteer but has 'had to sit on [her] hands' to stop herself even though this means it will 'likely close' because she thinks that libraries are too important to be run by untrained, voluntary staff.[89] In London, Angie, a staunch Labourite and lifelong trade unionist, was lobbying her local council to see if 'it is possible to legally ring-fence any money … to protect libraries'.[90] Women's experiences in childhood as 'daughters of the state' made them feel more valued and entitled to engage in the public sphere, and this feeling was developed through education and employment in the welfare state. What emerges from the interviews is that, in retirement, women are searching for ways to exercise their agency and retain a sense of power in society.

Politics as the welfare state

Women of this generation were not universally supportive of each aspect of the welfare state (or necessarily wanted it expanded). Rather, the evidence presented here shows that, when asked about politics, the state rather than the market is implicitly central to their understanding of what politics *is* and its influence on their own lives. It is telling that, throughout the 2010s, Conservative governments have shown 'unusual indulgence' to aspects of the welfare state used primarily by 'the country's over-sixties, whose benefits – triple-locked pensions, universal winter fuel payments, bus passes and the like – were carefully protected'.[91] The answers to a question asked towards the end of each interview are central to the analysis here: 'What would be the first thing that you would do if you were prime minister now?' The lines of discussion it sparked were revealing about the continued relevance of the welfare state to women of this generation and their fears that it was being dismantled. One interviewee even referenced returning to the 'template of Attlee' in her response.[92] Handing back the state control of services they had lost – 'renationalization' – was mentioned frequently.[93] Some, such as Anita and India, went further in imploring the state to intervene and enact radical economic redistribution. Women of this generation are stepping in to fill in gaps in social welfare provision. They are doing so in part because they are concerned about the impact of a contracted welfare state on their younger family members.

As during the discussion of childhood, the NHS was central, and maintaining it was women's clear political priority. Maureen was anxious about the future of the NHS and made an explicit connection between past and present in expressing her concerns about ageing in this system:

> You feel as if you're just shoved along in the NHS now … Burnham's [British Labour politician, and previous Health Secretary] got the right idea – of social care all the way through so they're all linked, doctors, hospitals, nurses, care – everything. There needs to be that for quality of life otherwise you're going back to before the NHS when my father-in-law's mother fell – she'd got seven boys and she fell in the yard taking in the washing … got an infection, had to have her leg off and they wouldn't even give her crutches![94]

Susannah (b.1940) also placed significant emphasis in her response on the social care aspect of the health service, stating that she wants 'Britain to have more provision of that'.[95] Rummery has noted that the social care budget was cut by 20 per cent under the coalition policy of fiscal austerity, making it one of the hardest hit areas of spending.[96] Other interviewees explicitly noted that they would happily pay increased taxes if they knew it would directly benefit the NHS.[97] Working in the NHS also influenced opinions about this. For example, Elizabeth (b.1939) feared that not enough of the public understood just how much of the health service had been privatized through private finance initiatives.[98] Public opinion of the NHS was surprisingly resilient during the attacks on the welfare state in the 1980s and 1990s.[99] The way in which these women saw the NHS as genuinely universal may point to its ability to endure.

Women were more conflicted in their views about the contemporary social security system. Those who themselves, or who had a relative who had, needed benefits were more inclined to be supportive. Kathy was diagnosed with breast cancer during a period of self-employment in 2000 and was shocked to find how little money she was entitled to considering how much national insurance she had paid during her working life. She remembered angrily saying to the man behind the counter at the social security office, 'What's all this bullshit about!?' He replied: 'Forget it – nobody's getting much.'[100] When Rita was made redundant in the mid-2000s she was similarly shocked to find out how little NI-related Jobseeker's Allowance she was entitled to. She ultimately decided not to claim because the amount was so low relative to the 'shame' she felt about collecting it. At the time of our interview, Angie was supplementing the income of her daughter, a single mother in her forties, because her benefits were not enough to live on.[101] She explained: 'The way it is now it's not actually possible for someone to survive just on benefits. So, the government knows that anybody that's on benefits is either fiddling in some way, they're doing paid work under the radar or they're being supported by their family.[102] Both Angie and Bridget (who, as we have seen, spent a period receiving unemployment benefit) wanted people to be able to envisage that someone they love could lose their job or become unwell, requiring state benefits.

In contrast, Barbara (b.1941) expressed concern that the 'benefits system was too lax' and invoked the figure of the 'chav mum'[103] having children in order to claim benefits and therefore putting a strain on the system. She added the caveat that perhaps 'I shouldn't judge too much because I've always had a good income'.[104] Joy (b.1939) worried that immigration had placed too much pressure on public services in recent years. She also stated her belief in the welfare state and added: 'It's dreadful that people are using food banks now.'[105] Although one interviewee, Clara (b.1939), expressly stated that the welfare state was 'unifying',[106] there is a sense here of the boundaries of welfare provision being used to define and exclude particular types of undesirable citizens. It is possible to view Barbara's and Joy's positions as still holding closely to the idea that the state should provide welfare but that resources need to be allocated carefully. This is a classic liberal view of welfare provision, which Thane has argued was a hallmark of the British welfare state.[107]

Born in 1945 to a working-class family in Oxford, Eileen's experience demonstrates that there were contradictions in the way that the welfare state made women feel throughout their lifetimes. Eileen's primary source of income had been social security benefits since the birth of her daughter in 1975. She referred to herself as part of the 'underclass' because 'I'm from that strata that lives off the state'.[108] 'Underclass' is a term associated with the neoliberal turn of the 1980s, and John Welshman noted that it was 'extremely influential in debates' about poverty during that decade.[109] Eileen's daughter is also a single mother who stays at home to look after her children. When her daughter recently made the decision to have another child, Eileen explained that her friends said to her, 'Oh your daughter is taking the mickey a bit, you know.' They were really annoyed in a way because she doesn't have a job either.[110] Eileen explained that she could 'understand their point of view' and 'in some ways agrees with it'. Eileen deployed her extensive campaigning for the NHS and her restrained usage of its services to emphasize her own moral standing in the face of the humiliation she felt from being on benefits. She constructed a complex moral economy, in which 'selfish' women who have multiple children and 'needlessly take all these resources from the NHS' are more of a 'drain' on society than those such as her, on benefits.

The respondents to a 2018 Mass Observation directive underscore complicated attitudes to the welfare state from women of this generation across the political spectrum. The directive asked respondents to state their political party alignment alongside their views of welfare. Although the women offered different opinions on the welfare state, there was a shared 'liberal' approach to it, similar to that expressed by Barbara and Joy – that the welfare state was precious, and an unquestioned element of British life, but that its resources were finite and how to fund it was a central question. Much more anxiety was expressed to the directive about how to pay for the welfare state than among younger respondents and more convergence of views about the state existed than among younger women of differing political persuasions. Post-war women expressed serious concern about the cost and who is eligible for support but made clear arguments that national – or local – government should provide these services rather than private companies. For example, a 77-year-old 'lifelong' Tory voter praised 'cradle to grave' provision, referring to her post-war childhood and indicating how different it was to that of her parents. The respondent wrote that 'people are falling through the social safety net' but simultaneously that 'unfortunately there are many people out there who take everything they can get – often not putting anything back in'.[111] Another Tory voter of a similar age stated that 'I really can't imagine this country without it … because it's been there all my life, perhaps we take it for granted, it's vital for some people, people who couldn't manage without it'.[112] This matters because it shows that there is no contradiction between a high number of post-war women voting Conservative,[113] but still representing a generation defined by and broadly in support of the welfare state.

Concerns about reduction in available council housing arose frequently in relation to the question asking the women to imagine themselves as prime minister. Many interviewees had lived in council houses in their younger years but now viewed this as shameful.[114] Two women did not want to meet in their homes because they were owned by the council, and another woman spoke of her feelings of 'failure' that, while she had achieved social mobility, she had not been 'savvy' enough to buy her own home when she had the chance.[115] The social expectation that post-war generations should, by definition, own their own homes and be financially comfortable weighed heavily on these women.[116] Women who did not live in council houses at the time of their interview had during childhood expressed feelings of estrangement from their own past because of the degradation of council housing in political discourse and policy.[117] Rita stated that, when she looks at the portrayal of council estates and the people that live there, she thinks, 'Is that me? Is that really my history?'[118] However, strong support was expressed for significantly increased provision of council housing. Chrissie outlined her view:

> Housing is just a joke. I don't think they should have ever sold council housing off. And my mum was in a council house, but I still don't believe they should have sold them off. I mean she didn't buy hers, and I can see the argument that if you've paid all that rent which she'd done for years you've paid for your house. But there has to be somewhere for people to live. It's ridiculous they've sold them off. And ridiculous that they've not been rebuilding. And all these houses that are empty they could do things with.[119]

Others articulated fears about the housing prospects of their own children.[120] Theresa succinctly explained that 'the younger generation have got no choice of owning a house because you can't get a mortgage any more, and they have got no chance of a council house because they have all been bought'.[121] She expressed guilt that she did not have any property for her son to inherit. Council housing is a key area in which public opinion has shifted significantly across these women's lifetimes.

Women of this generation internalized the idea that they had little choice but to pass on as much capital as possible to their children and grandchildren. Lesley explained that her son, who was in his mid-thirties at the time of our interview, was unable to find a permanent job as a research scientist in higher education and was 'still being exploited by private sector landlords'.[122] She and her husband were saving money to give him towards the deposit for a flat. Lesley felt that this was 'unfair' on those who did not have parents who were able to assist them but could not see any other way her son could get on the property ladder.[123] Likewise, Angie was struggling with anxiety about how much financial support she should provide for her extended family. She had built up capital in the home she had bought in London in the 1980s:

> I've looked at equity release schemes, and I've thought wouldn't it be nice to give money to the kids and grandkids now when they need it. But equity release schemes are so dodgy – I've looked at all of them but the biggest problem is that it doesn't allow me the freedoms I need in terms of my own future. Because without being selfish, if there's no welfare state to look after me when I'm old and I want to live independently, and there is no kind of social service network that will help to support me independently, then I might have to pay for somebody to live in. I want the flexibility to do that. I don't want my children to have to look after me. And I'd have to move out of London; I don't want to move out of London. Because my kids don't live in London. I don't want that, I want to be

able to live independently for the rest of my life if I can, but that might mean quite a lot of support.[124]

Similarly, Rita and Bridget, both single mothers, wrestled with the decision of whether to reduce their own standards of living in retirement so that they could pass on some capital to their adult children.[125] The contraction of the welfare state placed a significant amount of responsibility on the shoulders of women to fill the gap in the social safety net for their own families.

Alongside aiming to provide financial capital, women supported their children to earn money by stepping in to take active roles as grandmothers. This was sometimes a pleasurable activity for women but is also frequently an intensely practical choice to offer their domestic labour to help the family economy. For example, Maureen's daughter has four children, and she looks after the youngest child in the daytime to make it financially viable for her daughter to return to special needs teaching.[126] Maureen stated that her daughter's job is very 'stressful' but that she is 'committed' and wants to do a Master's degree when she can afford it so that she can achieve promotion.[127] In a similar vein, Sylvia said that she was providing childcare for one of her daughters in the school holidays to give her space to finish the monograph she needed to produce in order to secure a permanent position in academia.[128] Sylvia compared the opportunities that had been open to her as a young mother working in higher education with the lack of those available to her daughter, who held even more advanced qualifications.[129] Notably, one interviewee, Frances, had recently become a co-chair of a new charity for grandparents, which had merged with an older organization set up by Michael Young.[130] She was using her expertise as educator and politician to lobby the government to ensure that grandparents' voices are represented in the policy-making process. A piece of research commissioned by the charity found that 1 million mothers would be at risk of leaving the workforce if they did not have childcare support from their own parents and a further 1.7 million would consider reducing their hours.[131] Looking after grandchildren is a notable example of women of the welfare state generation enacting the 'caring' aspects of their dual sense of self outlined in earlier chapters.

Ultimately, women born between the late 1930s and early 1950s felt that the spiralling cost of housing, alongside reduction in public sector jobs and increases in university tuition fees, was harming the prospects of younger generations. One Mass Observer, Claudia (b.1948), who had experienced social mobility into 'the academic middle class', lamented that Britain is 'dreadfully unfair – much more so than when I was growing up'. She explained:

Education is one route that is increasingly shut off to people like me whose families came from different backgrounds – the levels of debt that students have to accept, the transition of universities into businesses. The cuts in health and social welfare, the meteoric rise of housing values and the absence of council housing.[132]

Claudia acknowledges here that she benefitted from the expanded welfare state and that it enabled her social mobility. In doing so, she challenges the discourse of meritocracy, which argues that individual endeavour and aspiration determine advancement. Ruth echoed Claudia's comments, noting that 'my chance to move to London was because of having a big public sector that was well funded … it acted as a sort of social back-up for a lot of people … and there were great opportunities. I think it's a great shame that it's not there anymore'.[133] Similarly, Sylvia highlighted that the fact that the education system was 'expanding' and 'free' while she was growing up prompted her own social mobility.[134] She spent her career in further and higher education and expressed concern about the cost of education for younger working-class people.[135] Jacqui (b.1943), from a working-class family in Scotland, stated that she dislikes the 'emphasis on individualism that has tainted a lot of [political] decision making'.[136] She described herself as 'furious' about tuition fees and explained that she felt the 'whole approach to higher education' needs to change, including bringing back 'polytechnics', which were 'valuable' to women of her generation. Even Diane, who came from a middle-class background, underscored that she had witnessed the social benefits of the welfare state and was concerned about the contemporaneous fraying of the social contract.[137] As a result of their own life experiences, women of this generation have a keen awareness of the importance of the state for enabling mobility. These women acknowledge a central truth of the welfare state that is often obscured in political discourse – as Mike Savage argues, 'an attack on the state is an attack on the main axis of middle-class formation'.[138]

Conclusion

Governmental efforts to raise living standards for pensioners since the turn of the millennium have enhanced the old age of women of the welfare state generation. They have been the beneficiaries of an increased state pension and improved access for women to state support in retirement. The high rates for women of this generation working in the public sector have also contributed to a more financially comfortable retirement for these women. Women's relatively improved financial position has been one of the key factors in their shift towards a more traditionally masculine form of retirement. In a similar manner to their male counterparts, women of the welfare state generation have increasingly wrestled with identity questions presented by the transition from work to retirement and the consequent 'limbo' of the 'third age'.

The educational and career opportunities offered to them by the welfare state, although gendered, have made it more difficult for them to give up paid work and status in the public sphere later in life. They want to continue making use of their expertise and not find themselves solely in caring roles at this stage in their lives. Women were also keen to engage in education that built on their existing knowledge base, which could represent a route into forms of self-employment. In addition, women born between the late 1930s and early 1950s contributed a significant amount of time and expertise to social welfare provision. This should be conceptualized as unpaid work rather than voluntary activity. Their contributions to civil society have been especially important at a time when the welfare state is contracting. As women who have grown up to expect a social safety net, much of their political activity in recent years has been directed at halting this trend.

In their reflections on contemporary politics, women demonstrated a shared belief that the welfare state is at the heart of politics, although they hold conflicting attitudes towards certain aspects of provision. The continued impact of growing up under the auspices of the welfare state and working in it during their adult lives is not *past* for these women, and they seek to extend the privilege of these experiences to their younger relatives This is particularly significant because it challenges the influential contemporary discourse that women of this generation seek to hoard the gains of the welfare state for themselves.

Conclusion

This book has made a historiographical contribution to how we conceptualize both the welfare state and women's relationship to it. In this regard, it builds on the work of second-wave feminist scholars, many of whom were of the welfare state generation, who defined the welfare state not only as a set of institutions but also as a gendered ideology which organized economic relations in the post-war period. A broad definition of the welfare state has been deployed throughout this book, incorporating the idea of it as educator and employer alongside providing a social safety net. Taking this approach has demonstrated how wide-ranging the impact of the expanded welfare state was on women of this generation and in turn shown the ways in which they shaped the state. This is all the more powerful because it emerged organically in oral history interviews with women.

The influence of the welfare state on these women in childhood was deep but often contradictory and fractured across gendered and classed lines. What the experience of this generation shows is that the welfare state could be a tool of both liberation and constraint. Material change imparted a sense of value in girls from a young age, and they felt more able to be vocal and articulate their needs than previous generations. It was significant that they were the first cohort of girls to receive a compulsory secondary education and the concomitant possibilities this allowed for testing the boundaries of prescribed gender roles. This was especially true for grammar school girls, whereas those who attended a secondary modern were less likely to feel as though their education offered them anything but the gendered norm. The way that the state intervened to sort children into different schools cast a long shadow, particularly in the recollections of girls from working-class homes where the passing or failing of the eleven-plus had the power to divide families and leave lasting scars in the relationship between siblings that were often still raw in older age.

One of the most important findings of this book is that growing up under the auspices of the welfare state gave women more confidence to take risks and to adapt to changing historical circumstances. This is an intangible impact of the welfare state that is hard to measure through quantitative source material. When the state significantly expanded again in the late 1960s, women grasped the opportunities in the diversified education system and professional welfare roles. Even though many women had married and become mothers, the changes arose at a time when they were restless for change. Just as they had not made rigid plans when they left school and had tried different things out, women of this generation re-entered education without career or mobility strategies. The moment of flexibility in the education system for mature students was particularly significant. When interviewed, younger women often reflect on their mother's experience of being able to return to education and compare it to contemporary Britain. One woman born in the 1970s stated that 'now we only have one shot at an education' so the stakes are very high – this means there is far more requirement to plan from a young age and take linear pathways.[1]

The secondary wave of welfare expansion was a major instrument of social mobility for women of this generation. This insight radically reorients how we think of social mobility in the post-war period, shifting the focus from the 'scholarship boy' experiencing long-range mobility to a more nuanced conception of short-range occupational mobility into public sector roles which were dependent on labour market demand. For women, the changes to the post-compulsory education system provided both educational *and* occupational opportunities, and this blurs the distinction between the propulsive power of educational or occupational expansion. Qualifications generally played a more important role in women's mobility than might have been expected, and they fulfil differing roles in this process: firstly, qualifications matter for the 'objective' proof that they provide of women's skills during recruitment and are often portable; secondly, they offer women something that cannot be taken away, unlike career progression or marital status.

Women's social mobility does not conform to the model of marital mobility. They are the authors of their own mobility journeys, although these journeys are always situated in a wider historical context. To say that women have agency in their own mobility is not to say that 'aspiration', 'hard work' or 'pulling yourself up by your bootstraps' is what produces social mobility. There has to be structural expansion and a material environment which makes experimentation possible. Socially mobile women are more vulnerable to downward mobility and are often in a precarious position in their newer social class. Women of this generation were acutely aware of their class position from a young age and, in adulthood, defined their social class through their own endeavours in education and employment. There was no moment when they subsumed their own identity within their long-term relationships.

Employment was not an incidental part of women's identity: most saw themselves as both a worker in the public sphere and a carer in the private sphere. Women often described this dual role, and the difficulties of negotiating it, as a hallmark of their generation. Despite the changes in women's lives, the stickiness of gendered roles and the division of labour in the home largely remained intact. Working for the welfare state was one potential way of accommodating the roles of worker and carer because semi-professions such as nursing were a professionalization of domesticity. There was a high growth rate in part-time and flexible jobs in the welfare state during this period. As employees of the state, women transformed the way that it functioned in practice. They viewed their employment in the welfare state as inherently politicized and used their roles to make a political intervention in society even if they were not activists in the conventional sense. Many women sought to continue shaping welfare provision well into retirement, particularly in areas where they had professional expertise. As a result of these women's increased commitment to employment and rising opportunities, their experience of retirement has become more of a life-changing moment than for earlier generations which creates the need to negotiate a new identity.

The exposure of the fragility of the welfare state in the later twentieth century was jarring for women of this generation. It clashed with their sense that an expansive welfare state would always endure. The experience was particularly difficult as employees of the state who were subject to increased surveillance in the workplace and were granted less autonomy. This process – which I have defined as de-professionalization – disproportionately affected women and intersected with ideological questions about the extent to which caring work should be performed on an unpaid basis by women in the private sphere rather than provided by the welfare state. The historical moment of the late twentieth century is an important example of the ways that gendered progress tends to ebb and flow and that no generation of women experiences the type of linear change which is often associated with post-war women. Women's experience of de-professionalization is a vital missing component in historiographical understandings of the hollowing out of middle-class jobs in the twenty-first-century economy.

The study of ageing has shown how women's early experiences inflected their choices, but that they were also influenced by their later interactions with the state and the contemporary context. The concept of generation is increasingly salient in political debate, but it can sometimes be used as a proxy for social class. This book has demonstrated that generational experience always intersects with class and that in older age meaningful class differences remained between these women. Women conveyed a sense of themselves as collectively benefitting from the period in which they were born and the significance of the welfare state for encouraging social fluidity and advancement – even if they were also clear-eyed about the uneven distribution of advantages. Women of the welfare state generation wanted to pass these advantages to younger people in some form. Throughout this book, we have seen examples of women aiming to create conditions for others to flourish in both their work and personal lives.

This generation of women have always perceived the nuances of the welfare state's workings as something to be debated, contested and intervened in. While their allegiance to the maintenance of the welfare state remains strong, the echoes of long-held ambivalences are evident in the contemporary tensions between women of this generation who argue that the political terrain should largely be fought on arresting further decline and those who advocate for welfare state expansion. Following the twists and turns of the whole life course demonstrates that for women born in the mid-century the welfare state has been, and continues to be, experienced as a defining structure and the essence of what politics means.

Appendix: Interviewee biographies

Anita, b.1952: Born in Loughborough. Lower middle-class background. Father a personnel manager in private firms, the family moved around a lot for his work. Mother a housewife. Failed the 11+. Attended a comprehensive school in Shropshire. Sat A-Levels and left school at 18. Got pregnant during A-Level year. Married in 1970. Moved to Essex with her husband where he attended university. Separated in 1973. Started a one-year apprenticeship in lithography at a technical college (did not complete). Moved to Leeds in 1974 to work in a print shop. Started a foundation course in social and community studies at a further education college in Sheffield. Went on to do a degree in applied social studies at Sheffield polytechnic. Stayed in Sheffield. Worked as social worker and then became involved in community development. Met current partner *c.*1985 and had a second child in 1987. Owner-occupier. Identifies as middle class.

Ann, b.1939: Born in Sheffield. Working-class background. Father worked on the railways. Mother a housewife. Passed the 11+. Attended a 'secondary' grammar. Left school at fifteen. Took up clerical job in steel works, left at nineteen to become a medical secretary. Medical secretary for rest of career. Married in 1971, divorced in 1981. No children. Owner-occupier. Identifies as upper working-class.

Angie, b.1945: Born in Deal, town in Kent. Working-class background. Father a coal miner and official in the National Union of Mineworkers. Mother a housewife, had been a nurse prior to marriage. Passed 11+ exam. Initially sent to a secondary modern but at fifteen transferred to a girls' grammar (partly private) after the secondary modern school complained about her treatment. Got pregnant and left school at sixteen. Married in 1961, husband a miner. Had second daughter in 1963. Divorced in 1965. Struggled financially as lone mother, had to undertake casual work picking and packing vegetables. Remarried in late 1960s, husband in the military. Worked part time in a cinema and then went to nursing college in the early 1970s. Became a nurse and was a shop steward in her union. Alongside this took long-distance learning units with TUC. Started a degree at Ruskin in 1979 and moved to Oxford during term-time. Divorced in early 1980s. After graduating moved around the country for promotions within union structure. Settled in London to work as national union official. Owner-occupier. Identifies as middle class in terms of 'lifestyle and income' but 'feels' working class.

Barbara, b.1941: Born in Reading. Working-class background. Mother had been in service but became a housewife on marriage. Father trained as a cobbler but sat the civil service exam after being demobbed and worked the post office telephones. Failed the 11+. Attended a 'central school' a tier in the district between secondary moderns and grammar school. Left school at sixteen with three O-Levels and shorthand typing. Worked in higher and further education administration for whole career. Starting as shorthand typist and quickly being promoted to accounts office. Married in 1961. No children. Husband worked for the post office, also working-class background. Owner-occupier. Identifies as economically middle class, but still 'feels' working class.

Beth, b.1955: Born in Cardigan, West Wales. Family moved around a lot during her childhood. Moved to Sierra Leone in 1955, returned to live near Tunbridge Wells when she was six. Moved to a village near Maidstone when she was eleven. Middle-class background. Father a civil servant, later bought a farm. Mother a housewife, had been a nurse prior to marriage. Failed the 11+. Attended a secondary modern for one school year then parents moved her to a private convent school. Sat exams there at sixteen, then moved to a technical school for A-Levels. Did a two-year course in hotel reception at technical college in Bristol. Met husband while in Bristol, he was studying to become a surveyor at the local polytechnic. Married in 1977. Worked in various hotel and then secretarial roles. Moved around country for husband's promotions. Had three sons during 1980s. Gave up work until mid-1990s. Returned to work as part-time special needs assistant in primary school then took up secretarial roles. Moved to Oxford in 2001 and started working in university administration. Owner-occupier. Identifies as middle class.

Brenda, b.1938: Born in London. Working-class background. Father a furniture maker. Mother a housewife, although would take in sewing work in the home when money was tight. Failed the 11+. Attended a secondary modern. Left school at sixteen with 'a couple of' CSEs. Went to Tottenham technical college to study shorthand typing. Worked in various clerical roles. Then got a job working in outside news broadcast through sister's husband. Met husband, a biochemistry PhD student, and they married late 1950s. Had son in 1960. Moved to Nigeria in 1961 for husband's work. Had two daughters while living in

Nigeria. Returned to UK in 1964 and lived in Glasgow briefly, before spending more time in Africa. Left husband while in Africa and returned to London with the children in 1969. Got a job as researcher for a member of parliament. Moved to Oxford *c.*1970 because her husband had got a job at Oxford polytechnic and they wanted to try again. Started a degree in sociology, history and political theory at Ruskin in 1973. Permanently separated from husband during the course. Began working for the Commission for Racial Equality. Commuted to London until 1987. Worked as a county coordinator for UN shelter for homelessness in Oxfordshire. Council house tenant. Identifies as working class.

Bridget, b.1951: Born in Newcastle. Lower middle-class background. Parents divorced in 1962. Father a small business-owner. Mother a housewife, worked part time first in a bakery then in local civil service following separation. Passed 11+ exam. Attended a grammar school. Left school at fifteen. Worked in library for a year and then went to college to study for O-Levels. Got pregnant in 1969 and got married. Husband from a working-class background, did an apprenticeship in sound recording which led him to well-paid job in television. Had second child in 1972. Housewife while children were young but alongside studying for O-Levels and A-Levels. Started a degree in politics and history at University of Newcastle in 1977. Divorced in 1986. Unemployed for much of 1980s. Worked in a book shop and then took a clerical role in a trade union. Lives with current partner in his house in Birmingham. Identifies as 'comfortable' working class, believes divorce led to downward mobility.

Carol, b.1948: Born in Swansea. Working-class background. Father a building labourer (although did set up his own construction business in the 1960s). Mother a housewife. Passed the 11+. Attended a grammar school. Left school at eighteen, sat A-Levels. Went to teacher training college near Cardiff. Took temporary teaching job in London. Moved to Oxford for a teaching job in early 1970s. Became full-time activist in 1972. Met long-term partner in mid-1970s, he was from a middle-class background. Had daughter in 1981. Returned to take degree in social work at Oxford polytechnic. Social worker for rest of career. Council house tenant. Identifies as middle class.

Chrissie, b.1950: Born in Sheffield. Working-class background. Father a labourer at the steel works. Mother in service before marriage, became a housewife. Failed the 11+. Attended a secondary modern. Left at sixteen with some CSEs. Worked in a library, then went to work abroad as an au pair. Returned to education in early 1970s, starting with sitting O-Levels, then A-Levels. Started training as social worker in mid-1970s. Married in 1974. Husband a teacher. Worked briefly as social worker before giving it up to have two children in late

1970s. Started degree at Open University and then a teacher training course specializing in adult education. Became further education tutor. Left in early 1990s and set up a project called 'refugee education', alongside some work in community development. Owner-occupier. Identifies as middle class, but also refers to working-class roots.

Clara, b.1939: Born near Chesterfield. Middle-class background. Mother had qualified as barrister but gave it up permanently after having children. Father had a professional career (details unknown). Passed the 11+, attended grammar school for a couple of years then moved to a private boarding school. Left at eighteen after sitting A-Levels and went to UCL to study Law. Met future husband around the start of university. Took law exams in 1963. Married the same year. Articled with a firm in London. Had first child in 1965 and left law firm during pregnancy. Went back to work when baby was three months old to work mornings in a law firm owned by a family friend. Moved to Birmingham for husband's career and got a job in a law firm part time. Moved to America 2.5 years later for husband's career again, gave birth to fraternal twins while there. Returned to UK in 1969. Worked part time in a law firm in Aylesbury, then a more substantial role – still part time – in an Oxford law firm in 1975. Promoted to partner *c.*1978. Set up own firm in 1981. Separated from husband *c.*1985 and remarried in 1989 (he passed away in late 2000s). Sold law office *c.*2000, continued to work there as self-employed until retirement at sixty-five years of age. Continued to work in husband's bookshop at weekends which she then took over after he died. Owner-occupier. Identifies as middle class.

Cynthia, b.1941: Born in Sheffield. Working-class background. Father ambulance man in the steelworks. Mother housewife. Passed the 11+. Attended a grammar school. Left at sixteen with seven O-Levels. Became secretary in steelworks and trained as shorthand typist. Married in 1962, met husband at steelworks where he was an engineer. Had first son in 1965, second son in 1967. Gave up work when had children but started teacher training at Sheffield polytechnic in 1970. Became a primary schoolteacher and promoted to head of department. Left in 1990s and took job as secretary in local hospital. Owner-occupier. Identifies as lower middle class.

Dawn, b.1945: Born in Sheffield. Upper working-class background (identified family as 'on cusp of middle'). Father foreman at building firm. Mother a housewife. Passed 11+. Attended a grammar school. Left school at sixteen after O-Levels. Started working in Sheffield libraries. Studied to become a chartered librarian. Returned to study for a Master's in library studies at University of Sheffield in early 1980s. Promoted to manager of five public libraries in Rotherham in the 1990s. Never married, no children. Owner-occupier. Identifies as middle class.

Diane, b.1946: Born in Poole, grew up in Slough. Middle-class background. Father a dentist. Mother a housewife, had been a dancer prior to marriage. Passed the 11+. Received a scholarship to attend a private school. Left school at nineteen, following A-Levels and additional term for Oxbridge entrance exam preparation. Read for a degree in history at University of Oxford. Did a Master's degree at LSE in personnel management. Worked as personnel manager in industry through 1970s. Married in 1979, had met husband at university. Promoted to personnel executive. Stayed in business until 1996, based in London. Undertook consulting work for various businesses and employed by civil service advising on recruitment. Appointed principal of Oxbridge college in mid-2000s. No children. Owner-occupier. Identifies as upper middle class.

Eileen, b.1945: Born in Oxford. Working-class background. Both parents worked in a hotel: mother as maid, father doing odd jobs and bar work. Failed the 11+ exam. Attended a secondary modern and then was moved to a technical school. Left school at sixteen, unclear which qualifications received. Worked various clerical and service jobs to save up money for going abroad, repeated this cycle. Married in 1966, separated shortly afterwards but had to wait for divorce law to change in 1973. Had baby with new partner in 1975. Raised daughter as single parent. Income derived from social security benefits. Took Open University modules in maths. Council flat tenant. Identifies as 'underclass' or 'lower class'.

Elizabeth, b.1939: Born in Birmingham (family moved to Surrey after the war). Middle-class background. Father worked at Head Office of Central Electricity Board. Mother a housewife. Passed the 11+. Attended a girls' grammar school (chosen because strong in science otherwise would have been sent to a private school like her brother). Left school at eighteen. Started science degree at University of London followed by a Master's and PhD. Worked in labs. Travelled abroad for work. Married in late 1960s. Husband a doctor, middle-class background. Had two sons, born 1972 and 1974. Worked part time as senior research scientist in Oxford. Owner-occupier. Identifies as professional middle class.

Frances, b.1939: Born in East Keswick. Middle-class background. Father worked for various local councils as secretary for further education. Mother a housewife. Passed the 11+ (sat it a year early at nine which meant she was a year ahead for rest of education). Attended a private school. Left at eighteen, after sitting A-Levels and extra term for Oxbridge entrance exam preparation.

Read for a history degree at University of Oxford. Met husband at university and married in 1960. He was from a working-class background. Became a housewife. Had three children between 1962 and 1968. Moved to Liverpool for husband's job in extra-mural department of a university. Undertook a postgraduate certificate in primary education at Liverpool polytechnic in 1971. Primary schoolteacher during 1970s. Moved to Sheffield in 1974 for husband's work. Elected to the city council in 1980. Separated from husband in mid-1980s. Elected as a member of parliament in 1992. Stood down as MP just before 2005 General Election. Owner-occupier. Identifies as middle class.

India, b.1947: Born in Hertfordshire, family moved to Northern Ireland in early 1950s. Upper working-class/lower middle-class background (defines parents as 'on the cusp'). Father took teacher training course offered to soldiers after the war and became the headmaster of a primary school in rural Northern Ireland. Mother housewife, had been a mental health nurse prior to marriage. Passed the 11+. Had disrupted schooling 11–14 because the family was moving back and forward between England and Ireland due to parents' marriage breaking down. Settled with mum in Surrey at fourteen and attended girls' grammar school. Left school at eighteen after sitting A-levels. Did a degree in English Literature at the University of Warwick. Did supply-teaching in London to pay for travelling. Then started a certificate of Education at the University of Oxford. Met husband through mutual undergraduate friends and married in 1972. Moved to Nigeria for a year to work at a university with husband. Worked part time in FE college in London in mid-1970s. Had son in 1975. Separated from husband three months after birth of son. Moved to Leicester with son in late 1970s, taught in a secondary school full time. Moved again to Sheffield in 1985, to teach adult education. Married in mid-1980s. Left adult education to become freelance teacher in mid-1990s. Owner-occupier. Identifies as middle class.

Jacqui, b.1943: Born in Edinburgh. Lower middle-class background. Father a pharmacist. Mother a housewife, but did the accounts for her husband's pharmacy. Passed selective exam, followed Scottish system of moving schools for Highers at fifteen. Attended University of Edinburgh to take psychology and zoology. Met her future husband at university. Moved to Liverpool to take an applied social studies graduate course. Moved back to Edinburgh to be with partner and get married after she finished this course. Obtained job as a childcare officer in children's department, then took up a position with an adoption agency. Moved to Buckinghamshire in 1968 for her husband's career so she got a job as a social worker nearby. Had daughter in 1970. Gave up work but 'hated it' so went back to train for a new position in the merged local children's health and welfare departments part time in *c.*1973. Had serious bout of depression during 1970s and decided to resign from her role *c.*1980s. Divorced her husband. Did not want to return to social work, managed to obtain a part-time role at a publishing house in early 1980s (eventually became full time). Retired in 2003. Owner-occupier. Identifies as middle class (although notes that her divorce and career change had big impact on her sense of class status).

Jean, b.1950: Born in Leicester. Adopted. Working-class background. Father part-time social worker, part-time film projectionist. Mother a housewife, worked part time as a clerk while Jean at school. Passed the 11+. Left school at seventeen, had sat O-Levels. Trained as a nurse. Met husband during training and married in 1973. Husband painter and decorator, later retrained and became further education tutor. Had a daughter in 1975 and a son in 1977. Briefly gave up work while had children but worked as nurse for most 1970s and 1980s. Moved to the East Midlands. Left nursing in late 1980s and became a further education tutor. Owner-occupier. Identifies as middle class.

Joy, b.1939: Born in London. Working-class background. Father worked repairing trains on the London Underground. Mother a housewife, although worked in factory during the war. Passed the 11+. Attended a grammar school. Left school at sixteen with 'four or five O-Levels'. Undertook various jobs including dental nurse and spent time in hospital with TB. Returned to education. Sat art A-Level in early 1960s then began art college in 1962. Married in 1963. Husband was 'a bit more up the social scale'. He started a PhD at Leeds *c.*1965 and became an academic. Had twin boys in 1966. Moved to Sheffield in early 1970s. Worked part time doing technical drawing and later shop work. Started part-time degree in teaching at local polytechnic in early 1980s. Became a further education tutor. Owner-occupier. Identifies as middle class.

Kathy, b.1950: Born in London (moved to Essex while she was at primary school). Working-class background. Father a postman. Mother a housewife but started part-time shop work once children went to school. Passed 11+. Attended a grammar school. Sat A-Levels and left school at eighteen. Started at Westminster polytechnic but left after less than a term. Took a job at Greater London Council and then in departmental administration at further education college. Left FE in 1997 to open a bookshop. Started degree at Ruskin College, Oxford, in early 2000s but did not complete and returned to FE administration. Now lives in Bristol. Never married, no children. Owner-occupier. Identifies as middle class, but refers to continuing influence of working-class background.

Lesley, b.1950: Born in Bolton, family moved to Sheffield when she was five. Middle-class background. Father a grammar schoolteacher. Mother a housewife, held an undergraduate degree. Passed the 11+. Attended a direct grant school. Left school at eighteen after sitting A-Levels and staying on for extra term of Cambridge entrance exam preparation. Read for a degree in classics at University of Cambridge. Spent time in New Guinea teaching with VSO after university. Teacher trained at York St John in mid-1970s. Met husband there, married in 1981 but cohabited prior to this. Both taught in London. Had son in 1983. Moved to Stafford in 1986 for husband's work, he retrained as educational psychologist. Continued working part time then back to full time as primary schoolteacher. Owner-occupier. Identifies as middle class.

Linda, b.1954: Born in Sheffield. Working-class background. Father in the RAF, and the family moved to Singapore when he was posted there during late 1950s/early 1960s. Mother a housewife, then later went into retail. Parents divorced when they returned to Sheffield. Passed the 11+. Attended a grammar school. Left school at sixteen with 'about four' O-Levels. Worked in various clerical and waitressing jobs. Took a job as a clerical assistant in the civil service in Sheffield in 1974. Married in 1978, divorced in 1981. Was moving up the ladder when Thatcher stopped all promotions in mid-1980s. Moved to London to join the immigration department at a 'Big Four' accountancy firm. Married in 1992. Moved jobs to another firm. Divorced in 1995. Moved back to Sheffield and rejoined civil service in 2002. Started a degree at Sheffield Hallam. No children. Owner-occupier. Identifies as middle class, but refers to continuing influence of 'working-class roots'.

Lois, b.1947: Born in Sheffield. Working-class background. Father worked as welder in steelworks. Mother a housewife, intermittently did part-time work in factory. Lois failed the 11+. Attended a secondary modern. Left school at sixteen, sat O-Levels. Started work in local government administration, first in public health department, then arts department. Began a part-time Open University history degree 1972 alongside working full time. Never married, no children. Council flat tenant. Identifies as working class.

Marion, b.1942: Born in Burton-on-Trent. Upper middle-class background. Father a vicar and the family moved every few years because of his job, places included Wolverhampton and Welsh Borders. Mother a vicar's wife/housewife. Attended private school from primary until age of eighteen. Took a year out and did a commercial course at local polytechnic. Went to study biology (with zoology) at St Andrew's. Through contacts got the opportunity to get a two-year fellowship to do own research and be research assistant in Uganda. Returned to the UK to continue the research (and turn into a PhD), then got a job working on her microbiological specialism attached to a London hospital *c.*1968. Met her husband who was an engineer. They moved to Leeds and she got a job at the public health laboratory. Moved to Brazil for eighteen months while she was pregnant because of her husband's career. Returned to Leeds and had another child 1974. Went back to work part-time in early-to-mid 1980s, initially teaching evening classes. Then became a liaison officer for the Foreign office, but administered by central office of information in Leeds (hours ad hoc). Alongside this also had a part-time teaching role at a further education college and a part-time administration job at local polytechnic. Did all three while children were teenagers, until diagnosed with cancer. Stopped working in mid-2000s. Owner-occupier. Identifies as 'sort of' upper-middle class.

Maureen, b.1944: Born in Sheffield. Working-class background. Father an engineer. Mother 'unskilled, manual' prior to marriage, then a part-time cleaner and factory worker once children went to school. Passed the 11+. Attended a girls' grammar school. Left school at sixteen with eight O-Levels. Worked at a blood bank followed by secretarial roles. Married in 1966. Husband working-class worked at English Steel then became a driving instructor in the 1970s. Had three children between 1968 and 1972 and gave up work. Returned to education, taking A-Levels 1973–1977, then starting teacher training. Became a primary schoolteacher in 1980. Owner-occupier. Identifies primarily as middle class but with caveats due to working-class roots.

Nancy, b.1940: Born in Blackpool. Described as upper working-class or lower middle-class background. Father worked for a building firm but had money troubles. Mother a housewife. Passed the 11+ and attended grammar school. Sat A-Levels and left school at eighteen. Went to University of Leeds to study geography. Then attended the IOE to take PGCE in Education and was elected President of the Students' Union. Obtained teaching job at a comprehensive school in London. Went to teach at a college of education for mature students in late 1960s. Got a job as a deputy-headteacher at a comprehensive school in Bicester in 1972. While there she set up a group focused on reforming secondary education training. In 1978 she moved to take up a headship in London. In early 1980 she was asked by the ILEA to set up a new sixth form college. Left in 1983 to work for county hall setting up other sixth form colleges. Five years later she moved to take up a position as deputy education officer for Warwickshire County Council. Took retirement in 1996 and moved to Oxford. Then was invited to take up a chair at a university part time to set up research centre on schools, became involved with national enquiry on education and wrote a book on education policy. Never married, no children. Owner-occupier. Identifies as upper middle class now.

Penny, b.1948: Born in Ilford. Background on cusp between lower middle class and upper working class. Father a civil servant. Mother a housewife. Passed the 11+ and attended a grammar school until eighteen. Went to Cambridge to study English (first person in family to go to university). Did VSO after completing degree. In early 1970s undertook teacher training at Oxford and worked for a grammar school. Moved to East Asia to teach at an international school. Worked there for three years and then travelled for two years. Returned to England and got a job at a girls' private school in London. Lived in various countries abroad from 1982, settling as a head of department in early 1990s. Retired in late 2000s and moved back to UK. Owner-occupier. Never married, no children. Identifies as 'upper middle class education-wise' and 'middle-middle class' in terms of occupational 'status'.

Rita, b.1952: Born in Halifax. Working-class background. Father a semi-skilled engineer. Mother primarily a housewife, although intermittently worked part time in retail. Passed the 11+. Attended a grammar school. Left at sixteen, with 'about three' O-Levels. Worked in various jobs and travelled. Went back to college to study for A-Levels in early 1970s. Went travelling then moved to London. Started a degree at a polytechnic in London but did not complete. In 1977 started a Master's in film. Wrote and made own films. Worked as visiting lecturer in art schools and polytechnics in London. Met long-term partner in early 1980s. Had three children 1985-1991. Moved to Newcastle in mid-1980s for role in FE, then took position at Northumbria University. Moved to Sheffield in 1996 for promotion. Made redundant and then worked in various temporary jobs including supply teaching. Separated from partner in 2000. Owner-occupier. Identifies as middle class but with caveats.

Rose, b.1945: Born in Oxford. Working-class background. Father a picture framer. Mother a housewife, until her husband set up a picture framing business in late 1950s which she helped with. Failed the 11+. Attended a secondary modern school. Left at sixteen after sitting O-Levels. Did an Art pre-dip course in Oxford. Went to Brighton for a DipAD course and met partner there. Gained a place to study at the Slade in 1966. Taught at Wolverhampton College of Art after finishing at the Slade. She found this job tough, and while there both her parents died within a few months of each other. Had a nervous breakdown, and left job to spend three months in a mental health hospital. After leaving hospital, moved to London to be with partner and opened up a market stall selling clothes that she had made. In early 1970s, moved back to Oxford to open up a clothing shop with her partner. Were struggling for money during this period and lived in the back of the shop, but once received some inheritance money bought a cottage. Bought further rental properties during the 1970s. Had son in 1979. Suffered from post-natal depression. Closed shop *c.*1980 because business was difficult. Had daughter in 1986. Took up painting again and has sold pieces and done workshops with mental hospital patients. Owner-occupier. Unsure of class identity, states has 'middle-class interests … have moved light years away from my parents in terms of wealth'.

Ruth, b.1949: Born in Sheffield. Working-class background. Father a miner. Mother a housewife, then later a factory worker. Parents divorced when she was a child. Passed the 11+. Attended grammar school. Left at fifteen. Worked in clerical roles. Returned to study in early 1970s as social worker. Moved to London. Became a social worker. Made redundant in a restructuring process. Became a social work tutor but faced redundancy again towards end of career and took early retirement. Returned to Sheffield. No children, not married. Owner-occupier. Describes her class identity as 'confused'.

Sadie, b.1943: Born in Sheffield. Lower middle-class background. Father manager of type-writing company. Mother ran a small hotel. Parents were divorced. Just failed the 11+ first time and attended an 'Intermediate' school. Resat at thirteen and passed, moved to a grammar school. Left school at eighteen with two A-Levels. Started a degree in general studies at Leicester but left after one year. Returned to Sheffield and teacher-trained. Worked as primary schoolteacher. No children. Married in early 2000s. Owner-occupier. Identifies as middle class.

Sandra, b.1946: Born in Oxford. Working-class background. Father a guard on the Great Western Railway network. Mother a housewife, had been a nanny prior to marriage and intermittently did evening childcare. Passed the 11+. Attended a grammar school. Left school at seventeen (nearly eighteen). Moved to Winchester for nursing college. Met current partner while at Winchester, not married. He was a painter and decorator, but later retrained and became a lecturer. No children. Worked as nurse in various hospitals in south of England. Did Master's degree (details unknown). Made redundant during 1980s, took some interim jobs, then moved to Bournemouth to set up cafe with partner. Owner-occupier. Class identity ambiguous, believes line between working class and middle class has become 'blurred'.

Susannah, b.1940: Born in Sheffield. Upper middle-class background. Father a consultant. Mother had worked in a pathology lab but gave up work on marriage. Passed the 11+. Attended a girls' grammar school. Left school at nineteen, after A-Levels stayed on for Cambridge entrance exam preparation. Undertook degree at University of Cambridge followed by postgraduate medicine at University of London. Worked briefly as locum in a hospital before deciding to train in psychiatry in late 1960s. Married early 1970s. Husband an American psychiatrist, moved with him to America in 1974. Had two children in mid-1970s. In 1980s ran a consultation service in a hospital and did teacher training of other doctors. Hospital restructured in 1990s and divorced around same time. Took position as principal of Oxbridge college. Remarried early 2000s. Owner-occupier. Identifies as upper middle class.

Sylvia, b.1945: Born in Leyland. Working-class background. Father a union area shop steward. Mother a housewife, had been a hairdresser prior to marriage. Failed the 11+. Initially attended a secondary modern. School put her in for the 13+ exam which she passed and moved to a grammar school. Left school at seventeen. Went to art school in Manchester. Followed by a Master's in fine art in London. Married in 1968. Husband also from a working-class background, they met at art college. Started teaching on temporary contracts at art colleges and schools around London, continued to paint. Had two daughters during the 1970s. Took a permanent job in cultural studies at a higher education institution. Did a Master's in cultural studies in mid-1980s, and then was promoted. Owner-occupier. Identifies as economically middle-class, but not in terms of beliefs and attitudes.

Theresa, b.1941: Born in Liverpool. Working-class background (both parents born in the workhouse). Father's occupation unknown. Mother a housewife and occasional waitress. Failed the 11+. Attended a secondary modern. Left school at fifteen. Went to work as cook in the merchant navy where she met her husband. Married in 1968. Both left navy and opened a pub in Southampton. Sold pub. Had son in 1973. Moved to Portsmouth and worked in local government. Equal opportunities officer for TUC. Made redundant. Took up roles as a cook and in admin. Became ill with breast cancer so took voluntary retirement in early 1990s. Started a degree in women's studies at Ruskin College, Oxford. Divorced in mid-1990s. Council flat tenant. Identifies as working class economically, although thinks she has a degree of upward class mobility due to 'moving around and education'.

Notes

Chapter 1

1   See for example Celia Hughes, *Young Lives on the Left: Sixties Activism and the Liberation of the Self* (Manchester: Manchester University Press, 2015), pp.6–7; Mathew Thomson, *Lost Freedom: The Landscape of the Child and the British Post-War Settlement* (Oxford: Oxford University Press, 2013), pp.80–1; Emily Robinson, Camilla Schofield, Florence Sutcliffe-Braithwaite and Natalie Thomlinson, 'Telling Stories about Post-War Britain: Popular Individualism and the "Crisis" of the 1970s', *Twentieth Century British History*, 28/2 (2017), pp.277–8; Nadja Durbach, *The Politics of Food in Britain from the Workhouse to the Welfare State* (Cambridge: Cambridge University Press, 2020), p. 10.

2   Carolyn Steedman, *Landscape for a Good Woman* (London: Virago, 1986), p.122.

3   Carolyn Steedman, 'Writing the Self: The End of the Scholarship Girl', in Jim McGuigan (ed.), *Cultural Methodologies* (London: Sage, 1997), p.107. The key welfare state acts are usually considered to be Butler Education Act (1944), Family Allowances Act (1945), National Health Service Act (1946), National Insurance Act (1946) and Town Planning Act (1947).

4   Liz Heron, 'Introduction', in Liz Heron (ed.), *Truth Dare or Promise: Girls Growing Up in the Fifties* (London: Virago, 1985), p.1.

5   Heron, 'Introduction', p.1.

6   Heron, 'Introduction', p.6.

7   Histories of the welfare state have tended to take a top-down approach, focused on policy and parliamentary decision-making; see Chris Renwick, *Bread for All: The Origins of the Welfare State* (London: Allen Lane, 2017); Rodney Lowe, *The Welfare State in Britain since 1945* (Basingstoke: Macmillan, 1999); Gosta Esping-Andersen, *The Three Worlds of Welfare Capitalism* (Cambridge: Polity, 1990).

8   Katrina Navickas, 'A Return to Materialism? Putting Social History Back into Place' in Sasha Handley, Rohan McWilliam and Lucy Noakes (eds), *New Directions in Social and Cultural History* (London: Bloomsbury: 2018), pp.94–5.

9   Lynn Abrams, *Oral History Theory* (New York: Routledge, 2010); Lynn Abrams, 'Liberating the Female Self: Epiphanies, Conflict and Coherence in the Life Stories of Post-War British Women', *Social History*, 39/1 (2014), pp.14–35; Penny Summerfield, *Histories of the Self: Personal Narratives and Historical Practice* (London: Routledge, 2018); Penny Summerfield, 'Culture and Composure: Creating

Narratives of the Gendered Self in Oral History Interviews', *Cultural and Social History*, 1/1 (2004), pp.65–93.

10 Elizabeth Roberts, *A Woman's Place: An Oral History of Working-Class Women, 1890–1940* (Oxford: Basil Blackwell, 1984); Elizabeth Roberts, *Women and Families: An Oral History 1940–1970* (Oxford: Blackwell, 1995).

11 See the extensive contents, Roberts, *Women and Families,* pp.vii–x.

12 Roberts, *Women and Families,* p.1.

13 Selina Todd, 'Class, Experience and Britain's Twentieth Century', *Social History*, 39/4 (2014), p.491.

14 Nicholas Timmins, *The Five Giants: A Biography of the Welfare State* (London: HarperCollins, 2017), p.7.

15 Timmins, *The Five Giants,* p.7.

16 Renwick, *Bread for All*; Esping-Andersen, *Three Worlds of Welfare Capitalism.*

17 Pat Thane, *Divided Kingdom*: *A History of Britain 1900–Present* (Cambridge: Cambridge University Press, 2018), p.470. For the growing interest in older age, see also Nick Hubble, Jennie Taylor and Phillip Tew (eds), *Growing Old with the Welfare State: Eight British Lives* (London: Bloomsbury, 2019).

18 See for example George Stevenson, *The Women's Liberation Movement and the Politics of Class in Britain* (London: Bloomsbury, 2019); Florence Sutcliffe-Braithwaite, *Class, Politics and the Decline of Deference in England, 1968–2000* (Oxford: Oxford University Press, 2018); Selina Todd, *The People: The Rise and Fall of the Working Class, 1910–2010* (London: John Murray, 2014).

19 Todd, *The People*, p.245.

20 Chris Renwick, 'Eugenics, Population Research, and Social Mobility Studies in Early and Mid-Twentieth Century Britain', *The Historical Journal*, 59/3 (2016), p.865.

21 Peter Mandler, 'Educating the Nation III: Social Mobility', *Transactions of the Royal Historical Society*, 26 (2016), p.5.

22 Todd, *The People*, pp.216–35; see also Selina Todd, *Snakes and Ladders: The Great British Social Mobility Myth* (London: Vintage, 2021).

23 Mandler, 'Social Mobility', p.6.

24 Geoff Payne and Pamela Abbott (eds), *The Social Mobility of Women: Beyond Male Mobility Models* (Basingstoke: Falmer Press, 1990), p.11. Female sociologists such as Steph Lawler have undertaken excellent work on experiences of social mobility but focused less on how and when it occurs, 'Getting Out and Getting Away: Women's Narratives of Class Mobility', *Feminist Review*, 63/1 (1999), pp.3–24.

25 Pamela Abbott and Geoff Payne, 'Women's Social Mobility: Conventional Wisdom Reconsidered', in Geoff Payne and Pamela Abbott (eds), *The Social Mobility of Women: Beyond Male Mobility Models* (Basingstoke: Falmer Press, 1990), p.13.

26 Gill Jones, 'Marriage Partners and Their Class Trajectories', in Geoff Payne and Pamela Abbott (eds), *The Social Mobility of Women: Beyond Male Mobility Models* (Basingstoke: Falmer Press, 1990), p.102.

27 Jones, 'Marriage Partners', p.102.

28 Selina Todd, *Young Women, Work, and Family in England 1918–1950* (Oxford: Oxford University Press, 2005).

29 Dolly Smith Wilson, 'A New Look at the Affluent Worker: The Good Working Mother in Post-War Britain', *Twentieth Century British History*, 17/2 (2006), pp.206–29.

30 Sarah Aiston, 'A Good Job for a Girl? The Career Biographies of Women Graduates of the University of Liverpool Post-1945', *Twentieth Century British History*, 15/4 (2004), pp.385–6; Pat Thane, 'Girton Graduates: Earning and Learning, 1920s–1980s', *Women's History Review*, 13/3 (2004), pp.347–62.

31 Helen McCarthy, *Double Lives: A History of Working Motherhood* (London: Bloomsbury, 2020).

32 Pat Thane, 'Visions of Gender in the British Welfare State', in Gisela Bock and Pat Thane (eds), *Maternity and Gender Policies: Women and the Rise of the European Welfare States 1880s–1950s* (London: Routledge, 1991) p.99.

33 Susan Pedersen, *Family, Dependence and the Origins of the Welfare State: Britain and France, 1914–1945* (Cambridge: Cambridge University Press, 1993), p.176.

34 Seth Koven and Sonya Michel, 'Womanly Duties: Maternalist Politics and the Origins of Welfare States in France, Germany, Great Britain and the United States, 1880–1920', *American Historical Review*, 95/4 (1990), pp.1076–108.

35 Koven, Michel, 'Womanly Duties', p.1107.

36 Elizabeth Wilson, *Women and the Welfare State* (London: Tavistock Publications, 1977), p.9.

37 Frances Fox Piven, 'Ideology and the State: Women, Power, and the Welfare State', in Linda Gordon (ed.), *Women, the State and Welfare* (Madison: University of Wisconsin Press, 1990), pp.250–64.

38 Piven, 'Ideology and the State', p.255.

39 Piven, 'Ideology and the State', p.260.

40 Sheila Blackburn, 'How Useful Are Feminist Theories of the Welfare State?', *Women's History Review*, 4/3 (1995), p.375.

41 Blackburn, 'Feminist Theories', p.375.

42 Blackburn, 'Feminist Theories', p.375.

43 Karl Mannheim, *Essays on the Sociology of Knowledge: Collected Works Volume Five* (London: Routledge, 1997), p.310.

44 Mannheim, *Essays on the Sociology of Knowledge*, pp.297–8.

45 Robert Gildea, James Mark and Anette Warring (eds), *Europe's 1968: Voices of Revolt* (Oxford: Oxford University Press, 2013), p.9; see also Luisa Passerini, *Autobiography of a Generation: Italy 1968* (London: University Press of New England, 1996); Hughes, *Young Lives on the Left*; Anna Von Der Goltz, 'Generation

of 68ers: Age-Related Constructions of Identity and Germany's 1968', *Cultural and Social History*, 8/4 (2011), pp.473–91.

46   Hughes, *Young Lives on the Left*.

47   Stevenson, *The Women's Liberation Movement*; Jonathan Moss, *Women, Workplace Protest and Political Identity in England, 1968–85* (Manchester: Manchester University Press, 2019).

48   Mannheim, *Essays on the Sociology of Knowledge*, p.278.

49   Forty-two interviews were conducted for this project in total, primarily between September 2014 and March 2016, although a small second wave was conducted in summer 2019.

50   Phillida Bunkle, 'The 1944 Education Act and Second Wave Feminism', *Women's History Review*, 25/5 (2016), p.800.

51   Abrams, 'Liberating the Female Self', pp.14–35.

52   Betty Jerman, *The Lively-Minded Women: The First Twenty Years of the National Housewives' Register* (London: Heinemann, 1981); Mary Ingham, *Now We Are Thirty: Women of the Breakthrough Generation* (London: Eyre Methuen, 1981).

53   Lynn Abrams, 'Talking about Feminism: Reconciling Fragmented Research Frames', *Cultural and Social History*, 16/2 (2019), pp.205–24.

54   See for example Todd, *The People*; Abrams, 'Liberating the Female Self', pp.14–35; Claire Langhamer, *Women's Leisure in England, 1920–1960* (Manchester: Manchester University Press, 2000); Laura Paterson, '"I Didn't Feel Like My Own Person": Paid Work in Women's Narratives of Self and Working Motherhood', *Contemporary British History*, 33/3 (2019), pp.405–26.

55   See for example Angela Davis, 'Uncovering the Lives of Women in Post-War Oxfordshire: An Oral History Approach', *Rural History*, 19/1 (2008), pp.105–21; Kate Fisher, 'An Oral History of Birth Control Practice c.1925–1950: A Study of Oxford and South Wales' (unpublished DPhil thesis, University of Oxford, 1997).

56   See Simon Gunn, 'Spatial Mobility in Later Twentieth-Century Britain', *Contemporary British History* (Advanced Access, 2021), DOI:10/1080/13619462.2020.1858060.

57   Steph Lawler, *Mothering the Self: Mothers, Daughters, Subjects* (London: Routledge, 2000), p.176.

58   Beverley Bryan, Stella Dadzie and Suzanne Scafe, *Heart of the Race: Black Women's Lives in Britain* (London: Verso, 2018), pp.89–123; see also Jordanna Bailkin, *The Afterlife of Empire* (Berkeley: University of California Press, 2012).

59   Stephanie Spencer, *Gender, Work and Education in Britain in the 1950s* (Basingstoke: Palgrave Macmillan, 2005), p.165.

60   Kristina Minister, 'A Feminist Frame for the Oral History Interview', in Sherna Berger Gluck and Daphne Patai (eds), *Women's Words: The Feminist Practice of Oral History* (London: Routledge, 1991), pp.27–41.

61   Mike Savage, *Identities and Social Change in Britain since 1940: The Politics of Method* (Oxford: Oxford University Press, 2010); see also Jon Lawrence, *Me? Me? Me? The Search for Community in Post-War England* (Oxford: Oxford University Press, 2019).

62   Steedman, 'Writing the Self', p.107.

63   SxMOA2/1/71/3, Spring 2004 Directive; SxMOA2/1/105/1, Spring 2016 Directive; SxMOA2/1/111/1, Spring 2018 Directive, Mass Observation Archive, University of Sussex.

64   Claire Langhamer, *The English in Love: The Intimate Story of an Emotional Revolution* (Oxford: Oxford University Press, 2013), p.xv.

65   Langhamer, *The English in Love,* p.xvi.

Chapter 2

1   Interview with Dawn, September 2014.

2   Laura King, 'Future Citizens: Cultural and Political Conceptions of Children in Britain, 1930s–1950s', *Twentieth Century British History*, 27/3 (2016), pp.389–411.

3   King, 'Future Citizens', p.393.

4   Pat Thane, 'Family Life and "Normality" in Postwar Britain', in Richard Bessel and Dirk Schumann (eds), *Life after Death: Approaches to a Cultural and Social History of Europe during the 1940s and 1950s* (Cambridge: Cambridge University Press, 2003), pp.193–210.

5   Thane, 'Family Life', pp.206–7.

6   Lynn Abrams, 'Mothers and Daughters: Negotiating the Discourse on the "Good Woman" in 1950s and 1960s Britain', in Nancy Christies and Michael Gauvreau (eds), *Sixties and Beyond: De-Christianization in North America and Western Europe 1945–2000* (Toronto: University of Toronto Press, 2013), pp.60–83; Celia Hughes, *Young Lives on the Left: Sixties Activism and the Liberation of the Self* (Manchester: Manchester University Press, 2015), pp.38–41. Laura King has written about fatherhood in the post-war period, but not specifically about the father–daughter relationship, *Family Men: Fatherhood and Masculinity in Britain, c.1914–1960* (Oxford: Oxford University Press, 2015).

7   Carolyn Steedman, *Landscape for a Good Woman* (London: Virago, 1986), p.2.

8   Steedman, *Landscape*, p.122.

9   Carolyn Steedman, 'Landscape for a Good Woman', in Liz Heron (ed.), *Truth Dare or Promise: Girls Growing Up in the Fifties* (London: Virago, 1985), p.125.

10   Angela Carter, 'Truly, It Felt Like One Year', in Sara Maitland (ed.), *Very Heaven: Looking Back at the 1960s* (London: Virago, 1988), p.210.

11   Carter, 'One Year', p.210.

12 Interview with Bridget, May 2015.

13 Rodney Lowe, *Welfare State in Britain since 1945* (Basingstoke: Macmillan, 1999), p.167.

14 George Gosling, *Payment and Philanthropy in British Healthcare: 1918–48* (Manchester: Manchester University Press, 2017), p.2.

15 Gosling, *Payment and Philanthropy*, p.2.

16 Gosling, *Payment and Philanthropy*, p.5.

17 Interview with Jean, April 2015.

18 Interview with Jean.

19 See for example interviews with Jean, Sandra, April 2015, and Joy, April 2015.

20 Richard Titmuss, *Essays on the Welfare State* (London: Allen & Unwin, 1959), p.137. Titmuss contrasted the demand for the NHS exceeding government expectations with the fact that claims for sickness benefit had 'been substantially lighter than expected since 1948 to the extent of 15 to 20 per cent'.

21 Interview with Sandra.

22 Interview with Diane, April 2015.

23 Interview with Diane.

24 Interview with Susannah, January 2015.

25 Interview with Jacqui, July 2019.

26 Conservative Party, *1950 Conservative Party General Election Manifesto*, http://www.conservativemanifesto.com/1950/1950-conservative-manifesto.shtml.

27 Interview with Jean.

28 Andrew Seaton, 'Against the "Sacred Cow": NHS Opposition and the Fellowship for Freedom in Medicine, 1948–1972', *Twentieth Century British History*, 26/3 (2015), p.429.

29 Interview with Dawn, September 2014.

30 Interview with Dawn.

31 Interview with Dawn.

32 Interview with Joy.

33 Interview with Joy.

34 Interview with Joy.

35 Interview with Kathy, April 2015.

36 Interview with Kathy.

37 Interview with Rita, October 2015.

38 Interview with Rita.

39 Selina Todd, *The People: The Rise and Fall of the Working Class, 1910–2010* (London: John Murray, 2014), p.158.

40 Interview with Sandra, April 2015.

41 Interview with Lois, September 2014.

42 Interview with Lois.

43 Liz Heron, 'Dear Green Place', in Liz Heron (ed.), *Truth, Dare or Promise: Girls Growing Up in the Fifties* (London: Virago, 1985), p.153.

44 Interview with Rita.

45 Claire Langhamer, 'The Meanings of Home in Postwar Britain', *Journal of Contemporary History*, 40/2 (2005), p.342.

46 Pat Thane, *Foundations of the Welfare State* (London: Longman, 1996), p.243.

47 Lowe, *Welfare State*, p.250.

48 Interviews with Sandra and Nancy, August 2019.

49 Interview with Nancy.

50 Interview with Jean.

51 Interview with Carol, November 2014.

52 Interview with Carol.

53 Interview with Carol.

54 Interview with Carol.

55 Heron, 'Dear Green Place', p.156.

56 Jon Lawrence, *Me? Me? Me? The Search for Community in Post-War England* (Oxford: Oxford University Press, 2019), pp.41–71; Peter Willmott and Michael Young, *Family and Kinship in East London* (London: Routledge & Kegan Paul, 1957), p.186.

57 Richard Hoggart, *The Uses of Literacy: Aspects of Working-Class Life* (London: Chatto & Windus, 1957).

58 Todd, *The People*, p.174.

59 Interview with Lois.

60 Interview with Ruth, October 2015.

61 Interview with Rita. Young and Willmott noted that parents thought the estates were 'better for the kiddies' because of the health benefits of 'fresh air and fields', *Family and Kinship*, p.128.

62 Interview with Rita.

63 Todd, *The People*, p.178.

64 Interview with Maureen, April 2015.

65 Ben Jones, 'Slum Clearance, Privatization and Residualization: The Practices and Politics of Council Housing in Mid-Twentieth-Century England', *Twentieth Century British History*, 21/4 (2010), p.515.

66 Conservative Party, *1951 Conservative Party General Election Manifesto*, http://www.conservativemanifesto.com/1951/1951-conservative-manifesto.shtml.

67 Ben Jackson, 'Revisionism Reconsidered: Property-Owning Democracy and Egalitarian Strategy in Postwar Britain', *Twentieth Century British History*, 16/4 (2005), pp.416–40; Phil Child, 'Landlordism, Rent Regulation and the Labour Party in Mid-Twentieth Century Britain, 1950–64', *Twentieth Century British History*, 29/1 (2018), p.81.

68 Ina Zweiniger-Bargielowska has explored the gender gap in post-war voting and the success of the distinct appeals to women made by the Conservative Party

in the 1950s and 1960s, 'Explaining the Gender Gap: The Conservative Party and the Women's Vote 1945–1964', in Martin Francis and Ina Zweiniger-Bargielowska (eds), *The Conservatives and British Society, 1880–1990* (Cardiff: University of Wales Press, 1996), pp.194–224. It is important to note that not all women voted Conservative in this period – Rose is an example of an interviewee who hailed from a working-class background whose parents both voted Labour: 'They hated the Conservatives', interview with Rose, July 2019.

69   Interview with Joy.

70   Interview with Joy.

71   Interview with Jean.

72   Interview with Jean.

73   Hoggart, *Uses of Literacy*, p.29. Steedman vividly recalled her own mother's frustrations and longings, a significant symbol of which was to own a house, *Landscape*, p.43.

74   Carol Dyhouse, 'Family Patterns of Social Mobility through Higher Education in England in the 1930s', *Social History*, 34/4 (2001), p.869.

75   See interviews with Linda, April 2015, Ruth and Rita.

76   Interview with Ruth.

77   Jones, 'Slum Clearance', p.515.

78   Interview with Linda.

79   Peter Mandler, 'Educating the Nation I: Schools', *Transactions of the Royal Historical Society*, 24 (2014), p.11; Peter Mandler, *Crisis of the Meritocracy: Britain's Transition to Mass Education since the Second World War* (Oxford: Oxford University Press, 2020).

80   Todd, *The People*, p.219.

81   Mandler, 'Schools', p.13. Scotland had a different secondary school system to the rest of the country during this period but the competing aims of equal opportunity and selection were shared, Laura Paterson, Alison Pattie and Ian Deary, 'Social Class, Gender and Secondary Education in Scotland in the 1950s', *Oxford Review of Education*, 37/3 (2011), pp.383–401. Jacqui, who grew up in Scotland, recalled sitting an exam at eleven and then moving schools for Highers at fifteen years of age; interview with Jacqui.

82   There has recently been some corrective to the lack of attention granted to secondary modern schools – see for example Laura Tisdall, 'Inside the "Blackboard Jungle": Male Teachers and Male Pupils at English Secondary Modern Schools in Fact and Fiction, 1950–1959', *Cultural and Social History*, 12/4 (2015), pp.489–507.

83   Interview with Theresa, April 2015.

84   Ross McKibbin, *Classes and Cultures, England 1918–1951* (Oxford: Oxford University Press, 1998), p.212.

85   Interview with Lois, and Barbara, December 2014.

86   Interview with Chrissie, October 2015.

87   Interview with Jean.

88   Interview with Lesley, July 2015.

89   McKibbin, *Classes and Cultures*, p.226.

90   Interview with Lesley.

91   Mary Evans, *A Good School: Life at a Girls' Grammar School in the 1950s* (London: Women's Press, 1991), p.26.

92   Interview with Elizabeth, January 2015.

93   Interview with Elizabeth.

94   Interview with Elizabeth.

95   Interview with Susannah.

96   George Smith, 'Schools' in A. H. Halsey and Josephine Webb (eds), *Twentieth Century British Social Trends* (Basingstoke: Macmillan, 2000), p.188.

97   Gillian Avery, *The Best Type of Girl: A History of Girls' Independent Schools* (London: Deutsch, 1991).

98   Brian Jackson and Dennis Marsden, *Education and the Working Class: Some General Themes Raised by a Study of 88 Working-Class Children in a Northern Industrial City* (London: Routledge & Kegan Paul, 1962), p.42.

99   Mandler, 'Schools', p.14.

100 Interview with Beth, January 2015.

101 Interview with Beth.

102 Interview with Sadie, September 2014, and Anita, February 2015.

103 Interview with Sadie.

104 Interview with Anita.

105 See for example in interviews with Maureen, Rita and Theresa.

106 David Glass cited in Halsey, *Twentieth Century*, p.185.

107 Interview with Sylvia, April 2015.

108 Interview with Sylvia.

109 Interview with Sylvia.

110 Interview with Sylvia.

111 Interview with Rose.

112 John Goldthorpe, David Lockwood, Frank Bechhofer and Jennifer Platt, *The Affluent Worker in the Class Structure* (Cambridge: Cambridge University Press, 1969), pp.138–40.

113 Interview with Maureen.

114 Interview with Maureen.

115 Interview with Rita.

116 Jean Floud and A. H Halsey, 'Intelligence Tests, Social Class and Selection for Secondary Schools', *The British Journal of Sociology*, 8/1 (1957), pp.33–9.

117 Ben Jackson, *Equality and the British Left: A Study in Progressive Political Thought, 1900–64* (Manchester: Manchester University Press, 2007), p.166.

118 Jackson, *Equality and the British Left*, p.166.

119 Jackson and Marsden, *Education and the Working Class.*

120 Interview with Sylvia.

121 See interviews with Maureen, Sylvia, Kathy.

122 Interview with Kathy.

123 Jackson and Marsden, *Education and the Working Class*, p.217.

124 Interview with Sylvia.

125 See interviews with Linda, Rita and Ruth.

126 Interview with Carol.

127 Interview with Carol.

128 Heron, 'Dear Green Place', p.167.

129 Heron, 'Dear Green Place', p.168.

130 Carolyn Steedman, 'Writing the Self: The End of the Scholarship Girl', in Jim McGuigan (ed.), *Cultural Methodologies* (London: Sage, 1997), pp.117–18.

131 Steedman, 'Writing the Self', p.117.

132 Liz Heron, 'Dear Green Place', p.7, in Liz Heron (ed.), *Truth, Dare or Promise: Girls Growing Up in the Fifties* (London: Virago, 1985), p.7.

133 Interview with Brenda, November 2014.

134 Interview with Brenda.

135 Interview with Brenda.

136 Interview with Lois.

137 Interview with Sylvia.

138 Interview with Carol.

139 Interview with Rita.

140 Interview with Rita.

141 Interview with Linda.

142 Interview with Linda.

143 Interview with Linda.

144 Stephanie Spencer, *Gender, Work and Education in Britain in the 1950s* (Basingstoke: Palgrave Macmillan, 2005), pp.22–48.

145 Stephanie Spencer, 'Reflections on the "Site of Struggle": Girls' Experience of Secondary Education in the Late 1950s', *History of Education*, 33/4 (2004), p.446.

146 Interview with Barbara.

147 Interview with Barbara.

148 Interview with Eileen, December 2014.

149 Interview with Lois.

150 Interview with Rose.

151 Pat Thane, 'History and Policy', *History Workshop Journal*, 67/1 (2009), p.143.

152 Interview with Rita.

153 Irene Payne, 'A Working-Class Girl in a Grammar School', in Dale Spender and Elizabeth Sarah (eds), *Learning to Lose: Sexism and Education* (London: Women's Press, 1980), p.19.

154 Margaret Forster, *Hidden Lives: A Family Memoir* (London: Viking, 1995), pp.203–6.

155 Jackson, Marsden, *Education and the Working Class*, p.216.

156 Interview with Rita.

157 Interview with Joy.

158 Interview with Sylvia.

159 Interview with Sally Alexander, *Europe's 1968 Project*, conducted and held by John Davis.

160 Interview with Sally Alexander.

161 Phillida Bunkle, 'The 1944 Education Act and Second Wave Feminism', *Women's History Review*, 25/5 (2016), p.4.

162 Evans, *A Good School*, p.55.

163 Anette Kuhn, *Family Secrets: Acts of Memory and Imagination* (London: Verso, 2002), p.108.

164 Kuhn, *Family Secrets*, p.110.

165 Kuhn, *Family Secrets*, p.108.

166 Interview with Rita.

167 Interview with Sylvia.

168 Kuhn, *Family Secrets*, p.116.

169 Kuhn, *Family Secrets*, p.117.

170 Bev Skeggs, *Formations of Class and Gender: Becoming Respectable* (London: Sage, 1997).

171 Diane Reay, 'Social Mobility, a Panacea for Austere Times: Tales of Emperors, Frogs and Tadpoles', *British Journal of Sociology*, 34/5–6 (2013), p.672.

172 Interview with Carol.

173 Interview with Angie, May 2015.

174 Interview with Angie.

175 Roland Barthes, *Mythologies* (London: Cape, 1972).

Chapter 3

1 Lynn Abrams, 'Liberating the Female Self: Epiphanies, Conflict and Coherence in the Life Stories of Post-war British Women', *Social History*, 39/1 (2014), p.17.

2 Abrams, 'Liberating the Female Self', pp.14–35; Phillida Bunkle, 'The 1944 Education Act and Second Wave Feminism', *Women's History Review*, 25/5 (2016), pp.791–811; Sarah Aiston, 'A Good Job for a Girl? The Career Biographies of Women Graduates of the University of Liverpool Post-1945', *Twentieth Century British History*, 15/4 (2004), pp.361–87; Helena Mills, 'Using the Personal to Critique the Popular: Women's Memories of 1960s Youth', *Contemporary British History*, 30/4 (2016), pp.463–83; Selina Todd and Hilary Young, 'Baby-Boomers to

"Beanstalkers": The Making of the Modern Teenager in Post-War Britain', *Cultural and Social History*, 9/3 (2012), pp.451–67.

3   1961 Census – England and Wales Education Tables, 'Table 1: Population Aged 15 and Over by Age and Terminal Education Age', Official Papers (OP), Bodleian Libraries, University of Oxford, p.2.

4   Peter Mandler, 'Educating the Nation II: Universities', *Transactions of the Royal Historical Study*, 25 (2015), p.8.

5   Arthur McIvor, *Working Lives: Work in Britain since 1945* (Basingstoke: Palgrave Macmillan, 2013), p.21.

6   Carol Dyhouse, *Students: A Gendered History* (London: Routledge, 2006).

7   Mandler, 'Universities', p.5.

8   Mandler, 'Universities', pp.1–2.

9   Carolyn Steedman, *Landscape for a Good Woman* (London: Virago, 1986), p.15.

10 Geoff Payne, *The New Social Mobility: How the Politicians Got It Wrong* (Bristol: Policy Press, 2017), p.113.

11 McIvor, *Working Lives*, p.21.

12 Peter Mandler, 'Educating the Nation III: Social Mobility', *Transactions of the Royal Historical Society*, 26 (2016), p.7.

13 Michael Roper, *Masculinity and the British Organization Man since 1945* (Oxford: Oxford University Press, 1994), pp.1–15.

14 Amitai Etzioni (ed.), *The Semi-Professions and Their Organization: Teachers, Nurses, Social Workers* (New York: Free Press, 1969).

15 Etzioni, *The Semi-Professions*, pp.xiii–xiv.

16 Madeleine Arnot, Miriam David and Gaby Weiner, *Closing the Gender Gap: Postwar Education and Social Change* (Cambridge: Polity, 1999), p.58; the post-war expansion functioned to intensify pre-war trends towards professionalization in gendered welfare occupations; Mark Peel, *Miss Cutler and the Case of the Resurrected Horse: Social Work and the Story of Poverty in America, Australia and Britain* (Chicago: University of Chicago Press, 2011); Alison Oram, *Women Teachers and Feminist Politics 1900–1939* (Manchester: Manchester University Press, 1996).

17 Interview with Kathy, April 2015.

18 Interview with Joy, April 2015.

19 Selina Todd, *Young Women, Work, and Family in England 1918–1950* (Oxford: Oxford University Press, 2005), p.114.

20 Interview with Maureen, April 2015.

21 Interview with Maureen.

22 Dale Spender and Elizabeth Sarah (eds), *Learning to Lose: Sexism and Education* (London: Women's Press, 1980) p.7.

23 Spender and Sarah, *Learning to Lose*, p.19.

24 Diane Reay, 'Social Mobility, a Panacea for Austere Times: Tales of Emperors, Frogs and Tadpoles', *British Journal of Sociology*, 34/5–6 (2013), pp.660–77.

25 Interview with Cynthia, September 2014.

26 Interview with Rita, October 2015.

27 Interview with Rita.

28 Interview with Ruth, October 2015.

29 Interview with Ruth.

30 Annette Kuhn, *Family Secrets: Acts of Memory and Imagination* (London: Verso, 2002), p.118.

31 Brian Jackson and Dennis Marsden, *Education and the Working Class: Some General Themes Raised by a Study of 88 Working-Class Children in a Northern Industrial City* (London: Routledge & Kegan Paul, 1962), p.169.

32 Interview with Sylvia, April 2015.

33 Interview with Sylvia.

34 Interview with India, March 2016.

35 Interview with India.

36 Selina Todd, *The People: The Rise and Fall of the Working Class, 1910–2010* (London: John Murray, 2014), p.231.

37 Bunkle, 'The 1944 Education Act', p.791.

38 Interview with Frances, February 2015.

39 Interview with Elizabeth, January 2015.

40 Interview with Susannah, January 2015.

41 Dyhouse, *Students*, p.87.

42 Dyhouse, *Students*, p.87.

43 Carol Dyhouse, 'Signing the Pledge? Women's Investment in University Education and Teacher Training before 1939', *History of Education*, 26/2 (1997), p.208.

44 David Butler and Gareth Butler, *British Political Facts* (Basingstoke: Palgrave Macmillan, 2011), p.395.

45 R. Kelsall, *Women and Teaching: Report on an Independent Nuffield Survey Following Up a Large National Sample of Women Who Entered Teaching in England at Various Dates Pre-war and Post-war* (London: HMSO, 1963), p.24.

46 Kelsall, *Women and Teaching*, p.25.

47 Todd, *The People*, p.231.

48 W1813, Spring 2004 Directive, Mass Observation Archive, University of Sussex (MOA).

49 Interview with Carol, November 2014.

50 Interview with Carol.

51 Interview with Carol.

52 Valerie Walkerdine, 'Dreams from an Ordinary Childhood', in Liz Heron (ed.), *Truth Dare or Promise: Girls Growing Up in the Fifties* (London: Virago, 1985), p.70.

53 Walkerdine, 'Dreams', p.70.

54 E743, Spring 2004 Directive, MOA.

55 Arnot, David, and Weiner, *Closing the Gender Gap*, p.59.

56 Interview with Sylvia.

57 Interview with Sandra, April 2015.

58 Interview with Sandra.

59 Interview with Sandra.

60 Interview with Jean, April 2015.

61 Interview with Jean.

62 Interview with Sylvia.

63 Shirley Dex, 'Occupational Mobility over Women's Lifetime', in Geoff Payne and Pamela Abbott (eds), *The Social Mobility of Women: Beyond Male Mobility Models* (Basingstoke: Falmer Press, 1990), p.126.

64 Interviews with Lesley, July 2015, Angie, May 2015 and Rita.

65 Interview with Lois, September 2014.

66 Henrietta O'Connor and John Goodwin, '"She Wants to Be Like Her Mum?": Girls' Experience of the School-to-Work Transition in the 1960s', *Journal of Education and Work*, 17/1 (2004), p.105.

67 O'Connor and Goodwin, 'Girls' Experience', p.105.

68 Richard Parry, *United Kingdom Public Employment: Patterns of Change 1951–1976* (Glasgow: Centre for the Study of Public Policy, University of Strathclyde, 1980).

69 Laura Paterson, 'Women and Paid Work in Industrial Britain: c.1945–1971', (unpublished PhD thesis, University of Dundee, 2015), p.78.

70 Paterson, 'Women and Paid Work', p.78.

71 Parry, *United Kingdom Public Employment*, p.16.

72 Interview with Cynthia.

73 Interview with Cynthia.

74 Interview with Linda, April 2015.

75 Interview with Linda.

76 Interview with Eileen, December 2014.

77 Interview with Eileen.

78 Interview with Brenda, November 2014.

79 Parry, *United Kingdom Public Employment*, pp.15–22.

80 Geoff Payne, Judy Payne and Tony Chapman, 'The Changing Pattern of Early Career Mobility', in Payne and Abbott (eds), *The Social Mobility of Women: Beyond Male Mobility Models* (Basingstoke: Falmer Press, 1990), p.53.

81 Interview with Barbara, December 2014.

82 Interview with Barbara.

83 Interview with Ann, February 2015.

84 Interview with Ann.

85 Interview with Kathy, April 2015.

86 Interview with Lois.

87 Interview with Lois.

88 Interview with Dawn, September 2014.

89 Interview with Bridget, May 2015.

90   Interview with Bridget.

91   Kuhn, *Family Secrets*, p.118.

92   Kuhn, *Family Secrets*, p.118.

93   Kuhn, *Family Secrets*, p.122.

94   Arnot, David and Weiner, *Closing the Gender Gap*, p.59.

95   Interview with Joy, April 2015.

96   Interview with Joy.

97   Interview with Maureen.

98   Interview with Maureen.

99   Interview with Angie; F4605, Spring 2016 Directive, MOA.

100 Interview with Chrissie, October 2015.

101 Interview with Chrissie.

102 Interview with Eileen.

103 Interview with Rita.

104 Interview with Rita.

105 Dyhouse, *Students*, p.107.

106 Interview with Frances.

107 Interview with Diane, April 2015.

108 Interview with Diane.

109 Celia Hughes, *Young Lives on the Left: Sixties Activism and the Liberation of the Self* (Manchester: Manchester University Press, 2015), p.103.

110 Interview with India.

111 1961 Census – England and Wales Occupation Tables, 'Table 1: Occupation by Status', OP, pp.2–6; 1971 Census – Great Britain Qualified Manpower Tables, 'Table 6: Persons 18 Years of Age and over Economically Active by Educational Attainment, Sex and Occupation', OP, pp.32–35.

112 Interview with India.

113 Interview with India.

114 Interview with Penny, September 2019.

115 Steedman, *Landscape*, p.15.

116 Liz Heron, 'Introduction', p.7, in Liz Heron (ed.), *Truth, Dare or Promise: Girls Growing Up in the Fifties* (London: Virago, 1985), p.168.

117 Reay, 'Social Mobility: A Panacea for Austere Times', p.672.

118 Reay, 'Social Mobility: A Panacea for Austere Times', p.672.

119 Interview with Kathy.

120 Interview with Kathy.

121 Interview with Kathy.

122 Interview with Kathy.

123 Interview with Sadie, September 2014.

124 Interview with Sadie.

125 Interview with Sadie.

126 Interview with Jean.

127 Jennifer Dale and Peggy Foster, *Feminists and State Welfare* (London: Routledge & Kegan Paul, 1986), pp.28–9.

128 Foster and Dale, *Feminists*, p.29.

129 Interview with Jean.

130 Interview with Sandra.

131 Tessa Blackstone, 'The Plowden Report', *The British Journal of Sociology*, 18/3 (1967), p.295.

132 Interview with Carol.

133 Lawrence Black, '"Making Britain a Gayer and More Cultivated Country": Wilson, Lee and the Creative Industries in the 1960s', *Contemporary British History*, 20/3 (2006), p.324.

134 Todd, *The People*, p.243.

135 Interview with Carol.

136 Shelagh Delaney, *A Taste of Honey: A Play* (London: Metheun, 1959). Shelagh Delaney (b.1938) herself left school early and used writing as a means to carve out a different kind of life; Selina Todd, *Tastes of Honey: The Making of Shelagh Delaney and a Cultural Revolution* (London: Chatto & Windus, 2019).

137 Interview with Sylvia.

138 Interview with Sylvia.

139 Interview with Sylvia.

140 Interview with Rose, August 2019.

141 Interview with Rose.

142 Pat Thane, 'The Careers of Female Graduates of Cambridge University, 1920s–1970s', in D. Mitch, J. Brown and M. Van Leeuwan (eds), *Origins of the Modern Career* (Aldershot: Ashgate, 2004), p.220.

143 Dyhouse, *Students*, p.114.

144 Interviews with India and Lesley.

145 Interview with Lesley.

146 Interview with Penny.

147 Interview with Elizabeth.

148 Interview with Elizabeth.

149 Interview with Susannah.

150 Margaret Cook, *A Slight and Delicate Creature: The Memoirs of Margaret Cook* (London: Orion, 1999).

151 Cook, *Slight and Delicate*, p.97.

152 Interview with Clara, September 2019.

153 Interview with Clara.

154 Interview with Diane.

155 Interview with Diane.

156 Roper, *Masculinity*, p.34.

157 Interview with Diane.

158 Interview with Diane.

159 Pat Thane, 'Family Life and "Normality" in Postwar Britain', in Richard Bessel and Dirk Schumann (eds), *Life after Death: Approaches to a Cultural and Social History of Europe during the 1940s and 1950s* (Cambridge: Cambridge University Press, 2003), pp.193–210.

160 Interview with Maureen.

161 Interview with Barbara.

162 Claire Langhamer, *The English in Love: The Intimate Story of an Emotional Revolution* (Oxford: Oxford University Press, 2013), p.25.

163 Langhamer, *The English in Love*, p.56.

164 Ferdynand Zweig, *Women's Life and Labour* (London: Victor Gollancz, 1952), p.122.

165 Langhamer, *The English in Love*, p.57.

166 Population Investigation Committee Marriage Survey cited in Langhamer, *The English in Love*, p.57.

167 Interview with Sylvia.

168 Interview with Joy.

169 Interview with Joy.

170 Interview with Joy.

171 Interview with Anita, February 2015.

172 Interview with Anita.

173 Pat Thane and Tanya Evans, *Sinners? Scroungers? Saints?: Unmarried Motherhood in Twentieth-Century Britain* (Oxford: Oxford University Press, 2013), p.128.

174 Jane Lewis, 'The Failure to Expand Childcare Provision and to Develop a Comprehensive Childcare Policy in Britain during the 1960s and 1970s', *Twentieth Century British History*, 24/2 (2013), pp.249–74.

175 Interview with Angie.

176 Interview with Angie.

177 Interview with Angie.

178 Interview with Eileen.

179 See for example interviews with Cynthia, Rita and Ruth.

180 Interview with Frances.

181 It is important to note that some married working-class women needed to continue working for economic reasons in the interwar period: see Miriam Glucksmann, 'In a Class of Their Own? Women Workers in the New Industries in Interwar Britain', *Feminist Review*, 24 (1986), pp.7–37.

182 C. G. Brown and W. H. Fraser (eds), *Britain since 1707* (Harlow: Longman, 2010), p.609.

183 Helen Glew, *Gender, Rhetoric and Regulation: Women's Work in the Civil Service and the London County Council, 1900–1955* (Manchester: Manchester University Press, 2016), pp.179–208.

184 Helen McCarthy, 'Women, Marriage and Paid Work in Post-War Britain', *Women's History Review*, 26/1 (2017), p.48.

185 Interview with Kathy.

186 Interview with Kathy.

187 Interview with Kathy.

188 Interview with Jean.

189 Interview with Jean.

190 Interview with Jean.

191 Interview with Susannah.

192 Interview with Lesley.

193 Judith Hubback, *Wives Who Went to College* (London: Heinemann, 1957), p.2.

194 Hubback, *Wives*, p.99.

195 Arnot, David and Weiner, *Closing the Gender Gap*, p.58.

196 Simon Szreter, Ann Louise Kinmonth, Natasha Kriznik and Michael Kelly, 'Health, Welfare and the State – the Dangers of Forgetting History', *The Lancet*, 388/10061 (2016), pp.2734–5.

Chapter 4

1 Pat Thane, 'The History of the Gender Division of Labour in Britain: Reflections on "Herstory", in Accounting, The First Eighty Years', *Accounting Organisations and Society*, 17/3–4 (1992), p.309; see also Paul Bagguley and Sylvia Walby, *Gender Restructuring: A Comparative Analysis of Five Local Labour Markets: Working Paper 28* (Lancaster: University of Lancaster, 1988).

2 See for example Carol Dyhouse, *Students: A Gendered History* (London: Routledge, 2006); Peter Mandler, 'Educating Nation II: Universities', *Transactions of the Royal Historical Society*, 25 (2015), pp.1–26.

3 Dyhouse, *Students*, p.98.

4 For further explanation of NS-SEC, see Geoff Payne, *The New Social Mobility: How the Politicians Got It Wrong* (Bristol: Policy Press, 2017), pp.178–80.

5 Payne, *The New Social Mobility*, pp.129–34.

6 John Goldthorpe, David Lockwood, Frank Bechhofer and Jennifer Platt, *The Affluent Worker in the Class Structure* (Cambridge: Cambridge University Press, 1969); John Goldthorpe with Caitriona Llewellyn and Clive Payne, *Social Mobility and Class Structure in Modern Britain* (Oxford: Oxford University Press, 1980).

7 John Goldthorpe, 'Women and Class Analysis: In Defence of the Conventional View', *Sociology*, 17/4 (1983), pp.465–88.

8 Anthony Heath and Nicky Britten, 'Women's Jobs Do Make a Difference: A Reply to Goldthorpe', *Sociology*, 18/4 (1984), pp.475–90.

9   Peter Mandler, 'Comment: Social Mobility and the Historians', *Cultural and Social History*, 16/1 (2019), p.104.

10   Halsey, 'Further and Higher Education', p.251.

11   The lowest level of qualification recorded in these census tables was 'qualifications that generally satisfy the three requirements of: obtained at age 18 or over; above GCE "A" Level; below first degree level. This level includes most teaching and nursing qualifications', 1971 Census – Great Britain Qualified Manpower Tables, 'General Explanatory Notes', Official Papers (OP), Bodleian Libraries, University of Oxford, pp.v–vii.

12   1971 Census, Great Britain – Qualified Manpower Tables, 'Table 8: Persons 18–69 Years of Age Qualified at Levels A, B, or C by Sex, Age and by Level, Subject Group and Primary Subject', p.48; 1981 Census, Great Britain – Qualified Manpower Tables, 'Table 6: Usually Resident Population Aged 18 and Over Qualified at Level A, B or C. Level of Qualification by Subject Group and Primary Subject by Age and Sex', OP, p.52 (all figures have been rounded to the nearest thousand).

13   1971 Census – Great Britain Qualified Manpower Tables, 'Table 8', OP, p.52; 1981 Census, Great Britain – Qualified Manpower Tables, OP, p.58.

14   A. H. Halsey, 'Further and Higher Education', in A. H. Halsey and Josephine Webb (eds), *Twentieth-Century British Social Trends* (Basingstoke: Macmillan, 2000), p.243.

15   Julia Whitburn, Maurice Mealing and Caroline Cox, *People in Polytechnics: A Survey of Polytechnic Staff and Students 1972–3* (Guildford: Society for Research into Higher Education, 1976), p.61.

16   Miriam David, 'A Gender Agenda: Women and Family in the New ERA?', *British Journal of Sociology of Education*, 12/4 (1991), pp.441–5.

17   Stephanie Spencer, *Gender, Work and Education in Britain in the 1950s* (Basingstoke: Palgrave Macmillan, 2005), pp.30–7.

18   Women's Policy Group, 'Report of the Women's Policy Group 1962–3', CCO 60/4/7, Conservative Party Archive (CPA), Bodleian Libraries, University of Oxford, pp.7–8.

19   Women's National Advisory Committee, 'Training and Re-training Women for Professional Posts', CCO 500/9/21, CPA, p.3.

20   Ellen Jordan, '"Making Good Wives and Mothers": The Transformation of Middle-Class Girls' Education in Nineteenth-Century Britain', *History of Education Quarterly*, 31/4 (1991), pp.439–62.

21   Women's Policy Group, 'Report', CPA, p.8.

22   Stephen Brooke and Amy Black, 'The Labour Party, Women and the Problem of Gender 1951–1966', *Journal of British Studies*, 36/4 (1997), pp.419–52.

23   Study Group on Discrimination against Women, 'Discussion Notes on Planning for Women at Work', Box 48, Labour History Archive (LHA), People's History

Museum, Manchester, p.1. This association is also noted by Michael Neary, *Youth, Training and the Training State in the Twentieth Century* (Basingstoke: Macmillan, 1997).

24 Study Group on Discrimination against Women, 'Discrimination against Women', Box 48, LHA, p.6.

25 Study Group on Discrimination against Women, 'Discrimination', LHA, p.9.

26 Mandler, 'Universities', pp.1–2.

27 Halsey and Webb, 'Further and Higher Education', p.227.

28 Although they are often classed as part of 'the extended public sector', Richard Parry, *United Kingdom Public Employment: Patterns of Change 1951–1976* (Glasgow: Centre for the Study of Public Policy, University of Strathclyde, 1980), p.6.

29 Pat Thane, 'Labour and Welfare', in Duncan Tanner, Pat Thane and Nick Tiratsoo (eds), *Labour's First Century* (Cambridge: Cambridge University Press, 2000), p.107.

30 Mandler, 'Universities', p.7.

31 Mandler, 'Universities', p.7.

32 Committee of Directors of Polytechnics, *The Polytechnics: Visions into Reality* (London: Committee of Directors of Polytechnics, 1979), p.3.

33 Daniel Weinbren, *The Open University: A History* (Manchester: Manchester University Press, 2015), p.75.

34 Jennie Lee quoted in Weinbren, *The Open University*, p.238.

35 Interview with Eileen, December 2014.

36 Weinbren, *The Open University*, pp.245–6.

37 Interview with Rita.

38 Interview with Rita.

39 Interview with Joy, April 2015.

40 'Education: A Framework for Collapse', *Spare Rib*, 124 (1982), pp.22–3.

41 H1745, Spring 2004 Directive, Mass Observation Archive, University of Sussex (MOA).

42 Interview with Maureen, April 2015.

43 Interview with Lois, September 2014.

44 Interview with Lois.

45 See, for example, interview with Maureen and K798, Spring 2004 Directive, MOA.

46 Thane, 'Labour and Welfare', p.110.

47 Parry, *United Kingdom Public Employment*, p.8.

48 Parry, *United Kingdom Public Employment*, p.34.

49 Parry, *United Kingdom Public Employment*, p.18. The number of female full-timers grew as well, just at a lower rate: from 400,000 to 800,000.

50 Veronica Beechey and Tessa Perkins, *A Matter of Hours: Women, Part-time Work and the Labour Market* (Cambridge: Polity, 1987), p.9.

51 Interview with Lesley, July 2016.

52 1971 Census – Great Britain Qualified Manpower Tables, 'Table 8', OP, p.44 and p.48.

53 1981 Census – Great Britain Qualified Manpower Tables, 'Table 6', OP, p.46 and p.52.

54 1971 Census – Great Britain Qualified Manpower Tables, 'Table 8', OP, p.50; 1981 Census – Great Britain Qualified Manpower Tables, 'Table 6', OP, p.55.

55 Interview with Anita, February 2015.

56 Jennifer Dale and Peggy Foster, *Feminists and State Welfare* (London: Routledge and Kegan Paul, 1986), p.67.

57 Dyhouse, *Students*, p.108.

58 Sarah Aiston, 'A Good Job for a Girl? The Career Biographies of Women Graduates of the University of Liverpool Post-1945', *Twentieth Century British History*, 15/4 (2004), pp.361–87; Heron, 'Manpower Services Commission', p.30.

59 Liz Heron, 'Manpower Services Commission', *Spare Rib*, 81 (1979), pp.30–1.

60 Interview with Angie, May 2015.

61 Department of Adult Education, *Women, Class and Education* (Southampton: University of Southampton, 1981), p.2.

62 Department of Adult Education, *Women*, p.4.

63 Interview 128, H. Newby, and P. Thompson, *Families, Social Mobility and Ageing, an Intergenerational Approach, 1900–1988*. UK Data Service. SN: 4938 (2005), http://doi.org/10.5255/UKDA-SN-4938-1.

64 Interview with Rita, October 2015.

65 Interview with Sylvia, April 2015.

66 Erzsbet Bukodi, *Education, First Occupation and Later Occupational Attainment: Cross-Cohort Changes among Men and Women in Britain* (London: Centre for Longitudinal Studies at the Institute of Education, 2009), pp.11, 18.

67 Pat Thane, 'Women and the 1970s: Towards Liberation?' in Lawrence Black, Hugh Pemberton and Pat Thane (eds), *Reassessing 1970s Britain* (Manchester: Manchester University Press, 2013), p.178.

68 Janet Parr, *Identity and Education: The Links for Mature Women Students* (London: Routledge, 2000), p.vii.

69 Parr, *Identity and Education*, p.vii.

70 Interviews with India, March 2016; Jean, April 2015; Marion, August 2019; and Sylvia.

71 Interview with Chrissie, October 2015.

72 Interview with Chrissie.

73 Interview with Joy.

74 Parr, *Identity and Education*, pp.ix–x.

75 Interview with Rita.

76 Interview with Cynthia, September 2014.

77 Interview with Cynthia. In 1980 the Women and Employment Survey found that young childless women were less interested in working than mothers who had returned to the workplace: '[T]he pull of anticipated domesticity and motherhood

reduces young women's interest in working while the experience of being at home makes some women more interested in working,' Jean Martin and Ceridwen Roberts, *Women and Employment: A Lifetime Perspective* (London: HMSO, 1980), p.188.

78   Interview with Maureen.

79   See Helen Glew, *Gender, Rhetoric and Regulation: Women's Work in the Civil Service and the London County Council, 1900–1955* (Manchester: Manchester University Press, 2016).

80   Laura Tisdall, 'Education, Parenting and Concepts of Childhood in England, c.1945–1979', *Contemporary British History*, 31/1 (2017), p.39.

81   Interview 128, *Families, Social Mobility and Ageing*; see Laura Paterson for discussion of women feeling bored in the home in the post-war decades, '"I Didn't Feel Like My Own Person": Paid Work in Women's Narratives of Self and Working Motherhood', *Contemporary British History*, 33/3 (2019), pp.405–26.

82   Interview with Chrissie.

83   Interview with Angie.

84   Interview with Maureen.

85   Interview with Maureen.

86   Angela Davis and Laura King, 'Gendered Perspectives on Men's Changing Familial Roles in Postwar England, c.1950–1990', *Gender History*, 30/1 (2018), p.75; Sarah Stoller, 'Forging a Politics of Care: Theorizing Household Work in the Women's Liberation Movement', *History Workshop Journal*, 85 (2018), p.97.

87   Interview with Jean.

88   Jane Lewis and Patrick Wallis, 'Fault, Breakdown, and the Church of England's Involvement in the 1969 Divorce Reform', *Twentieth Century British History*, 11/3 (2000), pp. 308–32.

89   Interview with Eileen, December 2014.

90   Interview with Eileen.

91   Interview with Angie.

92   Interview with Brenda, November 2014.

93   Interview with Lois.

94   Dale Spender and Elizabeth Sarah (eds), *Learning to Lose: Sexism and Education* (London: Women's Press, 1988), p.19.

95   Interview with Ruth, October 2015.

96   Interview with Bridget, May 2015.

97   Interview with Bridget.

98   H1745, Spring 2004 Directive, MOA.

99   H1745, Spring 2004 Directive, MOA.

100 Mandler, 'Comment', p.105.

101 Interview with Dawn, September 2014.

102 Interview with Nancy, August 2019.

103 Interview with Nancy.

104 Interview with Nancy.

105 Geoff Payne and Pamela Abbott, 'Beyond Male Mobility Models', in Payne and Abbott (eds), *The Social Mobility of Women: Beyond Male Mobility Models* (Basingstoke: Falmer Press, 1990), pp.161–2.

106 Andrew Miles, *Social Mobility in Nineteenth- and Early Twentieth-Century England* (Basingstoke: Macmillan, 1999), pp.88–91.

107 Geoff Payne and Pamela Abbott, 'Beyond Male Mobility Models', p.162.

108 Rosemary Crompton and Kay Sanderson, 'Credentials and Careers: Some Implications of the Increase in Professional Qualifications amongst Women', *Sociology*, 20/1 (1988), p.30. Simon Gunn has recently argued that geographical movement, especially within a region, became particularly important for the professional middle class in the late twentieth century, 'Spatial Mobility in Later Twentieth-Century Britain', *Contemporary British History* (Advanced Access, 2021), DOI:10/1080/13619462.2020.1858060.

109 Interview with Jacqui, August 2019.

110 Interview with Maureen.

111 Christina de Bellaigue, Eve Worth, Charlotte Bennett, Karin Eli and Stanley Ulijaszek, 'Women, Mobility and Education in England and Wales: A New Analytical Approach' (forthcoming *Twentieth Century British History*).

112 Pamela Abbott and Roger Sapsford, 'Class Identification of Married Working Women: A Critical Replication of Ritter and Hargens', *The British Journal of Sociology*, 37/4 (1986), p.537.

113 Abbott and Sapsford, 'Class Identification', p.545.

114 Interview with Theresa, April 2015.

115 Interview with Jean.

116 Interview with Ruth.

117 H2639, Spring 2016 Directive, MOA.

118 H2639, Spring 2016 Directive, MOA.

119 H2639, Spring 2016 Directive, MOA.

120 Interview with Chrissie.

121 Interview with Maureen.

122 Steph Lawler, '"Getting Out and Getting Away": Women's Narratives of Class Mobility', *Feminist Review*, 63/1 (1999), pp.3–24.

123 Interviews with Chrissie and Maureen.

124 Interview with Kathy, April 2015.

125 Interview with Kathy.

126 Interview with Angie.

127 Interview with Angie.

128 Interview with Carol.

129 Interview with Rita.

130 Interview with Rita.

131 Interview with Barbara.

132 Interview with Cynthia.

133 Mandler, 'Comment', p.104.

Chapter 5

1   Veronica Beechey and Tessa Perkins, *A Matter of Hours: Women, Part-time Work and the Labour Market* (Cambridge: Polity, 1987), p.76.

2   Lawrence Black and Hugh Pemberton, 'Introduction: The Benighted Decade? Reassessing the 1970s', in Lawrence Black, Hugh Pemberton and Pat Thane (eds), *Reassessing the 1970s* (Manchester: Manchester University Press, 2013), p.4.

3   Ray Pahl, *Divisions of Labour* (Oxford: Basil Blackwell, 1984), p.82.

4   Duncan Gallie, 'The Labour Force', in A. H. Halsey and Josephine Webb (eds), *Twentieth-Century British Social Trends* (Basingstoke: Macmillan, 2000), p.310.

5   See for example Sue Bruley and Laurel Forster, 'Introduction: Historicising the Women's Liberation Movement', *Women's History Review*, 25/5 (2016), pp.697–700; Phillida Bunkle, 'The 1944 Education Act and Second Wave Feminism', *Women's History Review*, 25/5 (2016), pp.791–811; George Stevenson, 'The Women's Movement and "Class Struggle": Gender, Class Formation and Political Identity in Women's Strikes, 1968–1978', *Women's History Review*, 25/5 (2016), pp.741–55; Lynne Segal, 'Jam Today: Feminist Impacts and Transformations in the 1970s' and Pat Thane, 'Women and the 1970s: Towards Liberation?', in Lawrence Black, Hugh Pemberton and Pat Thane (eds), *Reassessing the 1970s* (Manchester: Manchester University Press, 2013), pp.149–86. Much of the information we have about the British WLM comes from personal testimonies of women who were directly, and often centrally, involved with feminist activism. These accounts are invaluable resources, but their scope on the wider impact of the movement is limited.

6   Pat Thane, 'What Difference Did the Vote Make? Women in Public and Private Life in Britain since 1918', *Historical Research*, 76/192 (2003), pp.279–80.

7   Emily Robinson, Camilla Schofield, Florence Sutcliffe-Braithwaite and Natalie Thomlinson, 'Telling Stories about Post-War Britain: Popular Individualism and the "Crisis" of the 1970s', *Twentieth Century British History*, 28/2 (2017), p.292; see also Jack Saunders, 'Emotions, Social Practices and the Changing Composition of Class, Race and Gender in the National Health Service, 1970–79: "Lively Discussion Ensued"', *History Workshop Journal*, 88 (2019), pp.204–28.

8   Linda Gordon, 'The New Feminist Scholarship on the Welfare State', in Linda Gordon (ed.), *Women, the State and Welfare* (Madison: University of Wisconsin Press, 1990), p.10.

9　Sheila Blackburn, 'How Useful Are Feminist Theories of the Welfare State?', *Women's History Review*, 4/3 (1995), p.370.

10　Blackburn, 'How Useful Are Feminist Theories?', p.370.

11　Helen McCarthy, 'Social Science and Married Women's Employment in Post-War Britain', *Past and Present*, 23 (2016), pp.269–305.

12　McCarthy, 'Social Science', pp.271–2.

13　Bunkle, '1944 Education Act', p.798.

14　Elizabeth Wilson, *Women and the Welfare State* (London: Tavistock Publication, 1977), p.9.

15　Hilary Land, 'Who Cares for the Family?', *Journal of Social Policy*, 7/3 (1978), p.258.

16　Wilson, *Women and the Welfare State*, p.14.

17　Wilson, *Women and the Welfare State*, p.141.

18　Land, 'Who Cares for the Family?', p.278.

19　Blackburn, 'How Useful are Feminist Theories?', pp.369–94.

20　William Beveridge, *Social Insurance and Allied Services* (London: HMSO, 1942), p.49.

21　Beveridge, *Social Insurance*, p.49.

22　Jose Harris, *William Beveridge: A Biography* (Oxford: Oxford University Press, 1997), pp.394–5.

23　Hilary Land, 'An Analysis of the Meaning of Women's Work as Manifested in the British Income Maintenance Schemes', *International Sociology*, 1/3 (1986), p.245.

24　Land, 'An Analysis of the Meaning of Women's Work', p.253.

25　Land, 'An Analysis of the Meaning of Women's Work', p.254.

26　Mary McIntosh, 'The State and the Oppression of Women', in Annette Kuhn and AnnMarie Wolpe (eds), *Feminism and Materialism: Women and Modes of Production* (London: Routledge & Kegan Paul, 1978), pp.277–8.

27　Jennifer Dale and Peggy Foster, *Feminists and State Welfare* (London: Routledge & Kegan Paul, 1986), p.125.

28　Wilson, *Women and the Welfare State*, p.180.

29　Mary McIntosh, 'Feminism and Social Policy', *Critical Social Policy*, 1 (1980), p.38.

30　Carole Pateman, 'The Patriarchal Welfare State', in Amy Gutmann (ed.), *Democracy and the Welfare State* (Princeton: Princeton University Press, 1988), p.257.

31　Pateman, 'The Patriarchal Welfare State', p.256.

32　See, for example, Blackburn, 'How Useful Are Feminist Theories?'.

33　McIntosh, 'Feminism and Social Policy', p.34.

34　McIntosh, 'Feminism and Social Policy', p.34.

35　Pateman, 'The Patriarchal Welfare State', p.256.

36　Pateman, 'The Patriarchal Welfare State', p.246.

37　C. Cockburn, J. Holloway, D. Mackenzie, J. McDonald, N. McInnes, J. Mitchell, N. Murray and K. Polanshek, *In and against the State: Discussion Notes for Socialists* (London: London Edinburgh Weekend Return Group, 1979).

38   Cockburn, Holloway, MacKenzie, McDonald, McInnes, Mitchell, Murray and
     Polanshek, *In and Against the State*, p.6.
39   Cockburn, Holloway, MacKenzie, McDonald, McInnes, Mitchell, Murray and
     Polanshek, *In and Against the State*, p.i.
40   Cockburn, Holloway, MacKenzie, McDonald, McInnes, Mitchell, Murray and
     Polanshek, *In and Against the State*, p.3.
41   Cockburn, Holloway, MacKenzie, McDonald, McInnes, Mitchell, Murray and
     Polanshek, *In and Against the State*, p.3.
42   Cockburn, Holloway, MacKenzie, McDonald, McInnes, Mitchell, Murray and
     Polanshek, *In and Against the State*, p.9. Working for the state had a measurable
     influence on women's political affiliation during the post-war decades: unlike
     their male equivalents, there was a clear movement of female public sector
     workers away from the Conservative Party. This resulted from the welfare nature
     of their state roles, which placed them at the frontline of service delivery. Mike
     Savage, James Barlow, Peter Dickens and Tony Fielding, *Property, Bureaucracy
     and Culture: Middle-Class Formation in Contemporary Britain* (London:
     Routledge, 1992), p.218.
43   Interview with Jacqui, July 2019.
44   Interview with Sylvia, April 2015.
45   Interview with Chrissie, October 2015; Gill (b.1950) did choose to become
     involved in 'feminist politics' but was made to feel that what she thought did 'not
     count' by the 'middle-class women playing at being the proletariat', interview with
     Gill, April 2015.
46   Interview with Chrissie.
47   Interview with Rose, July 2019.
48   Helen McCarthy, *Double Lives: A History of Working Motherhood* (London:
     Bloomsbury, 2020), p.324.
49   Interview with Jean, April 2015.
50   Interview with Jean.
51   Interview with Susannah, January 2015.
52   Interview with Susannah.
53   Margaret Cook, *Slight and Delicate Creature: The Memoirs of Margaret Cook*
     (London: Orion, 1999), p.137.
54   Cook, *Slight and Delicate*, p.137.
55   Interview with Susannah.
56   Interview with Diane, April 2015.
57   Interview with Diane.
58   Interview with Diane.
59   Interview with Clara, September 2019.
60   Interview with Clara.
61   Interview with Elizabeth, January 2015.

62 Interview with Elizabeth.

63 Interview with Susannah.

64 Interview with Susannah.

65 Interview with Diane.

66 Interview with Diane.

67 Sheila Lewenhak, *Women and Trade Unions: An Outline History of Women in the British Trade Union Movement* (London: Benn, 1977), p.291.

68 Interview with Anita, February 2015.

69 Lewenhak, *Women and Trade Unions,* p.288.

70 Interview with Anita.

71 Interview with Anita.

72 Sarah Boston, *Women Workers and the Trade Unions* (London: Lawrence & Wishart Ltd., 2015), p.308.

73 Interview with Angie, May 2015.

74 Interview with Angie.

75 Interview with Angie.

76 Interview with Theresa, April 2015.

77 Richard Parry, *United Kingdom Public Employment: Patterns of Change, 1951–1976* (Glasgow: Centre for the Study of Public Policy, University of Strathclyde, 1980), p.35.

78 Parry, *United Kingdom Public Employment*, p.ii.

79 See for example interviews with Joy, April 2015 and Jean.

80 Interview with Jean.

81 Interview with Barbara, December 2014.

82 Brian Harrison, *Finding a Role? The United Kingdom, 1970–1990* (Oxford: Oxford University Press, 2011), p.458.

83 Cook, *Slight and Delicate,* p.125.

84 Boston, *Women Workers,* p.300.

85 Women working multiple jobs to make up full-time hours was quite common among women of this generation in the later twentieth century. Marion had three part-time jobs during this period: 'It was just stupid. I had teenage children, I was trying to be super mum, super wife', interview with Marion, August 2019.

86 Interview with Rita, October 2015.

87 Interview with Rita.

88 Interview with Lesley, July 2015.

89 Interview with Cynthia, September 2014.

90 Interview with Cynthia.

91 Mary Ingham, *Now We Are Thirty: Women of the Breakthrough Generation* (London: Eyre Methuen, 1981), p.147.

92 Interview with Dawn, September 2014.

93 Interview with Dawn.

94 Daniel Walkowitz, 'Women With(out) Class: Social Workers in the Twentieth-Century United States', *Women's History Review*, 14/2 (2005), pp.323–44.

95 Interview with Chrissie. Notably, Carolyn Steedman – progenitor of the phrase 'daughters of the state' – described feeling 'alienated' from the contemporary labour and liberation movements but did choose to use her position as a university lecturer to make a political intervention in society with her academic and autobiographical text, *Landscape for a Good Woman*.

96 Interview with Chrissie.

97 Interview with Chrissie; Alison Oram and Hilda Kean have argued that, during the early twentieth century, female teachers' politicization and sense of having a voice within the public sphere were intrinsically linked to the fact that they were employed by the state, '"Men Must Be Educated and Women Must Do It": The National Federation (Later Union) of Women Teachers and Contemporary Feminism 1910–1930', *Gender and Education*, 2/2 (1990), p.150.

98 Interview with Frances, February 2015.

99 Interview with Frances.

100 Celia Hughes, 'Left Activism, Succour and Selfhood: The Epistolary Friendship of Two Revolutionary Mothers in 1970s Britain', *Women's History Review*, 23/6 (2014), p.881.

101 Interview with Sylvia.

102 Interview with Carol.

103 Interview with Nancy, August 2019.

104 Judith Hubback, *Wives Who Went to College* (London: Heinemann, 1957), p.6.

105 Stephanie Spencer, *Gender, Work and Education in Britain in the 1950s* (Basingstoke: Palgrave Macmillan, 2005), p.194

106 Spencer, *Gender, Work and Education*, p.194.

107 Edmund Neill, 'Conceptions of Citizenship in Twentieth Century Britain', *Twentieth Century British History*, 17/3 (2006), p.425.

108 Joseph Maslen, 'Autobiographies of a Generation? Carolyn Steedman, Luisa Passerini and the Memory of 1968', *Memory Studies*, 6/1 (2013), p.31.

109 Hilary Land, 'Whatever Happened to the Social Wage?', in Caroline Glendinning and Jane Millar (eds), *Women and Poverty in Britain: The 1990s* (London: Harvester Wheatsheaf, 1992), p.47.

110 Interview with Brenda, November 2014.

111 Interview with Brenda.

112 Interview with Anita.

113 Interview with Anita.

114 Interview with Ruth, October 2015.

115 Interview with Ruth.

116 Selina Todd, 'Family, Welfare and Social Work in Post-War England, c.1948–1970', *English Historical Review*, 129 (2014), pp.362–87.

117 Interview with Carol, November 2014.

118 Interview with Carol.

119 Interview with Anita.

120 Interview with Nancy.

121 Interview with Sylvia, April 2015.

122 Interview with Sylvia.

123 Interview with Sylvia.

124 Interview with Sylvia.

125 Interview with Sylvia.

126 Interview with Rita.

127 Interview with Rita.

128 Interview with Rita.

129 Interviews with Maureen, April 2015 and Lesley, July 2015.

130 Madeleine Arnot, Miriam David and Gaby Weiner, *Closing the Gender Gap: Postwar Education and Social Change* (Cambridge: Polity, 1999), p.66–7.

131 Arnot, David and Weiner, *Closing the Gender Gap*, p.73.

132 Dale Spender and Elizabeth Sarah (eds), *Learning to Lose: Sexism and Education* (London: Women's Press, 1980).

133 Pippa Brewster, 'School Days, School Days' and Irene Payne, 'A Working-Class Girl in a Grammar School', in Dale Spender and Elizabeth Sarah (eds), *Learning to Lose: Sexism and Education* (London: Women's Press, 1980), pp.5–19.

134 Arnot, David and Weiner, *Closing the Gender Gap*, pp.72–3.

135 Jane Martin, 'Gender, Education and Social Change: A Study of Feminist Politics and Practices in London, 1870–1990', *Gender and Education*, 25/1 (2013), p.70.

Chapter 6

1   Howard Glennerster, *British Social Policy since 1945* (Oxford: Blackwell, 2000), p.176.

2   Department of Health, *Working for Patients*, Cm555 (London: HMSO, 1989), p.100.

3   Glennerster, *British Social Policy*, p.191.

4   Further key acts include: Local Government Act 1988, Social Security Act 1989, Education Act 1992, Education Act 1993.

5   Wendy Brown, *Undoing the Demos: Neoliberalism's Stealth Revolution* (New York: Zone Books, 2015), pp.30–1.

6   Department of Health, *Working for Patients*, p.19.

7   Ben Rogaly and Becky Taylor, *Moving Histories of Class and Community: Identity, Place and Belonging in Contemporary England* (Basingstoke: Palgrave Macmillan, 2009).

8   Jonathan Cribb, Richard Disney and Luke Sibieta, *The Public Sector Workforce: Past, Present and Future* (London: Institute for Fiscal Studies, 2015), p.17.

9   Rodney Lowe, *The Welfare State in Britain since 1945* Basingstoke: Macmillan, 2005), p.331.

10 Mike Savage, James Barlow, Peter Dickens and Tony Fielding, *Property, Bureaucracy and Culture: Middle-Class Formation in Contemporary Britain* (London: Routledge, 1992), p.75.

11 Brown, *Undoing the Demos*, p.105.

12 Brown, *Undoing the Demos*, p.105.

13 E. H. H. Green, *Ideologies of Conservatism: Conservative Political Ideas in the Twentieth Century* (Oxford: Oxford University Press, 2002), p.277.

14 Ben Jackson, 'Free Markets and Feminism: The Neo-Liberal Defence of the Male Breadwinner Model in Britain c.1980–1997', *Women's History Review* (2019), pp.297–9.

15 Lynn Abrams, 'Liberating the Female Self: Epiphanies, Conflict and Coherence in the Life Stories of Post-War British Women', *Social History*, 39/1 (2014), p.18.

16 Abrams, 'Liberating the Female Self', p.35.

17 Linda McDowell, *Working Lives: Gender, Migration and Employment in Britain, 1945–2007* (Chichester: John Wiley & Sons Inc., 2013), p.158.

18 Ben Jackson and Robert Saunders, 'Varieties of Thatcherism', in Ben Jackson and Robert Saunders (eds), *Making Thatcher's Britain* (Cambridge: Cambridge University Press, 2012), p.15.

19 Interview with Eileen, December 2014.

20 Jackson and Saunders, 'Varieties', p.15.

21 Lowe, *Welfare State*, p.324.

22 Stephen Lee, *Aspects of British Political History, 1914–1995* (London: Routledge, 1996), pp.234–5.

23 Florence Sutcliffe-Braithwaite, 'Neo-Liberalism and Morality in the Making of Thatcherite Social Policy', *The Historical Journal*, 55/2 (2012), p.516.

24 Lee, *Aspects of British Political History*, p.343.

25 Interview with Eileen.

26 Interview with Bridget, April 2015.

27 Interview with Bridget.

28 Interview with Bridget.

29 Hilary Land, 'Whatever Happened to the Social Wage?', in Caroline Glendinning and Jane Millar (eds), *Women and Poverty in Britain: The 1990s* (London: Harvester Wheatsheaf, 1992), p.47.

30 Ray Pahl, *Divisions of Labour* (Oxford: Basil Blackwell, 1984), p.303.

31 Linda, quoted in Pahl, *Divisions of Labour*, pp.303–4.

32 Interview with Jean, April 2015.

33 Interview with Jean.

34 Interview with Jean.

35 Interview with Maureen, April 2015.

36 Interview with Theresa, April 2015.

37 Interview with Chrissie, October 2015.

38 Interview with Chrissie.

39 Interview with Lois, September 2014; Daisy Payling, '"Socialist Republic of South Yorkshire": Grassroots Activism and Left-Wing Solidarity in 1980s Sheffield', *Twentieth Century British History*, 25/4 (2014), pp.602–27.

40 Interview with Lois.

41 In 1979, 48 per cent of women and 45 per cent of men voted Tory. In 1983, this figure was 45 per cent for each sex and by 1987 the percentage of women had dropped below men to 44 per cent, Pippa Norris and Joni Lovenduski (eds), *Gender and Party Politics* (London: Sage 1993), p.39.

42 Lee, *Aspects of British Political History*, pp.344–5.

43 Harold Perkin, *The Rise of Professional Society: England since 1880* (London: Routledge, 2002), pp.2–3.

44 Perkin, *Rise of Professional Society*, pp.359–63.

45 Eric Evans, *Thatcher and Thatcherism* (London: Routledge, 2004), p.67.

46 Lowe, *Welfare State*, pp.330–1.

47 Interview with Elizabeth, January 2015.

48 Interview with Sandra, April 2015.

49 Interview with Maureen.

50 Interview with Sandra.

51 Interview with Nancy, August 2019.

52 Interview with Nancy.

53 Interview with Elizabeth.

54 Interview with Jean.

55 See, for example, Giles Radice, *Equality and Quality: A Socialist Plan for Education* (London: Fabian Society, 1986).

56 Lowe, *Welfare State*, p.336.

57 W1813, Spring 2004 Directive, Mass Observation Archive, University of Sussex (MOA).

58 Department of Education and Science, *Better Schools*, Cmnd 9469, (London: HMSO, 1985), p.15.

59 W1813, Spring 2004 Directive, MOA.

60 Matthew Hilton, 'Politics Is Ordinary: Non-governmental Organizations and Political Participation in Contemporary Britain', *Twentieth Century British History*, 22/2 (2011), pp.252–3.

61 Paul Wilding, 'The Welfare State and the Conservatives', *Political Studies*, XLV (1997), p.718.

62 Hilton, 'Politics Is Ordinary', pp.252–3; Mike Savage, 'Affluence and Social Change in the Making of Technocratic Middle-Class Identities: Britain 1939–1955', *Contemporary British History*, 22/4 (2008), pp.457–76.

63 Adrian Barton, 'New Labour's Management, Audit and "What Works" Approach to Controlling the "Untrustworthy" Professions', *Public Policy and Administration*, 23/3 (2008), p.265.

64 Frank Mort, 'Social and Symbolic Fathers and Sons in Postwar Britain', *Journal of British Studies*, 38/3 (1999), pp.353–84.

65 Mort, 'Social and Symbolic', pp.365–6.

66 Michael Roper, *Masculinity and the British Organization Man since 1945* (Oxford: Oxford University Press, 1994), p.1.

67 Roper, *Masculinity*, p.77. Claire Langhamer has explored the false dichotomy between the rational and the emotional in the workplace in 'Feelings, Women and Work in the Long 1950s', *Women's History Review*, 26/1 (2017), pp.77–92.

68 Roper, *Masculinity*, p.223.

69 Department of Health, *Working for Patients*, p.20.

70 Department of Education and Science, *Better Schools*, p.44.

71 Department of Education and Science, *Better Schools*, p.7.

72 Margaret Cook, *A Slight and Delicate Creature: The Memoirs of Margaret Cook* (London: Orion, 1999), p.188. The Griffiths Report of 1983 outlined plans for an increased percentage of staff to be managers, Justin Waring, 'Looking Back (and Forwards) at General Management: 30 Years on from the Griffiths Report', *Journal of Health Service Research and Policy*, 18/4 (2013), pp.249–50.

73 Lowe, *Welfare State*, p.333.

74 Department of Health, *Working for Patients*, p.61.

75 Savage, Barlow, Dickens and Fielding, *Property*, pp.74–5.

76 Interview with Lois.

77 Cook, *Slight and Delicate*, p.188.

78 Interview with Barbara, December 2014.

79 Interviews with Ann, February 2015, Dawn, September 2014.

80 Stephen Brooke, '"Living in New Times": Historicizing 1980s Britain', *History Compass*, 12/1 (2014), p.23.

81 Interview with Barbara.

82 Interview with Marion, August 2019.

83 Interview with Marion.

84 Cook, *Slight and Delicate*, p.188.

85 Interview with Carol, November 2014.

86 Interview with Carol.

87 Cook, *Slight and Delicate*, p.189.

88 Lynne McTaggart, 'Doctors in Distress', *The Sunday Times Magazine* (22 January 1989), pp.17–23.

89 McTaggart, 'Doctors in Distress', p.19.

90 McTaggart, 'Doctors in Distress', p.17.

91   Madeleine Arnot, Miriam David and Gaby Weiner, *Closing the Gender Gap: Postwar Education and Social Change* (Cambridge: Polity, 1999), p.99.

92   Mary Langan, 'Who Cares? Women in the Mixed Economy of Care', in Mary Langan and Lesley Day (eds), *Women, Oppression and Social Work* (London: Routledge, 1992), p.77.

93   Savage, Barlow, Dickens and Fielding, *Property*, p.218.

94   Department of Health, *Working for Patients*, pp.15–19.

95   Savage, Barlow, Dickens and Fielding, *Property*, p.197.

96   Interview with Jean.

97   Interview with Nancy.

98   Interview with Nancy.

99   Ruth Eley, 'Women in Management in Social Services Departments', in Christine Hallet (ed.), *Women and Social Service Departments* (Hemel Hempstead: Harvester Wheatsheaf, 1989).

100 Interview with Rita, October 2015.

101 Interview with Sylvia, April 2015.

102 Land, 'Whatever Happened to the Social Wage?', p.52.

103 Land, 'Whatever Happened to the Social Wage?', p.46.

104 Interview with Jacqui, July 2019.

105 Interview with Jacqui.

106 Interview with Jean.

107 Interview with Rita.

108 Interview with Ruth, October 2015.

109 Langan, 'Who Cares', p.75.

110 Langan, 'Who Cares', p.75.

111 Interviews with Maureen and Cynthia.

112 Lowe, *Welfare State*, p.336.

113 Interview with Cynthia.

114 Interview with Cynthia.

115 Interview with Ann.

116 Interview with Maureen.

117 J. Douglas, J. Ross and H. Simpson, *All Our Future: A Longitudinal Study of Secondary Education* (London: P. Davies, 1968); Department of Education and Science, *Better Schools*.

118 B2969, Spring 2018 Directive, MOA.

119 Ursula Huws, *Your Job in the 80s: A Woman's Guide to New Technology* (London: Pluto Press, 1982).

120 Huws, *Your Job in the 80s*, pp.68–9.

121 Huws, *Your Job in the 80s*, p.69.

122 Interview with Jean.

123 Interview with Jean.

124 Carole Leathwood, 'Treat Me as a Human Being – Don't Look at Me as a Woman: Femininities and Professional Identities in Further Education', *Gender and Education*, 17/4 (2005), p.398.

125 Leathwood, 'Treat Me as a Human Being', p.390.

126 Interview with Kathy, April 2015.

127 Beverley Bryan, Stella Dadzie and Suzanne Scafe, *Heart of the Race: Black Women's Lives in Britain* (London: Verso, 2018), p.270.

128 Interview with Lesley, July 2015.

129 W1813, Spring 2004 Directive, MOA.

130 Interview with Maureen.

131 Interview with Rita.

132 Department of Education and Science, *Better Schools*, p.50.

133 Department of Education and Science, *Better Schools*, p.55.

134 Interview with Maureen.

135 Wilding, 'The Welfare State', p.722.

136 Damian Grimshaw, 'New Labour Policy and the Gender Pay Gap', in Claire Annesley, Francesca Gains and Kirstein Rummery (eds), *Women and New Labour: Engendering Policy and Politics?* (Bristol: Policy Press, 2007), pp.147–8.

137 Martin Powell, 'Introduction', in Martin Powell (ed.), *Modernising the Welfare State: The Blair Legacy* (Bristol: Policy Press, 2008), p.10.

138 Barton, 'New Labour', p.267.

139 Cribb, Disney and Sibieta, *Public Sector Workforce*, p.12.

140 Selina Todd, *The People: The Rise and Fall of the Working Class, 1910–2010* (London: John Murray, 2014), pp.322–6; Jim Tomlinson, 'De-Industrialization Not Decline: A New Meta-Narrative for Post-War British History', *Twentieth Century British History*, 27/1 (2016), pp.76–99.

141 Cynthia Cockburn, *Women, Trade Unions and Political Parties* (London: Fabian Society, 1987), p.5.

142 Interview with India, March 2016.

143 Interview with India.

144 Interview with India.

145 Interview with Jean.

146 Interview with Ruth.

147 Interview with Penny, September 2019.

148 Interview with Penny.

149 Interview with Penny.

150 Interview with Sandra.

151 Interview with Sandra.

152 Interview with Sandra.

153 Interviews with Ruth and Rita.

154 Steph Lawler, 'Getting Out and Getting Away: Women's Narratives of Class Mobility', *Feminist Review*, 63/1 (1999), p.7.

155 Steph Lawler, *Mothering the Self: Mothers, Daughters, Subjects* (London: Routledge, 2000), p.174.

156 Lawler, 'Getting out and Getting Away', p.15.

157 Lawler, 'Getting out and Getting Away', p.16.

158 Lawler, 'Getting out and Getting Away', p.16.

159 Penny Summerfield, 'Culture and Composure: Creating Narratives of the Gendered Self in Oral History Interviews', *Cultural and Social History*, 1/1 (2004), pp.65–93.

160 Interview with Susannah, January 2015.

161 Interview with Susannah.

162 Interview with Diane, April 2015.

163 Interview with Diane.

164 Interview with Linda, April 2015.

165 Interview with Linda.

166 Interview with Linda.

167 McDowell, *Working Lives*, p.161.

168 Interview with Maureen.

169 Interview with Anita, February 2015.

170 Valerie Walkerdine, 'Reclassifying Upward Mobility: Femininity and the Neo-Liberal Subject', *Gender and Education*, 15/3 (2003), pp.241–2.

171 Liz Heron (ed.), *Truth, Dare or Promise: Girls Growing up in the Fifties* (London: Virago, 1985); Carolyn Steedman, *Landscape for a Good Woman* (London: Virago, 1986).

172 Liz Heron, http://www.lizheron.co.uk/?doing_wp_cron=1561639872.55176901817 32177734375.

173 Liz Heron, 'Introduction' in Liz Heron (ed.), *Truth, Dare or Promise: Girls Growing Up in the Fifties* (London: Virago, 1985), p.2.

174 Heron, 'Introduction', p.5.

175 Carolyn Steedman, 'Writing the Self: The End of the Scholarship Girl', in Jim McGuigan (ed.), *Cultural Methodologies* (London: Sage, 1997), p.107.

176 Steedman, 'Writing the Self', p.107.

177 Valerie Hey, 'Joining the Club? Academia and Working-Class Femininities', *Gender and Education*, 15/3 (2003), p.320.

178 Hey, 'Joining the Club?', p.320.

179 Jon Lawrence and Florence Sutcliffe-Braithwaite, 'Thatcher and the Decline of Class Politics', in Ben Jackson and Robert Saunders (eds), *Making Thatcher's Britain* (Cambridge: Cambridge University Press, 2012), p.146.

180 Valerie Walkerdine, 'Subjectivity and Social Class: New Directions for Feminist Psychology', *Feminism & Psychology*, 6/3 (1996), p.356.

181 Todd, *The People*, p.338.

182 Valerie Hey, 'Northern Accent and Southern Comfort: Subjectivity and Social Class', in Pat Mahony and Christine Zmroczek (eds), *Class Matters: 'Working-Class' Women's Perspectives on Social Class* (London: Taylor & Francis, 1997), p.140.

183 Pat Mahony and Christine Zmroczek, 'Why Class Matters', in Pat Mahony and Christine Zmroczek (eds), *Class Matters: 'Working-Class' Women's Perspectives on Social Class* (London: Taylor & Francis, 1997), p.5.

184 Mahony and Zmroczek, 'Why Class Matters', p.5.

185 Mahony and Zmroczek, 'Why Class Matters', p.5.

186 Walkerdine, 'Subjectivity and Social Class', p.356.

187 Linda McDowell, 'Border Crossings: Reflections on Women's Lives in Twentieth Century Britain', *Gender, Place and Culture*, 21/2 (2014), p.160.

Chapter 7

1   Jennie Bristow, 'The Making of "Boomergeddon": The Construction of the Baby Boomer Generation as a Social Problem in Britain', *The British Journal of Sociology*, 67/4 (2016), p.576; Pat Thane, *Divided Kingdom: A History of Britain 1900 to Present* (Cambridge: Cambridge University Press, 2018).

2   Paul Thompson, 'I Don't Feel Old: Subjective Ageing and the Search for Meaning in Later Life', *Ageing and Society*, 12/1 (1992), p.24.

3   For discussion of this, see Charlotte Greenhalgh, *Aging in Twentieth-Century Britain* (Oakland: University of California Press, 2018), pp.12–13.

4   Wendy Webster, *Imagining Home: Gender, 'Race' and National Identity 1945–64* (London: UCL Press, 1998), p.xxii.

5   Pat Thane, *Old Age in English History: Past Experiences and Present Issues* (Oxford: Oxford University Press, 2000); Pat Thane, 'Women and Ageing in the Twentieth Century', *L'Homme*, 17/1 (2006), pp.59–74.

6   Thane, 'Women and Ageing', p.59.

7   Pat Thane, 'Older People and Equality', in Pat Thane (ed.), *Unequal Britain: Equalities in Britain since 1945* (London: Continuum, 2010), p.16.

8   Thane, 'Women and Ageing', p.74.

9   See for example, Selina Todd, *The People: The Rise and Fall of the Working Class, 1910–2010* (London: John Murray, 2014), p.344.

10 Howard Glennerster, *British Social Policy since 1945* (Oxford: Blackwell, 2000), pp.211–12.

11 Claire Annesley, Francesca Gains and Kirstein Rummery, 'New Labour: Towards an Engendered Politics and Policy?', in Claire Annesley, Francesca Gains and Kirstein Rummery (eds), *Women and New Labour: Engendering Policy and Politics?* (Bristol: Policy Press, 2007), pp.234–5.

12 Interview with Bridget, May 2015.

13 Kirstein Rummery, 'Caring Citizenship and New Labour: Dilemmas and Contradictions for Disabled and Older Women', Claire Annesley, Francesca Gains

and Kirstein Rummery (eds), *Women and New Labour: Engendering Policy and Politics?* (Bristol: Policy Press, 2007), p.175.

14 Interview with Rita, October 2015.

15 As early as 1998, the Labour government produced a comprehensive green paper on pension reform as part of their aim to reduce pensioner poverty but did not act on many of the proposals, Department of Social Security, *A New Contract for Welfare: Partnership in Pensions*, Cm 4179 (London: TSO, 1998).

16 Glennerster, *Social Policy*, pp.214–15.

17 Thane, *Old Age in English History*, p.384.

18 Pat Thane, 'The "Scandal" of Women's Pensions in Britain: How Did It Come About?', *History and Policy* (2006), http://www.historyandpolicy.org/policy-papers/papers/the-scandal-of-womens-pensions-in-britain-how-did-it-come-about.

19 Thane, 'The "Scandal" of Women's Pensions in Britain'.

20 Thane, 'The "Scandal" of Women's Pensions in Britain'.

21 Interview with Frances, February 2015.

22 Interview with Frances.

23 Interview with Frances.

24 Interview with Frances.

25 The Pensions Commission, *A New Pension Settlement for the Twenty-First Century: The Second Report of the Pensions Commission* (London: HMSO, 2005), p.40.

26 Kirstein Rummery, 'Equalities: The Impact of Welfare Reform and Austerity by Gender, Disability and Age', in Hugh Bochel and Martin Powell (eds), *The Coalition Government and Social Policy: Restructuring the Welfare State* (Bristol: Policy Press, 2016), pp.316-17.

27 Department of Social Security, *A New Contract for Welfare*, p.29.

28 Interview with Diane, April 2015.

29 The Pensions Commission, *A New Pension Settlement for the Twenty-First Century*, p.60.

30 The Pensions Commission, *A New Pension Settlement for the Twenty-First Century*, p.276.

31 S2207, Spring 2016 Directive, Mass Observation Archive, University of Sussex (MOA).

32 Interview with Cynthia, September 2014.

33 Interview with Bridget.

34 Peter Laslett, *A Fresh Map of Life: The Emergence of the Third Age* (London: Weidenfeld & Nicolson, 1989).

35 Laslett, *A Fresh Map of Life*, p.141.

36 Thane, 'Older People and Equality', p.17.

37 Thane, 'Older People and Equality', p.18.

38 For this reason, the 2007 Pension Act only slowly raised the pension age, Thane, 'Older People and Equality', p.18.

39 Andrew Thorpe, *A History of the British Labour Party* (London: Palgrave, 2015), pp.259–60.

40 Thane, 'Older People and Equality', pp.18–19.

41 Chris Philipson, Rebecca Leach, Annemarie Money and Simon Biggs, 'Social and Cultural Constructions of Ageing: The Case of the Baby Boomers', *Sociological Research Online*, 13/5 (2008), DOI: 10.5153/sro.1695.

42 Interview with Lois, September 2014.

43 Interview with Lois.

44 Interview with Angie, May 2015.

45 Interview with Angie.

46 Interview with Angie.

47 Interview with Angie.

48 Interview with Jean, April 2015.

49 Interview with Jean.

50 Interview with Jean.

51 Interview with Jean.

52 Interview with Maureen, April 2015.

53 Interview with Maureen.

54 Interview with Chrissie, October 2015.

55 Interview with Rita.

56 Interviews with Diane and Susannah, January 2015.

57 Pat Thane, 'The "Big Society" and the "Big State": Creative Tension or Crowding Out?', *Twentieth Century British History* 23/3 (2012), p.411.

58 Thane, 'The "Big Society" and the "Big State"', p.427.

59 John Welshman, *Underclass: A History of the Excluded 1880–2000* (London: Hambledon Continuum, 2006), p.195.

60 The government set itself a target 'to increase voluntary and community sector activity, including increasing community participation, by 5 per cent by 2006', Home Office, *2003 Home Office Citizenship Survey: People, Families and Communities* (London: Author, 2004), p.177.

61 Department for Communities and Local Government, *Community Action in England: A Report on the 2009–10 Citizenship Survey* (London: Home Office, 2011), p.80.

62 See for example Department for Communities and Local Government, *2007–08 Citizenship Survey: Volunteering and Charitable Giving Topic Report* (London: Author, 2009), pp.15–17.

63 Interview with Anita, February 2015.

64 Pete Alcock, 'Voluntary Action, New Labour and the Third Sector', in James McKay and Matthew Hilton (eds), *The Ages of Voluntarism: How We Got to the Big Society* (Oxford: Oxford University Press, 2011), pp.165–6.

65 Hugh Bochel and Martin Powell, 'Introduction', in Hugh Bochel and Martin Powell (eds), *The Coalition Government and Social Policy: Restructuring the Welfare State* (Bristol: Policy Press, 2016), p.11.

66 Interview with Ann, February 2015.

67 Interview with Sandra, April 2015.

68 For detailed definition of the 'Big Society' concept, see Matthew Hilton, Nick Crowson, Jean-Francois Mouhot and James McKay, *Historical Guide to NGOs in Britain: Charities, Civil Society and the Voluntary Sector since 1945* (Basingstoke: Palgrave Macmillan, 2012), pp.283–4.

69 Thane, 'The "Big Society" and the "Big State"', p.429.

70 Interview with Theresa, April 2015.

71 Interview with Theresa.

72 Interview with Theresa.

73 Matthew Hilton, 'Politics Is Ordinary: Non-governmental Organisations and Political Participation in Contemporary Britain', *Twentieth Century British History*, 22/2 (2011), pp.230–68.

74 Interview with India, March 2016.

75 Interview with Anita.

76 F4605, Spring 2016 Directive, MOA.

77 Nigel Meager and Peter Bates, 'Self-Employment in the United Kingdom during the 1980s and 1990s', in Richard Arum and Walter Muller (eds), *The Re-emergence of Self-Employment: A Comparative Study of Self-Employment Dynamics and Social Inequality* (Princeton: Princeton University Press, 2004), pp.134–65.

78 Meager and Bates, 'Self-Employment in the United Kingdom during the 1980s and 1990s', p.137.

79 The figures for older women attending further and higher education are not collected in the Higher Education Statistics or in the Census. We know that the numbers of those attending over sixty were rising in the 2000s, Justin Parkinson, 'Learning in Retirement', http://news.bbc.co.uk/1/hi/education/4054259.stm.

80 Interview with Linda, April 2015.

81 Interview with Sylvia, April 2015.

82 Interviews with Jean and Lois.

83 Interview with Angie.

84 Interview with Nancy, August 2019.

85 Interview with Ruth, October 2015.

86 Interview with Ruth.

87 NatCen Social Research, 'British Social Attitudes 34: Role of Government', http://www.bsa.natcen.ac.uk/latest-report/british-social-attitudes-34/role-of-government.aspx. This report also found that an increasing number of those over the age of sixty-five are happy for welfare spending to be directed away from pension increases to other forms of welfare provision.

88 Interview with Cynthia.

89   Interview with Cynthia.

90   Interview with Angie.

91   Tim Bale, *The Conservative Party: From Thatcher to Cameron* (Cambridge: Polity, 2016), p.395. Focusing exclusively on these metrics obscures the fact that real-term incomes fell for pensioners under the coalition and older people suffered significantly from cuts to welfare services, Rummery, 'Equalities', pp.316–17.

92   Interview with Theresa.

93   See interviews with Kathy, Bridget and Sandra.

94   Interview with Maureen.

95   Interview with Susannah, January 2015.

96   Rummery, 'Equalities', p.311.

97   Interviews with Jean and Sandra.

98   Interview with Elizabeth, January 2015.

99   Ben Jackson and Robert Saunders, 'Varieties of Thatcherism', in Ben Jackson and Robert Saunders (eds), *Making Thatcher's Britain* (Cambridge: Cambridge University Press, 2012), p.15.

100 Interview with Kathy.

101 Interview with Angie.

102 Interview with Angie.

103 For discussion of this term see Imogen Tyler, 'Chav Mum, Chav Scum: Class Disgust in Contemporary Britain', *Feminist Media Studies*, 8/1 (2008), pp.17–34.

104 Interview with Barbara, December 2014.

105 Interview with Joy, April 2015.

106 Interview with Clara, September 2019.

107 Thane, *Old Age in English History*, p.384.

108 Interview with Eileen, December 2014.

109 Welshman, *Underclass*, p.183.

110 Interview with Eileen.

111 F3641, Spring 2018 Directive, MOA, University of Sussex.

112 R1025, Spring 2018 Directive, MOA.

113 Yougove found that of women over 65 who voted, 64 per cent of them voted Conservative in the 2019 General Election, https://yougov.co.uk/topics/politics/articles-reports/2019/12/17/how-britain-voted-2019-general-election.

114 Ben Jones, 'The Uses of Nostalgia: Autobiography, Community Publishing and Working-Class Neighbourhoods in Post-War England', *Cultural and Social History*, 7/3 (2010), p.356.

115 Interview with Carol, November 2014.

116 Bristow, 'The Making of "Boomergeddon"', pp.575–91.

117 Jones, 'The Uses of Nostalgia', p.356.

118 Interview with Rita.

119 Interview with Chrissie.

120 Interviews with Lesley, July 2015, Carol and Sandra.

121 Interview with Theresa.

122 Interview with Lesley.

123 Interview with Lesley.

124 Interview with Angie.

125 Interview with Rita.

126 Interview with Maureen.

127 Interview with Maureen.

128 Interview with Sylvia.

129 Interview with Sylvia.

130 Interview with Frances.

131 Grandparents Plus, https://kinship.org.uk/report/state-of-the-nation-2017-survey-report/.

132 S4743, Spring 2016 Directive, MOA.

133 Interview with Ruth.

134 Interview with Sylvia.

135 Interview with Sylvia.

136 Interview with Jacqui, July 2019. Jon Lawrence has recently found that using evidence from personal testimony can challenge notions of the hegemonic triumph of 'individualism' in contemporary society, *Me? Me? Me? The Search for Community in Post-War England* (Oxford: Oxford University Press, 2019), p.229.

137 Interview with Diane.

138 Mike Savage, James Barlow, Peter Dickens and Tony Fielding, *Property, Bureaucracy and Culture: Middle-Class Formation in Contemporary Britain* (London: Routledge, 1992), p.205.

Chapter 8

1   Interview with Rebecca, May 2019.

Bibliography

Unpublished sources

Author's oral history interviews

All names are pseudonyms

Angie, May 2015
Anita, February 2015
Ann, February 2015
Barbara, December 2014
Beth, January 2015
Brenda, November 2015
Bridget, May 2015
Carol, November 2014
Chrissie, October 2015
Clara, September 2019
Cynthia, September 2014
Dawn, September 2014
Diane, April 2015
Eileen, December 2014
Elizabeth, January 2015
Frances, February 2015
India, March 2016
Jacqui, July 2019
Jean, April 2015
Joy, April 2015
Kathy, April 2015
Lesley, July 2015
Linda, April 2015
Lois, September 2014
Marion, August 2019
Maureen, April 2015
Nancy, August 2019
Penny, September 2019
Rebecca, May 2019
Rita, October 2015
Rose, July 2019

Ruth, October 2015
Sadie, September 2014
Sandra, April 2015
Susannah, January 2015
Sylvia, April 2015
Theresa, April 2015

Conservative Party Archive, Bodleian Libraries, University of Oxford

CCO 60/4/7: Women's Policy Group, 1962–3

CCO 60/4/9: Women's National Advisory Committee Working Party on Employment of Women, 1963–4

CCO 500/9/4: Equal Guardianship of Infants, 1967

CCO 500/9/21: Women's National Advisory Committee Parliamentary Sub-Committee, 1968–9

CCO 500/9/22: Women's National Advisory Committee Working Party on the Rights of Wives, 1968

Labour History Archive, People's History Museum, Manchester

Box 1: National Labour Women's Advisory Committee Minutes, 1951–68
Box 48: Study Group on Discrimination against Women Minutes, 1967–72

Mass Observation Archive, University of Sussex

SxMOA2/1/71/3, Spring 2004 Directive (Going to University)
SxMOA2/1/105/1, Spring 2016 Directive (Social Mobility)
SxMOA2/1/111/1, Spring 2018 (Welfare State and Charity)

Official Papers, Bodleian Libraries, University of Oxford

1951 Census – England and Wales Occupation Tables
1961 Census – England and Wales Occupation Tables
1961 Census – England and Wales Education Tables
1961 Census – Great Britain General Report
1961 Census – Great Britain Summary Tables

1971 Census – Great Britain Qualified Manpower Tables
1981 Census – Great Britain Qualified Manpower Tables
1991 Census – Great Britain Qualified Manpower Tables

Europe's 1968 Project, Oral History Transcripts Held by the Interviewer John Davis

Interview with Hilary Wainwright
Interview with Marjorie Mayo
Interview with Roberta Hunter-Henderson
Interview with Sally Alexander
Interview with Stef Pixner

Families, Social Mobility and Ageing, an Intergenerational approach, Interviews held by the UK Data Service

Newby, H., Thompson, P., *Families, Social Mobility and Ageing, an Intergenerational Approach, 1900–1988*. UK Data Service. SN: 4938 (2005), http://doi.org/10.5255/UKDA-SN-4938-1
Interview numbers:
004 074 117
025 079 128
036 084 136
039 092 141
045 096

Printed Primary Sources

Please note that due to the contemporary nature of this book and its themes, there is not always a clear boundary between what constitutes a printed primary and secondary text. Sources are divided based on how they are primarily used in this book.

Abbott, Pamela, 'Women's Social Class Identification: Does Husband's Occupation Make a Difference?', *Sociology*, 21/1 (1987), pp.91–103
Abbott, Pamela and Sapsford, Roger, 'Class Identification of Married Working Women: A Critical Replication of Ritter and Hargens', *The British Journal of Sociology*, 37/4 (1986), pp.535–49
Bailey, Roy and Brake, Mike (eds), *Radical Social Work* (London: Edward Arnold, 1975)

Bagguley, Paul and Walby, Sylvia, *Gender Restructuring: A Comparative Analysis of Five Local Labour Markets: Working Paper 28* (Lancaster: University of Lancaster, 1988)

Beechey, Veronica and Perkins, Tessa, *A Matter of Hours: Women, Part-Time Work and the Labour Market* (Cambridge: Polity, 1987)

Beveridge, William, *Social Insurance and Allied Services* (London: HMSO, 1942)

Carter, Angela, 'Truly, It Felt Like One Year', in Sara Maitland (ed.), *Very Heaven: Looking Back at the 1960s* (London: Virago, 1988), pp.209–16

Cockburn, Cynthia, *Women, Trade Unions and Political Parties* (London: Fabian Society, 1987)

Cockburn, C., Holloway., J., Mackenzie, D., McDonald, J., McInnes, N., Mitchell, J., Murray, N. and Polanshek, K., *In and against the State: Discussion Notes for Socialists* (London: London Edinburgh Weekend Return Group, 1979)

Cook, Margaret, *A Slight and Delicate Creature: The Memoirs of Margaret Cook* (London: Orion, 1999)

Conservative Party, 1950 *Conservative Party General Election Manifesto*, http://www.conservativemanifesto.com/1950/1950-conservative-manifesto.shtml, accessed February 2021

Conservative Party, 1951 *Conservative Party General Election Manifesto*, http://www.conservativemanifesto.com/1951/1951-conservative-manifesto.shtml, accessed February 2021

Cribb, Jonathan, Disney, Richard and Sibieta, Luke, *The Public Sector Workforce: Past, Present and Future* (London: Institute for Fiscal Studies, 2015)

Curtis, Chris and McDonnell, Adam, 'How Britain Voted in the 2019 General Election', https://yougov.co.uk/topics/politics/articles-reports/2019/12/17/how-britain-voted-2019-general-election, accessed February 2021

Dale, Jennifer and Foster, Peggy, *Feminists and State Welfare* (London: Routledge & Kegan Paul, 1986)

Delaney, Shelagh, *A Taste of Honey: A Play* (London: Metheun, 1959)

Department of Adult Education, *Women, Class and Education* (Southampton: University of Southampton, 1981)

Department for Communities and Local Government, *2007–08 Citizenship Survey: Volunteering and Charitable Giving Topic Report* (London: Author, 2009)

Department for Communities and Local Government, *Community Action in England: A Report on the 2009–10 Citizenship Survey* (London: Author, 2011)

Department of Education and Science, *Better Schools*, Cmnd 9469 (London: HMSO, 1985)

Department of Health, *Working for Patients*, Cm555 (London: HMSO, 1989)

Department of Social Security, *A New Contract for Welfare: Partnership in Pensions*, Cm 4179 (London: HMSO, 1998)

Douglas, J., Ross, J. and Simpson H., *All Our Future: A Longitudinal Study of Secondary Education* (London: P. Davies, 1968)

'Education: A Framework for Collapse', *Spare Rib*, 124 (1982),pp.22–3

Etzioni, Amitai (ed.), *The Semi-Professions and Their Organization: Teachers, Nurses, Social Workers* (New York: Free Press, 1969)

Evans, Mary, *A Good School: Life at a Girls' Grammar School in the 1950s* (London: Women's Press, 1991)

Floud, Jean and Halsey, A. H., 'Intelligence Tests, Social Class and Selection for Secondary Schools', *The British Journal of Sociology*, 8/1 (1957), pp.33–9

Forster, Margaret, *Hidden Lives: A Family Memoir* (London: Viking, 1995)

Glass, David, *Social Mobility in Britain* (London: Routledge & Kegan Paul, 1954)

Goldthorpe, John, Lockwood, David, Bechhofer, Frank and Platt, Jennifer, *The Affluent Worker in the Class Structure* (Cambridge: Cambridge University Press, 1969)

Goldthorpe, John, Llewellyn, Caitriona and Payne, Clive, *Social Mobility and Class Structure in Modern Britain* (Oxford: Oxford University Press, 1980)

Goldthorpe, John, 'Women and Class Analysis: In Defence of the Conventional View', *Sociology*, 17/4 (1983), pp.465–88

Grandparents Plus, https://kinship.org.uk/report/state-of-the-nation-2017-survey-report/, accessed February 2021

Hallet, Christine, (ed.), *Women and Social Service Departments* (Hemel Hempstead: Harvester Wheatsheaf, 1989)

Heath, A. and Britten N., 'Women's Jobs Do Make a Difference: A Reply to Goldthorpe', *Sociology*, 18/4 (1984), pp.475–90

Heron, Liz, 'Manpower Services Commission', *Spare Rib*, 81 (1979), pp.30–1

Heron, Liz (ed.), *Truth, Dare or Promise: Girls Growing Up in the Fifties* (London: Virago, 1985)

Heron, Liz, 'Truth, Dare or Promise', www.lizheron.co.uk/category/non-fiction/, accessed February 2021

Hey, Valerie, 'Joining the Club? Academia and Working-Class Feminists', *Gender and Education*, 15/3 (2003), pp.319–35

Hoggart, Richard, *The Uses of Literacy: Aspects of Working-Class Life* (London: Chatto & Windus, 1957)

Home Office, *2003 Home Office Citizenship Survey: People, Families and Communities* (London: Author, 2004)

Hubback, Judith, *Wives Who Went to College* (London: Heinemann, 1957)

Huws, Ursula, *Your Job in the 80s: A Woman's Guide to New Technology* (London: Pluto Press, 1982)

Ingham, Mary, *Now We Are Thirty: Women of the Breakthrough Generation* (London: Eyre Methuen, 1981)

Jackson, Brian and Marsden, Dennis, *Education and the Working Class: Some General Themes Raised by a Study of 88 Working-Class Children in a Northern Industrial City* (London: Routledge & Kegan Paul, 1962)

Jerman, Betty, *The Lively-Minded Women: The First Twenty Years of the National Housewives' Register* (London: Heinemann, 1981)

Joseph, George, *Women at Work* (Oxford: P. Allan, 1983)

Kelsall, R., *Women and Teaching: Report on an Independent Nuffield Survey Following Up a Large National Sample of Women Who Entered Teaching in England at Various Dates Pre-War and Post-War* (London: HMSO, 1963)

Kuhn, Annette, *Family Secrets: Acts of Memory and Imagination* (London: Verso, 2002)

Labour Party, *Labour Party 1945 General Election Manifesto*, 1945 Labour Party Manifesto (labour-party.org.uk), accessed February 2021

Land, Hilary, 'Who Cares for the Family?', *Journal of Social Policy*, 7/3 (1978), pp.257–84

Land, Hilary, 'An Analysis of the Meaning of Women's Work as Manifested in the British Income Maintenance Schemes', *International Sociology*, 1/3 (1986), pp.243–58

Langan, Mary, 'Who Cares? Women in the Mixed Economy of Care' in Mary Langan and Lesley Day (eds), *Women, Oppression and Social Work* (London: Routledge, 1992), pp.67–91

Mahony, Pat and Zmroczek, Christine (eds), *Class Matters: 'Working-Class' Women's Perspectives on Social Class* (London: Taylor & Francis, 1997)

Mannheim, Karl, *Essays on the Sociology of Knowledge: Collected Works Volume Five* (London: Routledge, 1997)

Martin, Jean and Roberts, Ceridwen, *Women and Employment: A Lifetime Perspective* (London, HMSO, 1980)

McIntosh, Mary, 'The State and the Oppression of Women', in Annette Kuhn and AnnMarie Wolpe (eds), *Feminism and Materialism: Women and Modes of Production* (London: Routledge & Kegan Paul, 1978), pp.254–89

McIntosh, Mary, 'Feminism and Social Policy', *Critical Social Policy*, 1/1 (1981), pp.32–42

McTaggart, Lynne, 'Doctors in Distress', *The Sunday Times Magazine* (22 January 1989), pp.17–23

NatCen Social Research, 'British Social Attitudes 34: Role of Government', http://www.bsa.natcen.ac.uk/latest-report/british-social-attitudes-34/role-of-government.aspx, accessed February 2021

Oakley, Ann, *Father and Daughter: Patriarchy, Gender and Social Science* (Bristol: Policy Press, 2014)

Pahl, Ray, *Divisions of Labour* (Oxford: Basil Blackwell, 1984)

Parkinson, Justin, 'Learning in Retirement', http://news.bbc.co.uk/1/hi/education/4054259.stm, accessed February 2021

Parr, Janet, *Identity and Education: The Links for Mature Women Students* (London: Routledge, 2000)

Parry, Richard, *United Kingdom Public Employment: Patterns of Change 1951–1976* (Glasgow: Centre for the Study of Public Policy, University of Strathclyde, 1980)

Pateman, Carole, 'The Patriarchal Welfare State', in Amy Gutmann (ed.), *Democracy and the Welfare State* (Princeton: Princeton University Press, 1988), pp.231–60

The Pensions Commission, *A New Pension Settlement for the Twenty-First Century: The Second Report of The Pensions Commission* (London: HMSO, 2005)

Philips, Anne and Taylor, Barbara, 'Sex and Skill: Notes towards a Feminist Economics', *Feminist Review*, 6/1 (1980), pp.79–88

Radice, Giles, *Equality and Quality: A Socialist Plan for Education* (London: Fabian Society, 1986)

Rowbotham, Sheila, Segal, Lynne and Wainwright, Hilary, *Beyond the Fragments: Feminism and the Making of Socialism* (London: Merlin Press, 1981)

Sage, Lorna, *Bad Blood* (London: Forth Estate, 2001)

Segal, Lynne, *Making Trouble: Life and Politics* (London: Serpent's Tail, 2007)

Spender, Dale and Sarah, Elizabeth (eds), *Learning to Lose: Sexism and Education* (London: Women's Press, 1980)

Steedman, Carolyn, *Landscape for a Good Woman* (London: Virago, 1986)

Taylor, Barbara, *The Last Asylum: A Memoir of Madness in Our Times* (London: Hamish Hamilton, 2014)

Titmuss, Richard, *Essays on the Welfare State* (London: Allen & Unwin, 1959)

Walkerdine, Valerie, 'Subjectivity and Social Class: New Directions for Feminist Psychology', *Feminism and Psychology*, 6/3 (1996), pp.355–60

Whitburn, Julia, Mealing, Maurice and Cox, Caroline, *People in Polytechnics: A Survey of Polytechnic Staff and Students, 1972–3* (Guildford: Society for Research into Higher Education, 1976)

Willmott, Peter and Young, Michael, *Family and Kinship in East London* (London: Routledge & Kegan Paul, 1957)

Wilson, Elizabeth, *Women and the Welfare State* (London: Tavistock, 1977)

Zweig, Ferdynand, *Women's Life and Labour* (London: Victor Gollancz, 1952)

Secondary Sources

Books

Avery, Gillian, *The Best Type of Girl: A History of Girls' Independent Schools* (London: Deutsch, 1991)

Abrams, Lynn, 'Mothers and Daughters: Negotiating the Discourse on the "Good Woman" in 1950s and 1960s Britain', in Nancy Christie and Michael Gauvreau (eds), *Sixties and beyond: De-Christianization in North America and Western Europe 1945–2000* (Toronto: University of Toronto Press, 2013), pp.60–83

Abrams, Lynn, *Oral History Theory* (New York: Routledge, 2010)

Alcock, Pete, 'Voluntary Action, New Labour and the Third Sector', in James McKay and Matthew Hilton (eds), *The Ages of Voluntarism: How We Got to the Big Society* (Oxford: Oxford University Press, 2011), pp.159–79

Annesley, Claire, Gains, Francesca and Rummery, Kirstein (eds), *Women and New Labour: Engendering Policy and Politics?* (Bristol: Policy Press, 2007)

Arnot, Madeleine, David, Miriam and Weiner, Gaby, *Closing the Gender Gap: Postwar Education and Social Change* (Cambridge: Polity, 1999)

Bailkin, Jordanna, *The Afterlife of Empire* (Berkeley: University of California Press, 2012)

Bale, Tim, *The Conservative Party from Thatcher to Cameron* (Cambridge: Polity, 2016)

Barthes, Roland, *Mythologies* (London, Cape, 1972)

Beckett, Andy, *When the Lights Went Out: Britain in the Seventies* (London: Faber, 2009)

Black, Lawrence and Pemberton, Hugh (eds), *An Affluent Society? Britain's Post-War 'Golden Age' Revisited* (Aldershot: Ashgate, 2007)

Black, Lawrence, *Redefining British Politics: Culture, Consumerism and Participation, 1954–70* (Basingstoke: Palgrave Macmillan, 2010)

Black, Lawrence, Pemberton, Hugh and Thane, Pat (eds), *Reassessing 1970s Britain* (Manchester: Manchester University Press, 2013)

Bochel, Hugh and Powell, Martin (eds), *The Coalition Government and Social Policy: Restructuring the Welfare State* (Bristol: Policy Press, 2016)

Boston, Sarah, *Women Workers and the Trade Unions* (London: Lawrence & Wishart Ltd, 2015)

Briar, Celia, *Working for Women? Gendered Work and Welfare Policies in Twentieth Century Britain* (London: UCL Press, 1997)

Brown, C. G. and Fraser, W. H. (eds), *Britain since 1707* (Harlow: Longman, 2010)

Brown, Wendy, *Undoing the Demos: Neoliberalism's Stealth Revolution* (New York: Zone Books, 2015)

Bryan, Beverley, Dadzie, Stella and Scafe, Suzanne, *Heart of the Race: Black Women's Lives in Britain* (London: Verso, 2018)

Bukodi, Erzsbet, *Education, First Occupation and Later Occupational Attainment: Cross-Cohort Changes among Men and Women in Britain* (London: Centre for Longitudinal Studies at the Institute of Education, 2009)

Butler, David and Butler, Gareth, *British Political Facts* (Basingstoke: Palgrave Macmillan, 2011)

Clarke, John, Cochrane, Allan and Smart, Carol, *Ideologies of Welfare: From Dreams to Disillusion* (London: Routledge, 1992)

Crompton, Rosemary, *Women and Work in Modern Britain* (Oxford: Oxford University Press, 1997)

Davis, Angela, *Modern Motherhood: Women and Family in England, 1945–2000* (Manchester: Manchester University Press, 2012)

De Bellaigue, Christina, *Educating Women: Schooling and Identity in England and France, 1800–1867* (Oxford: Oxford University Press, 2007)

Devine, Fiona, *Affluent Workers Revisited: Privatism and the Working Class* (Edinburgh: Edinburgh University Press, 1992)

Dex, Shirley, *Women's Attitudes towards Work* (Basingstoke: Macmillan, 1988)

Durbach, Nadja, *Many Mouths: The Politics of Food from the Workhouse to the Welfare State* (Cambridge: Cambridge University Press, 2020)

Dyhouse, Carol, *Students: A Gendered History* (London: Routledge, 2006)

Esping-Anderson, Gosta, *The Three Worlds of Welfare Capitalism* (Cambridge: Polity, 1990)

Evans, Eric, *Thatcher and Thatcherism* (London: Routledge, 2004)

Fielding, Steven, *The Labour Party: Continuity and Change in the Making of 'New' Labour* (Basingstoke: Palgrave Macmillan, 2003)

Foucault, Michel, *Discipline and Punish: The Birth of the Prison* (London: Penguin Books, 1991)

Gamarnikow, Eva, Morgan, David, Purvis, June and Taylorson, Daphne (eds), *Gender, Class and Work* (London: Heinemann Educational Books, 1983)

Gildea, Robert, Mark, James and Warring, Anette (eds), *Europe's 1968: Voices of Revolt* (Oxford: Oxford University Press, 2013)

Glendinning, Caroline and Millar, Jane (eds), *Women and Poverty in Britain: The 1990s* (London: Harvester Wheatsheaf, 1992)

Glennerster, Howard, *British Social Policy since 1945* (Oxford: Blackwell, 2000)

Glew, Helen, *Gender, Rhetoric and Regulation: Women's Work in the Civil Service and the London County Council, 1900–55* (Manchester: Manchester University Press, 2016)

Gluck, Sherner Berger and Patai, Daphne (eds), *Women's Words: The Feminist Practice of Oral History* (London: Routledge, 1991)

Gordon, Linda (ed.), *Women, the State and Welfare* (Madison: University of Wisconsin Press, 1990)

Gosling, George, *Payment and Philanthropy in British Healthcare: 1918–48* (Manchester: Manchester University Press, 2017)

Green, E. H. H., *Ideologies of Conservatism: Conservative Political Ideas in the Twentieth Century* (Oxford: Oxford University Press, 2002)

Greenhalgh, Charlotte, *Aging in Twentieth Century Britain* (Oakland: University of California Press, 2018)

Hall, Phoebe, Land, Hilary, Parker, Roy and Webb, Adrian (eds), *Change, Choice and Conflict in Social Policy* (Aldershot: Gower, 1986)

Halsey, A. H. and Webb, Josephine (eds), *Twentieth-Century British Social Trends* (Basingstoke: Macmillan, 2000)

Handley, Sasha, McWilliam, Rohan and Noakes, Lucy, *New Directions in Social and Cultural History* (London: Bloomsbury, 2018)

Harris, Jose, *William Beveridge: A Biography* (Oxford: Oxford University Press, 1997)

Harrison, Brian, *Finding a Role? The United Kingdom 1970–1990* (Oxford: Oxford University Press, 2011)

Hilton, Matthew, Crowson, Nick, Mouhot, Jean-Francois and McKay, James, *A Historical Guide to NGOs in Britain: Charities, Civil Society and the Voluntary Sector since 1945* (Basingstoke: Palgrave Macmillan, 2012)

Hubble, Nick, Taylor, Jennie and Tew, Phillip, *Growing Old with the Welfare State: Eight British Lives* (London: Bloomsbury, 2019)

Hughes, Celia, *Young Lives on the Left: Sixties Activism and the Liberation of the Self* (Manchester: Manchester University Press, 2015)

Jackson, Ben, *Equality and the British Left: A Study in Progressive Political Thought, 1900–64* (Manchester: Manchester University Press, 2007)

Jackson, Ben and Saunders, Robert (eds), *Making Thatcher's Britain* (Cambridge: Cambridge University Press, 2012)

King, Laura, *Family Men Fatherhood and Masculinity in Britain, c.1914–1960* (Oxford: Oxford University Press, 2015)

Langhamer, Claire, *Women's Leisure in England, 1920–1960* (Manchester: Manchester University Press, 2000)

Langhamer, Claire, *The English in Love: The Intimate Story of an Emotional Revolution* (Oxford: Oxford University Press, 2013)

Laslett, Peter, *A Fresh Map of Life: The Emergence of the Third Age* (London: Weidenfeld & Nicholson, 1989)

Lawler, Steph, *Mothering the Self: Mothers, Daughters, Subjects* (London: Routledge, 2000)

Lawrence, Jon, *Me? Me? Me? The Search for Community in Post-War England* (Oxford: Oxford University Press, 2019)

Lee, Stephen, *Aspects of British Political History, 1914–1995* (London: Routledge, 1996)

Lewenhak, Sheila, *Women and Trade Unions: An Outline History of Women in the Trade Union Movement* (London: Benn, 1977)

Lewis, Jane, *Women in Britain since 1945: Women, Family, Work and the State in the Post-War Years* (Oxford: Blackwell, 1992)

Lowe, Rodney, *The Welfare State in Britain since 1945* (Basingstoke: Macmillan, 1999)

Mandler, Peter, *Crisis of the Meritocracy: Britain's Transition to Mass Education since the Second World War* (Oxford: Oxford University Press, 2020)

McCarthy, Helen, *Double Lives: A History of Working Motherhood* (London: Bloomsbury, 2020)

McDowell, Linda, *Working Lives: Gender, Migration and Employment in Britain, 1945–2007* (Chicester: John Wiley & Sons Inc., 2013)

McIvor, Arthur, *Working Lives: Work in Britain since 1945* (Basingstoke: Palgrave Macmillan, 2013)

McKibbin, Ross, *Classes and Cultures: England 1918–1951* (Oxford: Oxford University Press, 1998)

Meager, Nigel and Bates, Peter, 'Self-Employment in the United Kingdom during the 1980s and 1990s', in Richard Arum and Walter Muller (eds), *The Reemergence of Self-Employment: A Comparative Study of Self-Employment Dynamics and Social Inequality* (Princeton: Princeton University Press, 2004), pp.134–65

Miles, Andrew, *Social Mobility in Nineteenth- and Early Twentieth-Century England* (Basingstoke: Macmillan, 1999)

Moss, Jonathan, *Women, Workplace Protest and Political Identity in England, 1968–85* (Manchester: Manchester University Press, 2019)

Neary, Michael, *Youth, Training and the Training State in the Twentieth Century* (Basingstoke: Macmillan, 1997)

Norris, Pippa and Lovenduski, Joni (eds), *Gender and Party Politics* (London: Sage, 1993)

Oram, Alison, *Women Teachers and Feminist Politics: 1900–1939* (Manchester: Manchester University Press, 1996)

Passerini, Luisa, *Autobiography of a Generation: Italy 1968* (London: University Press of New England, 1996)

Payne, Geoff and Abbott, Pamela (eds), *The Social Mobility of Women: Beyond Male Mobility Models* (Basingstoke: Falmer, 1990)

Payne, Geoff, *The New Social Mobility: How the Politicians Got It Wrong* (Bristol: Policy Press, 2017)

Pedersen, Susan, *Family, Dependence, and the Origins of the Welfare State: Britain and France, 1914–1945* (Cambridge: Cambridge University Press, 1993)

Peel, Mark, *Miss Cutler and the Case of the Resurrected Horse: Social Work and the Story of Poverty in America, Australia and Britain* (Chicago: University of Chicago Press, 2011)

Perkin, Harold, *The Rise of Professional Society: England since 1880* (London: Routledge, 2002)

Powell, Martin (ed.), *Modernising the Welfare State: The Blair Legacy* (Bristol: Policy Press, 2008)

Renwick, Chris, *Bread for All: The Origins of the Welfare State* (London: Allen Lane, 2017)

Roberts, Elizabeth, *A Woman's Place: An Oral History of Working-Class Women, 1890–1940* (Oxford: Basil Blackwell, 1984)

Roberts, Elizabeth, *Women and Families: An Oral History 1940–1970* (Oxford: Blackwell, 1995)

Rogaly, Ben and Taylor, Becky, *Moving Histories of Class and Community: Identity, Place and Belonging in Contemporary England* (Basingstoke: Palgrave Macmillan, 2009)

Roper, Michael, *Masculinity and the British Organization Man since 1945* (Oxford: Oxford University Press, 1994)

Savage, Mike, *The Dynamics of Working-Class Politics: The Labour Movement in Preston 1880–1940* (Cambridge: Cambridge University Press, 1987)

Savage, Mike, Barlow, James, Dickens, Peter and Fielding, Tony, *Property, Bureaucracy and Culture: Middle-Class Formation in Contemporary Britain* (London: Routledge, 1992)

Savage, Mike, *Identities and Social Change in Britain since 1940: The Politics of Method* (Oxford: Oxford University Press, 2010)

Savage, Mike, Cunningham, Niall, Devine, Fiona, Friedman, Sam, Laurison, Daniel, McKenzie, Lisa, Miles, Andrew, Snee, Helen and Wakeling, Paul, *Social Class in the 21st Century* (London: Pelican, 2015)

Sennett, Richard, *The Corrosion of Character: The Personal Consequences of Work in the New Capitalism* (New York: Norton, 1998)

Skeggs, Bev, *Formations of Class and Gender: Becoming Respectable* (London: Sage, 1997)

Smith, Harold (ed.), *War and Social Change: British Society in the Second World War* (Manchester: Manchester University Press, 1986)

Spencer, Stephanie, *Gender, Work and Education in Britain in the 1950s* (Basingstoke: Palgrave Macmillan, 2005)

Steedman, Carolyn, 'Writing the Self: The End of the Scholarship Girl', in Jim McGuigan (ed.), *Cultural Methodologies* (London: Sage, 1997), pp.106–25

Stevenson, George, *The Women's Liberation Movement and the Politics of Class in Britain* (London: Bloomsbury, 2019)

Summerfield, Penny, *Reconstructing Women's Wartime Lives: Discourse and Subjectivity in Oral Histories of the Second World War* (Manchester: Manchester University Press, 1998)

Summerfield, Penny, *Histories of the Self: Personal Narratives and Historical Practice* (London: Routledge, 2018)

Sutcliffe-Braithwaite, Florence, *Class, Politics and the Decline of Deference in England 1968–2000* (Oxford: Oxford University, 2018)

Tanner, Duncan, Thane, Pat and Tiratsoo, Nick (eds), *Labour's First Century* (Cambridge: Cambridge University Press, 2000)

Taylor, Yvette, *Working-Class Lesbian Life: Classed Outsiders* (Basingstoke: Palgrave Macmillan, 2007)

Thane, Pat, 'Visions of Gender in the Making of the British Welfare State: The Case of Women in the British Labour Party and Social Policy, 1906–1945', in Gisela Bock and Pat Thane (eds), *Maternity and Gender Policies: Women and the Rise of the European Welfare States 1880s–1950s* (London: Routledge, 1991), pp.93–118

Thane, Pat, *The Foundations of the Welfare State* (London: Longman, 1996)

Thane, Pat, *Old Age in English History: Past Experiences, Present Issues* (Oxford: Oxford University Press, 2000)

Thane, Pat, 'Family Life and "Normality" in Postwar Britain', in Richard Bessel and Dirk Schumann (eds), *Life after Death: Approaches to a Cultural and Social History of Europe during the 1940s and 1950s* (Cambridge: Cambridge University Press, 2003), pp.193–210

Thane, Pat, 'The Careers of Female Graduates of Cambridge University, 1920s–1970s', in D. Mitch, J. Brown and M. Van Leeuwan (eds), *Origins of the Modern Career* (Aldershot: Ashgate, 2004), pp.207–24

Thane, Pat, 'The "Welfare State" and the Labour Market', in Nicholas Crafts, Ian Gazeley and Andrew Newell, (eds), *Work and Pay in Twentieth-Century Britain* (Oxford: Oxford University Press, 2007), pp.179–200

Thane, Pat (ed.), *Unequal Britain: Equalities in Britain since 1945* (London: Continuum, 2010)

Thane, Pat, *Divided Kingdom: A History of Britain 1900-Present* (Cambridge: Cambridge University Press, 2018)

Thane, Pat and Evans, Tanya, *Sinners? Scroungers? Saints? Unmarried Motherhood in Twentieth-Century England* (Oxford: Oxford University Press, 2012)

Thomson, Mathew, *Lost Freedom: The Landscape of the Child and the British Post-War Settlement* (Oxford: Oxford University Press, 2013)

Thorpe, Andrew, *A History of the British Labour Party* (London: Palgrave, 2015)

Tickner, Lisa, *Hornsey 1968: The Art School Revolution* (London: Frances Lincoln, 2008)

Timmins, Nicholas, *The Five Giants: A Biography of the Welfare State* (London: Harper Collins, 2017)

Todd, Selina, *Young Women, Work and Family in England 1918–1950* (Oxford: Oxford University Press, 2005)

Todd, Selina, *The People: The Rise and Fall of the Working Class, 1910–2010* (London: John Murray, 2014)

Todd, Selina, *Tastes of Honey: The Making of Shelagh Delaney and a Cultural Revolution* (London. Chatto & Windus, 2019)

Todd, Selina, *Snakes and Ladders: The Great British Social Mobility Myth* (London: Vintage, 2021)

Vinen, Richard, *Thatcher's Britain: The Politics and Social Upheaval of the 1980s* (London: Simon & Schuster, 2009)

Webster, Wendy, *Imagining Home: Gender, 'Race' and National Identity 1945–64* (London: UCL Press, 1998)

Welshman, John, *Underclass: A History of the Excluded 1880–2000* (London: Hambledon Continuum, 2006)

Zweiniger-Bargielowska, Ina, 'Explaining the Gender Gap: The Conservative Party and the Women's Vote', in Martin Francis and Ina Zweiniger-Bargielowska (eds), *The Conservatives and British Society 1880–1990* (Cardiff: University of Wales Press, 1996), pp.194–224

Articles

Abrams, Lynn, 'Liberating the Female Self: Epiphanies, Conflict and Coherence in the Life Stories of Post-War British Women', *Social History*, 39/1 (2014), pp.14–35

Abrams, Lynn, Hazley, Barry, Wright, Valerie and Kearns, Ade, 'Aspiration, Agency and the Production of New Selves in a Scottish New Town, c.1947–2016', *Twentieth Century British History*, 29/4 (2018), pp.576–604

Abrams, Lynn, 'Talking about Feminism: Reconciling Fragmented Research Frames', *Cultural and Social History*, 16/2 (2019), pp.205–24

Aiston, Sarah, 'A Good Job for a Girl? The Career Biographies of Women Graduates of the University of Liverpool Post-1945', *Twentieth Century British History*, 15/4 (2004), pp.361–87

Alexander, Sally, 'Generational Memory and 20th-Century Lives', *Families, Relationships and Societies*, 3/3 (2014), pp.491–4

Barclay, Katie, Carr, Rosalind, Elliot, Rose and Hughes, Annemarie, 'Introduction: Gender and Generations: Women and Life Cycles', *Women's History Review*, 20/2 (2011), pp.175–88

Barton, Adrian, 'New Labour's Management, Audit and "What Works" Approach to Controlling the "Untrustworthy" Professions', *Public Policy and Administration*, 23/3 (2008), pp.263–77

Bivens, Roberta, 'Picturing Race in the British National Health Service, 1948–1988', *Twentieth Century British History*, 28/1 (2017), pp.83–109

Black, Lawrence, '"Making Britain a Gayer and More Cultivated Country": Wilson, Lee and the Creative Industries in the 1960s', *Contemporary British History*, 20/3 (2006), pp.323–42

Blackburn, Sheila, 'How Useful Are Feminist Theories of the Welfare State?', *Women's History Review*, 4/3 (1995), pp.369–94

Blackstone, Tessa, 'The Plowden Report', *The British Journal of Sociology*, 18/3 (1967), pp.291–302

Bristow, Jennie, 'The Making of "Boomergeddon": The Construction of the Baby Boomer Generation as a Social Problem in Britain', *The British Journal of Sociology*, 67/4 (2016), pp.575–91

Britten, Nicky, 'Models of Intergenerational Class Mobility: Findings from the National Survey of Health and Development', *The British Journal of Sociology*, 32/2 (1981), pp.224–38

Brooke, Stephen and Black, Amy 'The Labour Party, Women and the Problem of Gender 1951–1966', *Journal of British Studies*, 36/4 (1997), pp.419–52

Brooke, Stephen, 'Gender and Working-Class Identity in Britain during the 1950s', *Journal of Social History*, 34/4 (2001), pp.773–95

Brooke, Stephen, 'Living in "New Times": Historicizing 1980s Britain', *History Compass*, 12/1 (2014), pp.20–32

Browne, Sarah, '"A Veritable Hotbed of Feminism": Women's Liberation in St Andrews, Scotland, c.1968–c.1979', *Twentieth Century British History*, 23/1 (2012), pp.100–23

Bruegel, Irene and Kean, Hilda, 'The Moment of Municipal Feminism: Gender and Class in 1980s Local Government', *Critical Social Policy*, 15/ 44–45 (1995), pp.147–69

Bruley, Sue and Forster, Laurel, 'Introduction: Historicising the Women's Liberation Movement', *Women's History Review*, 25/5 (2016), pp.696–700

Bunkle, Phillida, 'The 1944 Education Act and Second Wave Feminism', *Women's History Review*, 25/5 (2016), pp.791–811

Butler, Lise, 'Michael Young, The Institute of Community Studies, and the Politics of Kinship', *Twentieth Century British History*, 26/2 (2015), pp.203–24

Bukodi, Erzsebet, Goldthorpe, John, Joshi, Heather and Waller Lorraine, 'Why Have Relative Rates of Class Mobility Become More Equal among Women in Britain?', *British Journal of Sociology*, 68/3 (2017), pp.512–33

Child, Phil, 'Landlordism, Rent Regulation and the Labour Party in Mid Twentieth Century Britain, 1950–64', *Twentieth Century British History*, 29/1 (2018), pp.79–103

Clapson, Mark, 'Working-Class Women's Experiences of Moving to New Housing Estates in England since 1919', *Twentieth Century British History*, 10/3 (1999), pp.345–65

Crane, Jennifer, '"Save Our NHS": Activism, Information-Based Expertise and the "New Times" of the 1980s', *Contemporary British History*, 33/1 (2019), pp.52–74

Crompton, Rosemary and Sanderson, Kay, 'Credentials and Careers: Some Implications of the Increase in Professional Qualifications amongst Women', *Sociology*, 20/1 (1988), pp.25–42

Cutler, Tony and Waine, Barbara, 'Managerialism Reformed? New Labour and Public Sector Management', *Social Policy and Administration*, 34/3 (2000), pp.318–32

David, Miriam, 'A Gender Agenda: Women and Family in the New ERA?', *British Journal of Sociology of Education*, 12/4 (1991), pp.433–46

Davidson, Ruth, 'Family Politics: Campaigning for Child Benefits in the 1980s', *Twentieth Century British History*, 31/1, (2018), pp.101–24

Davis, Angela, 'Uncovering the Lives of Women in Post-War Oxfordshire: An Oral History Approach', *Rural History*, 19/1 (2008), pp.105–21

Davis, Angela, 'A Critical Perspective on British Social Surveys and Community Studies and Their Accounts of Married Life c.1945–70', *Cultural and Social History*, 6/1 (2009), pp.47–64

Davis, Angela and King, Laura, 'Gendered Perspectives on Men's Changing Familial Roles in Postwar England, c.1950–1990', *Gender and History*, 30/1 (2018), pp.70–92.

Deem, Rosemary, Ozga, Jennifer and Prichard, Craig, 'Managing Further Education: Is It Still Men's Work Too?', *Journal of Further and Higher Education*, 24/2 (2000), pp.231–50

Driver, Stephen and Martell, Luke, 'New Labour, Work and the Family', *Social Policy and Administration*, 36/1 (2002), pp.46–61

Dyhouse, Carol, 'Signing the Pledge? Women's Investment in University Education and Teacher Training before 1939', *History of Education*, 26/2 (1997), pp.207–23

Dyhouse, Carol, 'Family Patterns of Social Mobility through Higher Education in England in the 1930s', *Journal of Social History*, 34/4 (2001), pp.817–42

Elliott, Jane, Dale, Angela and Edgerton, Muriel, 'The Influence of Qualifications on Women's Work Histories, Employment Status and Earnings at Age 33', *European Sociological Review*, 17/2 (2001), pp.145–68

Elliott, Jane and Lawrence, Jon, 'The Emotional Economy of Unemployment: A Re-analysis of Testimony from a Sheppy Family, 1978–1983', *Digital Representations*, 1/11 (2016), pp.1–11

Gallwey, April, 'The Rewards of Using Archived Oral Histories in Research: The Case of the Millennium Memory Bank', *Oral History*, 41/1 (2013), pp.37–50

Glucksmann, Miriam, 'In a Class of Their Own? Women Workers in New Industries in Inter-war Britain', *Feminist Review*, 24 (1986), pp.7–37

Gosling, George, 'Open the Other Eye: Payment, Civic Duty and Hospital Contributory Schemes in Bristol, c.1927–48', *Medical History*, 54/4 (2010), pp.475–94

Gosling, George, 'Gender, Money and Professional Identity: Medical Social Work and the Coming of the British National Health Service', *Women's History Review*, 27/2 (2018), pp.310–28

Green, Anna, 'Individual Remembering and "Collective Memory": Theoretical Presuppositions and Contemporary Debates', *Oral History*, 32/2 (2004), pp.35–44

Gunn, Simon, 'Spatial Mobility in Later Twentieth-Century Britain', *Contemporary British History* (Advanced Access, 2021), DOI: 10/1080/13619462.2020.1858060

Harris, Jose, 'Political Thought and the Welfare State 1870–1940: An Intellectual Framework for British Social Policy', *Past and Present*, 135/1 (1992), pp.116–41

Hays, Bernadette and Miller, Robert, 'The Silenced Voice: Female Social Mobility Patterns with Particular Reference to the British Isles', *The British Journal of Sociology*, 44/4 (1993), pp.653–72

Heggie, Vanessa, 'Women Doctors and Lady Nurses: Class, Education and the Professional Victorian Woman', *Bulletin of the History of Medicine*, 89/2 (2015), pp.267–92

Hilton, Matthew, 'Politics Is Ordinary: Non-governmental Organizations and Political Participation in Contemporary Britain', *Twentieth Century British History*, 22/2 (2011), pp.230–68

Hughes, Celia, 'Negotiating Ungovernable Spaces between the Personal and the Political: Oral History and the Left in Post-War Britain', *Memory Studies*, 6/1 (2013), pp.70–90

Hughes, Celia, 'Left Activism, Succour and Selfhood: The Epistolary Friendship of Two Revolutionary Mothers in 1970s Britain', *Women's History Review*, 23/6 (2014), pp.874–902

Jackson, Ben, 'Revisionism Reconsidered: Property-Owning Democracy and Egalitarian Strategy in Postwar Britain', *Twentieth Century British History*, 16/4 (2005), pp.416–40

Jackson, Ben, 'Free-Markets and Feminism: The Neo-Liberal Defence of the Male Breadwinner Model, c.1980–1997', *Women's History Review*, 28/2 (2019), pp.297–316

Jefferys, Kevin, 'British Politics and Social Policy during the Second World War', *The Historical Journal*, 30/1 (1987), pp.123–44

Jones, Ben, 'Slum Clearance, Privatization and Residualization: The Practices and Politics of Council Housing in Mid-Twentieth-Century England', *Twentieth Century British History*, 21/4 (2010), pp.510–39

Jones, Ben, 'The Uses of Nostalgia: Autobiography, Community Publishing and Working-Class Neighbourhoods in Post-War England', *Cultural and Social History*, 7/3 (2010), pp.355–74

Jordan, Ellen, '"Making Good Wives and Mothers": The Transformation of Middle-Class Girls' Education in Nineteenth-Century Britain', *History of Education Quarterly*, 31/4 (1991), pp.439–62

Joshi, Heather, 'The Opportunity Costs of Childbearing: More Than Mothers' Business', *Journal of Population Economics*, 11/2 (1998), pp.161–83

Joshi, Heather and Owen, Susan, 'How Long Is a Piece of Elastic? The Measurement of Female Activity Rates in British Censuses, 1951–1981', *Cambridge Journal of Economics*, 11 (1987), pp.55–74

Kean, Hilda and Oram, Alison, '"Men Must Be Educated and Women Must Do It": The National Federation (Later Union) of Women Teachers and Contemporary Feminism 1910–1930', *Gender and Education*, 2/2 (1990), pp.147–67

King, Laura, 'Future Citizens: Cultural and Political Conceptions of Children in Britain, 1930s–1950s', *Twentieth Century British History*, 27/3 (2016), pp.389–411

Koven, Seth and Michel, Sonya, 'Womanly Duties: Maternalist Politics and the Origins of Welfare States in France, Germany, Great Britain and the United States, 1880–1920', *American Historical Review*, 95/4 (1990), pp.1076–108

Langhamer, Claire, 'The Meanings of Home in Postwar Britain', *Journal of Contemporary History*, 40/2 (2005), pp.341–62

Langhamer, Claire, 'Feelings, Women and Work in the Long 1950s', *Women's History Review*, 26/1 (2017), pp.77–92

Lawler, Steph, '"Getting out and Getting Away": Women's Narratives of Class Mobility', *Feminist Review*, 63/1 (1999), pp.3–24

Lawler, Steph, 'Heroic Workers and Angry Young Men: Nostalgic Stories of Class in England', *European Journal of Cultural Studies*, 17/6 (2014), pp.701–20

Lawrence, Jon, 'Inventing the "Traditional Working Class": A Re-analysis of Interview Notes from Young and Willmott's *Family and Kinship in East London*', *The Historical Journal*, 59/2 (2016), pp.567–93

Leathwood, Carole, 'Treat Me as a Human Being – Don't Look at Me as a Woman: Femininities and Professional Identities in Further Education', *Gender and Education*, 17/4 (2005), pp.387–409

Lewis, Jane and Wallis, Patrick, 'Fault, Breakdown, and the Church of England's Involvement in the 1969 Divorce Reform', *Twentieth Century British History*, 11/3 (2000), pp.308–32

Lewis, Jane, 'The Failure to Expand Childcare Provision and to Develop a Comprehensive Childcare Policy in Britain during the 1960s and 1970s', *Twentieth Century British History*, 24/2 (2013), pp.249–74

Lister, Ruth, 'The Dilemmas of Pendulum Politics: Balancing Paid Work, Care and Citizenship', *Economy and Society*, 31/4 (2002), pp.520–32

Mandler, Peter, 'Educating the Nation I: Schools', *Transactions of the Royal Historical Society*, 24 (2014), pp.5–28

Mandler, Peter, 'Educating the Nation II: Universities', *Transactions of the Royal Historical Society*, 25 (2015), pp.1–26

Mandler, Peter, 'Educating the Nation III: Social Mobility', *Transactions of the Royal Historical Society*, 26 (2016), pp.1–23

Mandler, Peter, 'Educating the Nation IV: Subject Choice', *Transactions of the Royal Historical Society*, 27 (2017), pp.1–27

Mandler, Peter, 'Comment: Social Mobility and the Historians', *Cultural and Social History*, 16/1 (2019), pp.103–7

Martin, Jane, 'Gender, Education and Social Change: A Study of Feminist Politics and Practice in London, 1870–1990', *Gender and Education*, 25/1 (2013), pp.56–74

Maslen, Joseph. 'Autobiographies of a Generation? Carolyn Steedman, Luisa Passerini and the Memory of 1968', *Memory Studies*, 6/1 (2013), pp.23–36

Maynes, Mary Jo, 'Age as a Category of Historical Analysis: History, Agency, and Narratives of Childhood', *The Journal of the History of Childhood and Youth*, 1/1 (2008), pp.114–24

McCarthy, Helen, 'Whose Democracy? Histories of British Political Culture between the Wars', *The Historical Journal*, 55/1 (2012), pp.221–38

McCarthy, Helen, 'Social Science and Married Women's Employment in Post-War Britain', *Past and Present*, 233/1 (2016), pp.269–305

McCarthy, Helen, 'Women, Marriage and Paid Work in Post-War Britain', *Women's History Review*, 26/1 (2017), pp.46–61

McDowell, Linda, 'Border Crossings: Reflections on Women's Lives in Twentieth Century Britain', *Gender, Place and Culture*, 21/2 (2014), pp.152–73

Mills, Helena, 'Using the Personal to Critique the Popular: Women's Memories of 1960s Youth', *Contemporary British History*, 30/4 (2016), pp.463–83

Mold, Alex, 'Making the Patient-Consumer in Margaret Thatcher's Britain', *The Historical Journal*, 54/2 (2011), pp.509–28

Mort, Frank, 'Social and Symbolic Fathers and Sons in Postwar Britain', *Journal of British Studies*, 38/3 (1999), pp.353–84

Neill, Edmund, 'Conceptions of Citizenship in Twentieth Century Britain', *Twentieth Century British History*, 17/3 (2006), pp.424–38

O'Connor, Henrietta and Goodwin, John, '"She Wants to Be Like Her Mum?": Girls' Experience of the School-to-Work Transition in the 1960s', *Journal of Education and Work*, 17/1 (2004), pp.13–21

Paterson, Laura, '"I Didn't Feel Like My Own Person": Paid Work in Women's Narratives of Self and Working Motherhood, 1950–1980', *Contemporary British History*, 33/3 (2019), pp.405–26

Paterson, Lindsay, Pattie, Alison and Deary, Ian J., 'Social Class, Gender and Secondary Education in Scotland in the 1950s', *Oxford Review of Education*, 37/3 (2011), pp.383–401

Payling, Daisy, '"Socialist Republic of South Yorkshire": Grassroots Activism and Left-Wing Solidarity in 1980s Sheffield', *Twentieth Century British History*, 25/4 (2014), pp.602–27

Philipson, Chris, Leach, Rebecca, Money, Annemarie and Biggs, Simon, 'Social and Cultural Constructions of Ageing: The Case of the Baby Boomers', *Sociological Research Online*, 13/3 (2008) DOI: 10.5153/sro.1695

Reay, Diane, 'Social Mobility: A Panacea for Austere Times: Tales of Emperors, Frogs and Tadpoles', *British Journal of Sociology of Education*, 34/5–6 (2013), pp.660–77

Renwick, Chris, 'Eugenics, Population Research, and Social Mobility Studies in Early and Mid-Twentieth-Century Britain', *The Historical Journal*, 59/3 (2016), pp.845–67

Rees, Jeska, 'A Look Back at Anger: The Women's Liberation Movement in 1978', *Women's History Review*, 19/3 (2010), pp.337–56

Roberts, Helen and Woodward, Diana, 'Changing Patterns of Women's Employment in Sociology: 1950–80', *The British Journal of Sociology*, 32/4 (1981), pp.531–46

Robinson, Emily, Schofield, Camilla, Sutcliffe-Braithwaite, Florence and Thomlinson, Natalie, 'Telling Stories about Post-War Britain: Popular Individualism and the "Crisis" of the 1970s', *Twentieth Century British History*, 28/2 (2017), pp.268–304

Saunders, Jack, 'Emotions, Social Practices and the Changing Composition of Class, Race and Gender in the National Health Service, c.1970–79: "Lively Discussion Ensued"', *History Workshop Journal*, 88 (2019), pp.204–28

Savage, Mike, 'Affluence and Social Change in the Making of Technocratic Middle-Class Identities: Britain 1939–1955', *Contemporary British History*, 22/4 (2008), pp.457–76

Seaton, Andrew, 'Against the "Sacred Cow": NHS Opposition and the Fellowship for Freedom in Medicine, 1948–1972', *Twentieth Century British History*, 26/3 (2015), pp.424–49

Smith Wilson, Dolly, 'A New Look at the Affluent Worker: The Good Working Mother in Post-War Britain', *Twentieth Century British History*, 17/2 (2006), pp.206–29

Spencer, Stephanie, 'Reflections on the "Site of Struggle": Girls' Experience of Secondary Education in the Late 1950s', *History of Education*, 33/4 (2004), pp.437–49

Starkey, Pat, 'The Feckless Mother: Women, Poverty and Social Workers in Wartime and Post-War England', *Women's History Review*, 9/3 (2000), pp.539–57

Strange, Julie-Marie, 'Fatherhood, Providing, and Attachment in Late Victorian and Edwardian Working-Class Families', *The Historical Journal*, 55/4 (2012), pp.1007–27

Stevenson, George, 'The Women's Movement and "Class Struggle": Gender, Class Formation and Political Identity in Women's Strikes, 1968–78', *Women's History Review*, 25/5 (2016), pp.741–55

Stoller, Sarah, 'Forging a Politics of Care: Theorizing Household Work in the British Women's Liberation Movement', *History Workshop Journal*, 85/1 (2018), pp.95–119

Summerfield, Penny, 'Culture and Composure: Creating Narratives of the Gendered Self in Oral History Interviews', *Cultural and Social History*, 1/1 (2004), pp.65–93

Sutcliffe-Braithwaite, Florence, 'Neo-Liberalism and Morality in the Making of Thatcherite Social Policy', *The Historical Journal*, 55/2 (2012), pp.497–520

Szreter, Simon, Kinmonth, Ann Louise, Kriznik, Natasha and Kelly, Michael, 'Health, Welfare and the State – the Dangers of Forgetting History', *The Lancet*, 388/10061 (2016), pp.2734–5

Taylor, Becky, 'Their Only Words of English Were "Thank You": Rights, Gratitude and "Deserving" Hungarian Refugees to Britain in 1956', *Journal of British Studies*, 55/1 (2016), pp.120–44

Thane, Pat, 'The History of the Gender Division of Labour in Britain: Reflections on "Herstory" in Accounting: The First Eighty Years', *Accounting Organizations and Society*, 17/3–4 (1992), pp.299–312

Thane, Pat, 'What Difference Did the Vote Make? Women in Public and Private Life in Britain since 1918', *Institute of Historical Research*, 76/192 (2003), pp.268–85

Thane, Pat, 'Girton Graduates: Earning and Learning, 1920s–1980s', *Women's History Review*, 13/3 (2004), pp.347–62

Thane, Pat, 'The "Scandal" of Women's Pensions in Britain: How Did It Come About?', *History and Policy* (2006), http://www.historyandpolicy.org/policy-papers/papers/the-scandal-of-womens-pensions-in-britain-how-did-it-come-about, accessed February 2021

Thane, Pat, 'Women and Ageing in the Twentieth Century', *L'Homme*, 17/1 (2006), pp.59–74

Thane, Pat, 'History and Policy', *History Workshop Journal*, 67/1 (2009), pp.140–5

Thane, Pat, 'The "Big Society" and the "Big State": Creative Tension or Crowding Out?', *Twentieth Century British History*, 23/3 (2012), pp.408–29

Thomlinson, Natalie, 'The Colour of Feminism: White Feminists and Race in the Women's Liberation Movement', *History*, 97 (2012), pp.453–75

Thompson, Paul, '"I Don't Feel Old": Subjective Ageing and the Search for Meaning in Later Life', *Ageing and Society*, 12/1 (1992), pp.23–47

Tisdall, Laura, 'Inside the "Blackboard Jungle": Male Teachers and Male Pupils at English Secondary Modern Schools in Fact and Fiction, 1950–1959', *Cultural and Social History*, 12/4 (2015), pp.489–507

Tisdall, Laura, 'Education, Parenting and Concepts of Childhood in England, c.1945–c.1979', *Contemporary British History*, 31/1 (2017), pp.24–46

Todd, Selina, 'Affluence, Class and Crown Street: Reinvestigating the Post-War Working Class', *Contemporary British History*, 22/4 (2008), pp.501–18

Todd, Selina and Young, Hilary, 'Baby-Boomers to "Beanstalkers": Making the Modern Teenage in Post-War Britain', *Cultural and Social History*, 9/3 (2012), pp.451–67

Todd, Selina, 'Class, Experience and Britain's Twentieth Century', *Social History*, 39/4 (2014), pp.489–508

Todd, Selina, 'Family Welfare and Social Work in Post-War England, c.1948–c.1970', *The English Historical Review*, 129/537 (2014), pp.362–87

Tomlinson, Jim, 'De-Industrialization Not Decline: A New Meta-Narrative for Post-War British History', *Twentieth Century British History*, 27/1 (2016), pp.76–99

Tyler, Imogen, 'Chav Mum, Chav Scum: Class Disgust in Contemporary Britain', *Feminist Media Studies*, 8/1 (2008), pp.17–34

Vernon, James, 'The Local, the Imperial and the Global: Repositioning Twentieth Century British History and the Brief Life of Social Democracy', *Twentieth Century British History*, 21/3 (2010), pp.404–18

Von der Goltz, Anna, 'Generation of 68ers: Age-Related Constructions of Identity and Germany's 1968', *Cultural and Social History*, 8/4 (2011), pp.473–91

Walkerdine, Valerie, 'Reclassifying Upward Mobility: Femininity and the Neo-Liberal Subject', *Gender and Education*, 15/3 (2003), pp.237–48

Walkowitz, Daniel, 'Women With(out) Class: Social Workers in the Twentieth-Century United States', *Women's History Review*, 14/2 (2005), pp.323–44

Waring, Justin, 'Looking Back (and Forwards) at General Management: 30 Years on from the Griffiths Report', *Journal of Health Service Research and Policy*, 18/4 (2013), pp.249–50

Wilding, Paul, 'The British Welfare State: Thatcherism's Enduring Legacy', *Policy and Politics*, 20/3 (1992), pp.201–12

Wilding, Paul, 'The Welfare State and the Conservatives', *Political Studies*, XLV (1997), pp.716–26

Worth, Eve and Paterson, Laura, 'How Is She Going to Manage with the Children? Organizational Labour, Working and Mothering in Britain, c.1960–1990', *Past and Present*, Supplement 15 (2021), pp.318–43

Unpublished theses and papers

De Bellaigue, Christina, Worth, Eve, Bennett, Charlotte, Eli, Karin and Ulijaszek, Stanley, 'Women, Mobility and Education in England and Wales: A New Analytical Approach' (forthcoming *Twentieth Century British History*)

Fisher, Kate, 'An Oral History of Birth Control Practice c.1925–1950: A Study of Oxford and South Wales' (DPhil Thesis, University of Oxford, 1997)

Mills, Helena, 'The Experience and Memory of Youth in England, c.1960–c.1969' (DPhil Thesis, University of Oxford, 2017)

Paterson, Laura, 'Women and Paid Work in Industrial Britain: c.1945–1971' (PhD Thesis, University of Dundee, 2015)

Worth, Eve 'The Welfare State Generation: Women Born in Britain, c.1938–1952' (DPhil Thesis, University of Oxford, 2018)

Index

Boldface locators indicate figures; locators followed by 'n.' indicate endnotes

Milton Keynes UK
Ingram Content Group UK Ltd.
UKHW022214271223
435002UK00004B/63